WebGL GEMS

Beginner's Guide to Learning 3D Graphics with WebGL Shaders.

Also Includes 2D Game Development Insights.

WebGL GEMS is a tutorial book that was written to help readers get familiar with WebGL through working source code examples ready for practical application.

The book is written in 2 parts. The first larger part is all about standard WebGL implementation. The second part which is much shorter is dedicated to making 2D games in WebGL.

At first I wanted to create two separate books on 2D and 3D graphics in WebGL. But a decision was made to include both subjects. This way you get everything in one volume.

First part will discuss preliminary setup and everything you need to know about loading and drawing 3D objects on the screen using WebGL. We will cover programmable **shaders** and multiple shader loading techniques, **texture mapping**, scene illumination using **light** sources and camera movement to name a few. We'll also dive into a detailed discussion on matrices and learn how to use a common matrix library to accomplish common 3D transformations.

In the part of the book covering 3D we will demonstrate a very early version of Platypus Kart. A kart racing game. The entire source code will be provided explaining how every single element of the game works. This way you can make your own racing games by the time you finish reading this book.

The game Platypus Kart features several techniques for segment vs plane collision detection in 3D, texture mapping, loading models from URLs, creating your own shaders and much more.

The second part explains how to apply that knowledge to make 2D games. WebGL is often used for simulating 2D games by rendering polygons that always face the camera view. We're still operating entirely in 3D and this gives advantage to making games that look and feel like 2D platformers but gain so much more from programmable GLSL shaders and lighting effects.

At the end of this part we will take a look at 2D graphics implementation in WebGL. In part, this knowledge resulted from programming my own platformer game Autumn. These final chapters will explain how to approach building a 2D platformer created entirely in WebGL. Subjects include sprite sheets, character animation and collision detection. We won't spend much time on this, just the basic principles will be covered.

The rest of this chapter explains the content of this book from various vantage points for those who are previewing it using Amazon "Look Inside" feature. Also a few bits about me and my writing style to ease into the rest of the content.

If you are ready to start learning, you can skip right ahead to table of contents or **Gem 1 - JavaScript Canvas** which kicks off our discussion on initializing WebGL.

3D. The core of the book consists of tutorials supplemented by practical source code that you can copy and paste and start building your own projects on. Learn how to create your own 3D shaders, how to load 3D models, how WebGL handles light representation models and get to display 3D worlds on the screen using <canvas> tag.

This book will serve as a reference for those who are moving from OpenGL and native desktop applications to WebGL in browsers. It'll be helpful for porting applications written in C++ (or C#) by rewriting them in JavaScript language. It's also a resource for people who are just starting out making 3D graphics online and have chosen HTML <canvas> as their starting point, perhaps for making video games.

2D. Wait what? Isn't WebGL a 3D graphics library? That much is true but it would be unfair to write a WebGL book leaving out examples of 2D game creation. Platformer games are fun. And even though there is a great multitude of them out there, they are often one of the first choices for learning making video (or computer) games.

A good reason for moving to WebGL from regular canvas graphics is performance optimization. Many game developers learn <canvas> primarily for 2D graphics but later realize that its native performance isn't always enough.

When WebGL came about it gave canvas ability to render actual 3D primitives by talking directly to the GPU via OpenGL drivers for rendering thousands of polygons per animation frame. Desktop OpenGL-based implementations are still about 10 times faster than WebGL. After all browsers use shared resources where memory is non-exclusive to the WebGL application itself. But as browsers continue to improve it will only get better. It's definitely much faster than regular 2D canvas drawing functions.

Performance increase gained from initializing canvas in 3D mode can be beneficial for making 2D games. This is good news because to make 2D graphics in WebGL we need to fully understand construction of 3D primitives. This book covers both.

Book's Purpose

After reviewing technical documentation books for many years I've gained wisdom to strategically design a plan that makes my educational materials as beneficial to the learner as possible. It is my hope this book accomplishes that task.

The book assumes basic knowledge of HTML and JavaScript. I won't go into details of what a JavaScript variable, function and objects are. If you need to get back to speed on that I recommend my other books JavaScript Principles or jQuery Gems.

My goals with this book are outlined below.

1. Do not offend the reader by long explanations.
2. **Enlighten** with dense ones.
3. Provide educational material that gradually builds on knowledge from prior chapters.
4. Do not use filler text to increase perceived length of the book.
5. Provide accurate facts and **ready to use source code** examples. Include solutions for common problems found in game development.

WebGL has been around since 2011 but there hasn't been any dense tutorials that focus only on the important source code examples that accomplish practical tasks. This book tries to fill that chasm.

Moreover, WebGL Gems will help newcomers to the framework get started at an optimal pace through the learning curve. This period may or may not be steep based on your past experience with 3D graphics. In particular, OpenGL.

However, the book assumes absolutely no prior knowledge and gradually takes the reader from basic 3D principles straight to their counterpart implementations in cross-browser source code.

We'll cover how light works in WebGL and write some shaders. Although how light works in reality is a total mystery — because it behaves as a wave and particle at the same time — it's certainly possible to break it down into separate abstract components so we can actually implement it in a WebGL program.

This will help us generate realistic 3D scenery similar to the kind used in modern computer and video games like Mario Kart 8, for example.

Aside from all that my goal was nothing more but to create a valuable resource and a reference for those who are looking to learn how to write WebGL applications for making 2D or 3D game engines that work in web browsers.

As a tutorial writer for over 14 years I have developed an instinct to know that readers simply want working source code examples with direct explanations that focus on how to get things done.

I wrote my first OpenGL tutorials in 2003. Clear explanations that *gradually* deepen knowledge of the subject are very important. But when carelessly used they can only clutter chapter space.

In this book I try to balance theory with practical examples including source code that you can "copy and paste and it just works across all browsers." Due to sheer amount of knowledge required to just get started with something decent, I have made an attempt to try and organize this book to the best of my ability. But it might feel a little jumpy here and there. I've never seen a book cover all of the gaps in one volume. Writing a WebGL Bible wasn't one of my goals. I just wanted to write a book that pointed beginner game developers in the right direction. And hopefully I made the journey a bit more fun and less dull than standard technical material.

By the end of the book we will also have constructed a simple yet fully functional WebGL library that can be built upon and used as a starting point for your own projects. It is not perfect. But it's not so bad either.

For these reasons this book was strategically organized and split up into separate sections called "gems." Each gem is a condensed bit of knowledge and written out as a tutorial with complete, working source code included. Yet, the book flows from one chapter to the next, assuming that you've read the previous chapter before diving into the next.

Still, I tried my best to make it usable as a desk reference. I tried to make this book be "everything for everyone" as much as possible without making it way too loose or completely scattered. Hopefully by doing this I have gained a few readers that come from various backgrounds and experience levels.

WebGL For Game Development

Note that this book is primarily based on practical and real-world examples that almost everyone who wants to make games will stumble across given enough time. These concepts, covered through the lens of WebGL graphics programming library is what this book is mainly about. At first, to make the adventure a bit more fun I decided to include complete game examples and explanations of how they were made as well. But as I ran out of space, I realized that it would take an entire book on its own just to explain how to make a complete video game.

For this reason the demos in this book won't be professional games with impressive graphics. They are here only to exemplify how what we learned can be used for a particular purpose.

As you progress through the bag of gems, investigating each one in great detail you will gradually learn how to write programs and games in WebGL — one of the most exciting 3D graphics frameworks for browsers.

The first half of the book is based on several examples that gradually build up to a basic 3D kart racing game called Platypus Kart. It's a quirky name. I just thought it was kind of funny because male platypus has venom in the back of their feet that could be used as a metaphoric analogy for nitro injection!

It is in that part we will touch upon subjects such as:

1. **3D collision detection.**
2. Setting up kart following **camera view** with **LookAt** vector.
3. **Loading racing track** into our game in Blender's **PLY** format.

Toward the end we will use what was learned throughout the book to demonstrate simple principles behind building 2D platformer games.

Features will include:

1. Fast 2D WebGL graphics on canvas (of course.)
2. Framerate-independent, time-based animation.
3. Sprite Sheet animation.
4. Keyboard and mouse controls.
5. Playing sounds in JavaScript.

I chose these 5 subjects to be focus of the game at the end of this book because they are fundamental subjects involved in making a JavaScript game engine. I just tried to include as much additional insight as possible.

A game without sound just doesn't have the same feel. One element of a game enhances the experience as a whole. Also, at one point, you will want to know how to make an audio engine. But it'll already be provided here in this book together with a dynamic sound effect resource loader. You can copy and paste it and start playing sound in your own games.

Likewise, simply using **timeInterval** for fluid game animations isn't always enough and your character animations become visually unreliable. Especially when using even a small number of stretched and alpha-blended sprites the performance can become choppy. But more importantly timeInterval is not always acceptable on its own if you need extreme amount of precision when building your own physics engine. We will use **requestAnimationFrame** (which is implemented in most modern browsers) to achieve an optimal performance streamlined with the GPU.

Using frame-rate independent animation solves many problems and the only visual hiccups would be created are the ones coming from computer specs themselves and perhaps memory load from currently running application.

Frame rate independent animation makes your game engine as fast as possible given the specs of the machine your WebGL game is running on. This effectively shifts responsibility for additionally tweaking performance over to the player upgrading their machine. Which is not an unreasonable request.

And finally… this book is designed to build confidence in becoming a good 3D graphics programmer and getting better at making games in WebGL. By providing examples that help you learn its fundamental principles, I hope this book accomplishes this task.

Table Of Contents

Introduction

Writing about an extensive subject such as rendering 3D computer graphics is a difficult task. Not so much in regard to WebGL API alone, but 3D principles themselves. For example, if you've never dealt with 3D matrices or 3D vector libraries before, either one of which is can be a subject unto itself, this book will guide you through explanations of how and where they should be used. For example, a matrix can represent a camera view.

Likewise, if you've never worked with cross product or dot product formulas, while you will find their mathematical representation in this book, in 3D graphics they are often used to solve abstract problems. An example here could be, determining the direction of a tank turret. An issue that seems more intuitive rather than something that has anything to do with trigonometry. Some kind of basic understanding of the latter is semi-required.

There is simply a significant amount of knowledge required just to get started. And to stay true to book's name the author has chosen to focus on WebGL source code versus convoluted explanations of trigonometry and mathematical formulas. They are all very important. But we're looking for practical results here so you can get started making something happen in your own projects… if possible, sooner than you would have otherwise. At least, that's partial goal of this volume.

This choice to give primary focus to source code and examples was made simply because WebGL alone is a vast subject. It's best to conserve page space for writing about what's promised by the book's title. So many times we see a mismatch between content and the title and I wanted to avoid doing that as much as possible. I am myself an owner of several books that for one reason or another seem to follow that unruly pattern.

This book is primarily targeted at someone who is somewhat familiar with JavaScript, or at least looking to spend some serious time learning it. When learning WebGL it is crucial to understand JavaScript. In year 2017 JavaScript is the primary language for building web applications. But if you don't know it yet, this book will help you get there by (hopefully) not providing source code examples that are too overwhelming. I've taken time to ensure that most of the source code provided in this book is clean enough to read and understand. An attempt was made to avoid convoluted or "spaghetti" source code to improve the chances of getting lost while consuming.

I think when learning WebGL most readers will simply want examples of working source code that demonstrate how to actually get things done on a WebGL canvas followed by brief but dense and direct explanations. The API is already fairly well-explained online by Khronos Group and a multitude of tutorials written by 3D graphics enthusiasts and independent game developers. We live in an age where information on just about any technical topic is within 5 minute's reach.

In order to make games, however, you want to be able to load 3D models, move them around the world, set up a LookAt camera, load images and shaders asynchronously, figure out how to light your 3D scene and create objects that can collide with your game world terrain. You would need to at least write a collision detection function between a triangle and a line segment to get any reasonably interesting stuff going on. Which, by the way is covered in this book.

You cannot do much without a lighting system in WebGL. So directional and point light shaders will be explained as well. You can later use them as a starting point for even more intriguing effects. Or simply extend them into your own shader implementation by adjusting and tweaking its properties.

All of the above and probably a little more I'm forgetting is described in sufficient detail in this book. With a little artistic touch, once grappled, these techniques can be used to construct your own WebGL graphics rendering engine!

I tried as much as possible sticking to modular approach for teaching as you parse through this book. Each chapter or "gem" focusing on a particular issue. Breaking down the whole journey into smaller focused studies (without having to use an overwhelmingly technical language) helped me organize this book and provide a smooth learning progression through the subject.

In fact, getting just one important element of a game engine finished gradually brings it closer to becoming a viable platform for creating a KickStarter demo or trailer. That is, if you are someone who is interested in that kind of thing. Of course, you can simply use Unity or UE3 engine. But it is always nice to know how things actually work. Besides, making your own engine has other benefits. For example, avoiding licensing fees. Or having control over optimizations based on unique structure of your game's level design. Perhaps taking advantage of other opportunities.

Some of the subjects in this book are not directly related to WebGL. But they are included in order to help you move forward with developing your own game engine. Because of generally greater difficulty they can often become roadblocks to making that happen. I tried to make intelligent choices in determining what to include and what to exclude.

For example adding 3D collision detection to your game engine, while not trivial, is a tremendous help in imitating realistic traversal of scenery where objects don't just fall through the floor or pass through walls but remain steadily placed on solid surface. Or at least appear as if they were. Without implementing this feature you would be limited to just shaders and rendering. But I can't think of a single software package or a game that does not have collision detection implemented. This book will provide a fully working JavaScript function to get you started.

We will also take an incremental approach to learning 3D matrices. I will not go into deep mathematical derivations here. Rather I will show you abstract principles that matrices are used for and how to implement them in a practical situation. We'll break down the math behind matrices and their structure, but don't expect long-winded "proof"-like math formulas that take up several pages here. That's completely irrelevant to making games and in my experience reading many game development books they are often used as filler text. Which is something I tried to avoid as much as possible here. Instead, I'll focus on explanations of how something works perceptually.

3D game programming is pretty much like magic. This illusory aspect is one of the most fascinating concepts about video games, in my opinion. We're building an imitation of reality. And there is a lot of room for creative control to make truly interesting things take place on the computer screen. But it does take a long and narrow road to walk until we can get at least a color-shaded triangle appear on HTML canvas. This is why it's not uncommon for examples of just the basic shapes (triangles, cubes, spheres) to appear past half of the book's length.

Nonetheless, the book contains several intermediate-difficulty examples as well. For example, the kart racing example with camera set up in "chase" mode, which responds to velocity and direction of the racing model I quickly made up in Blender.

This book was named WebGL Gems because it's a collection of "gems". Each gem is a chapter of a book that focuses on an important concept. However, while the book is structured and can be used as a reference book, it is also organized to be read from start to finish in gradual progression. Each chapter builds on knowledge from a previous one.

I've been a tutorial writer and game developer since 2003 when I wrote my first OpenGL tutorials. But even now years later while writing this book I realize the monumental amount of knowledge it takes to get anything reasonably interesting done on the screen in the context of a 3D world.

Having said this, there is no way any single book volume can cover everything you need to know to make interactive video games. However, most of my effort while writing this book was spent on wisely using its space to communicate as many subjects as possible following the principle that if I am going to write about it, it should be supplemented with practical examples and source code.

Book's GitHub

To gain access to all source code examples from this book navigate to my WebGL project via my GitHub account page at:

github.com/gregsidelnikov/WebGLTutorials

Note: you may have to do some work setting it up on your development environment to get them to work. This is especially true to examples that require loading resources via a PHP script.

In addition in this book you will see few references to actual URLs with live demos where appropriate. The GitHub account contains absolutely all source code from this book.

Independent Publishing

This book was independently published by Greg Sidelnikov. As a tutorial writer and author of several books published by Learning Curve I couldn't have done this task by myself. While most of my knowledge on the subject of 3D graphics was picked up over a decade of programming and experimenting I have to give credit to many other authors of WebGL literature, tutorials and contributors to online forums and similar resources.

Namely:

1. Few members of the community at reddit.com/r/gamedev/ for help with answering technical and game development related questions.

2. And one at reddit.com/r/opengl for helping with accurate implementation of 3D collision detection algorithm.

3. Joey de Vries who appears to have written some of the best online OpenGL tutorials at www.learnopengl.com

4. A now outdated but nonetheless important OpenGL resource called NeHe GameDev that contains a lot of fundamental principles and source code in just about any language available.

5. Independent game developers in general who by showing that one person can make a completed game encourage others.

Book's Evolution

I wouldn't call it evolution but some things do change and take a different shape. Independent publishing is different from being published by say, Random House, Penguin or Packt. But there is one advantage I really like about publishing on your own and that is creative control. More precisely, the ability to update, improve and otherwise upgrade the book's material at any given moment.

As with any book published by Learning Curve, an independent book publishing company I've started in 2017, I've always tried to gradually improve all of my books over a period of time. This means that there is a possibility that even after you purchase this book it will continue to improve and released under a new edition. Things change. Even WebGL 2 is already around the corner.

Gradual improvement is a common process for any publication. This is what making a new edition of a book is all about.

I can't write a perfect book but hopefully it is a pretty good one. And with everyone's help I can continue improving this volume. If you find something is missing, or a piece of source code produces an error in a particular browser (or anything of the sort) please consider contacting me so I can take a note and put it on my to do list for next edition. Writing and editing is hard work. And while I try my best to provide a great reading experience for my readers, there are times when I might still need your help.

Before We Begin

It means a lot to me that someone's actually learning from materials I poured a lot of hours into with the one and only intent: to provide educational material. Thank you for obtaining a copy of WebGL Gems.

This is the longest book I have written as of yet. My goal as usual is to help you learn something faster than you would have otherwise. I don't know if I succeeded at this. Only time can tell. But I hope this book will prove to be instrumental in helping you make your own game engines and maybe even one day publish your own games!

Gem 1 - JavaScript Canvas

Before we go in depth on WebGL-related examples I'd like to first introduce you to JavaScript canvas. Even though canvas was not originally designed to support 3D graphics it's become crucial and a required output format for WebGL graphics in modern browsers.

The canvas element is an HTML tag tied to graphics capabilities that go beyond simple DOM element rendering. If you're an OpenGL programmer for the desktop computers on Windows OS, canvas can be thought of as the Win32's GDI of the browser.

Canvas was originally created to extend DOM functionality to draw pixels, images and basic geometric shapes on such as lines with variable thickness and color (fill and stroke components respectively,) rectangles, circles and color-filled shapes represented by n-sided polygons that can be filled in with a solid color.

The <canvas> tag is capable of being initialized in 2D and 3D modes. Initializing 2D Context

The canvas context must be initialized in either case whether we use it for 2D or 3D. Regardless, to initialize canvas we must use the getContext function on the HTML element with an attribute id that represents the canvas tag. In this case it's id = "view".

HTML:
<canvas id = "view"></canvas>

JavaScript:
```
var canvasId = "view";
var canvas = document.getElementById( canvasId );
var context = canvas.getContext('2d');
```

This is the important part: notice the '2d' string passed to getContext method.

The 2D mode is usually a non-WebGL but nonetheless hardware-accelerated area capable of rendering flat 2D images within the boundaries of the canvas element's area which are usually loaded from a *.png file on the hosting server.

The image loading process takes place within object constructors of type Image as follows:

```
var sprite = new Image( filename );
```

Executing this line of code automatically triggers the "onload" event on the image tag, when the image has fully finished downloading from the web server. In game engines these events are intercepted by a resource loading mechanism.

This is important because later on we will use images for texture mapping. The process is the same as it is when loading regular images into JavaScript page. I recommend writing at least a basic resource manager which displays a loading bar on the screen. An example of this will be shown toward the end of this book when we take a look at our game examples.

Nonetheless...

To draw an image on canvas, you would have to perform the following steps:

Create a <canvas id = 'view'></canvas> tag.
Initialize canvas from JavaScript by getting "2D context" object var context.
Load the image and wait until it's completed downloading from the server.
Display the image using native canvas function context.drawImage.

Downloading Resources

Attempting to draw an image on canvas before the image is fully downloaded will result in no image being drawn. This will usually not interrupt the program or throw an error which might puzzle some of the viewers of your application for a moment.

Because of this side effect inherent to all browsers, some kind of a progress bar display should be implemented. Once the image has finished loading it will start showing up on canvas for the first time and from then on.

You can create a basic progress bar using native canvas shapes, such as filled rectangles, so you don't have to wait for loading graphics for the progress bar itself.

If a graphics-based progress bar is a requirement for your game, you should load graphics that represent the progress bar separately without counting it as a resource.

Loading Multiple Types Of Resources Simultaneously

To display anything reasonably interesting in WebGL we will require loading a set consisting of files that contain different types of resources. So just to warn you ahead of time, we will be dealing with asynchronous multi-resource loaders that load up our 3D model data (racing track, for example), texture images, and shaders. We simply have to load one after another and test for the last resource loaded in each case.

Once all resources have finished loading, only then we will move forward to actually initializing our drawing loop for drawing a 3D scene which requires fully loaded resources. Because we are working in a browser and not a stand-alone native desktop (or Android, or OSX application) the process can become quickly convoluted and cause spaghetti code because resources are loaded asynchronously. Throughout this book we will gradually explore one way of waiting for all resources to be loaded in a nice and clean way.

Avoid writing complicated code. Think about everything you write as something you will do only once. Writing bad code will eventually cause discouragement when you realize that it just doesn't fit very well with the rest of your program as its complexity increases. But if you spend an extra hour and walk the second mile with it, you only have to do it once. If you're planning to operate your own indie game development company you can think of this as building your assets. Clean code makes a difference. Making an engine that is easy to read, understand and modify should be one of your goals.

But let's get back to initializing canvas. Part of this book is dedicated to making a 2D platformer game. But canvas in 2D mode isn't ideal for this purpose.

Original non-WebGL 2D canvas implementation also supports alpha-blending and transparency out of the box via the alpha channel of the PNG image. This can be good news, until you start using transparent alpha-blended sprites even in small-to-medium amounts. Unless clever optimization trickery is applied (take for example CrossCode game which did this brilliantly) this may not always be sufficient for dynamic in-game environments where a lot of things happen. Take explosions and hundreds of simultaneous animations, for example. WebGL canvas initialized in 3D context can help us achieve greater performance.

Initializing 3D Context

I demonstrated the 2D graphics capabilities of <canvas> tag just to show how to use the method getContext. But 2D is really not why you're reading this book. Although semi-important, we shouldn't dedicate more time than this on the standard 2D functionality that has nothing to do with WebGL. Let's initialize a 3D WebGL-enabled canvas.

Similar to the previous section <canvas> WebGL counterpart is initialized as follows:

HTML:
```
<canvas id = "view"></canvas>
```

JavaScript:
```
var canvasId = "view";
var canvas = document.getElementById( canvasId );
var context = canvas.getContext('webgl');
```

This time of course, instead of '2d' we pass 'webgl' to getContext function.

But things aren't this easy in the world of competing web browser vendors. When new libraries such as WebGL take time to adapt as absolute standards, each browser of course has its own special experimental string for initializing WebGL on canvas.

We must try to check for each one of them in ascending progression to make sure we are offering complete support for old browsers... or browsers missing an update. Below I provide a complete function for initializing WebGL in any browser:

```
// Get WebGL context, if standard is not available
// fall back on alternatives
function GetWebGLContext( canvas )
{
    // Standard
    return canvas.getContext("webgl") ||
    // Alternative; Safari, others
    canvas.getContext("experimental-webgl") ||
    // Firefox; mozilla
    canvas.getContext("moz-webgl") ||
    // Last resort;
    canvas.getContext("webkit-3d");
    // Safari, and maybe others
    // Note that "webgl" is not available as of Safari version <= 7.0.3
    // So we have to fall back to ambiguous alternatives for it,
    // and some other browser implementations.
}
```

Throughout the rest of this book to get WebGL context we'll do it as follows:

```
var gl = GetWebGLContext( canvas_object );
```

Gem 2 - Initializing WebGL

Initializing just the 3D canvas context is not enough without checking the system for compatibility with 3D graphics. Before 3D canvas is initialized we need to ensure whether we're in a browser that supports WebGL.

Source Code

The function below describes a complete WebGL initialization routine. Note that until anything happens, we first query window.WebGLRenderingContext object. If it exists, we can be sure that this browser supports WebGL.

```
function InitializeWebGL()
{
    // Handle to canvas tag
    var canvas = document.getElementById("gl");

    // WebGL rendering context
    var gl = null;

    // Available extensions
    var extensions = null;

    // ! used twice in a row to cast object
    // state to a Boolean value
    if (!!window.WebGLRenderingContext == true)
    {
        // Initialize WebGL rendering context, if available
        if ( gl = GetWebGLContext( canvas ) )
        {
            console.log("WebGL is initialized.");

            // Ensure WebGL viewport is resized
            // to match canvas dimensions
            gl.viewportWidth = canvas.width;
```

```
            gl.viewportHeight = canvas.height;

            // Output the WebGL rendering context object
            // to console for reference
            console.log( gl );

            // List available extensions
            console.log( extensions = gl.getSupportedExtensions() );

        } else
            console.log("Your browser doesn't support WebGL.");
    } else
        console.log("WebGL is supported, but disabled :-(");
}
```

If your browser supports WebGL this function will initialize WebGL and output supported GL extensions to console. Note that WebGL can also be supported but disabled. If this is the case you have to look into your browser configuration settings to enable it.

Gem 3 - Simplified WebGL Pipeline

Although we can easily start using WebGL functions now that the 3D canvas is initialized, it really helps to understand the underlying processes that take place from construction of 3D primitives to their rasterization on the screen via Frame Buffer. Frame buffers are memory locations associated with rendering graphics on the screen.

Just like OpenGL, WebGL adapts a similar graphics pipeline. To pick up some principles, let's take a closer look at how it is visually represented by this simplified WebGL pipeline diagram:

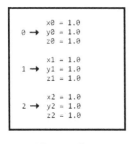 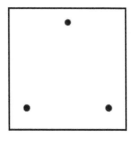  

Vertex Set   Vertex Shader   Fragment Shader   HTML canvas

I used a triangle here because it is the most basic primitive shape that demonstrates the whole WebGL pipeline visually. A single vertex, for example, would only be rendered as a single dot on the screen.

In first step we're preparing our 3D vertex set to represent a triangle. This set doesn't have to be limited to triangle shapes but it usually contains X,Y,Z representation of at least one vertex with an optional RGB value (not shown in this example for simplicity).

This vertex data is usually passed on to something called a shader which takes its name from being responsible for "shading" or filling the area of a triangle or some other primitive with pixel color values. This makes it appear as though it is illuminated by a light source, or at least has an image (texture) mapped across its area. Shaders give you access to a separate shading language that provides means for controlling in which way this process will take place. This gives a lot of room for improvisation and creating your own 3D effects.

There are different types of shaders. Two most common ones are **Vertex** and **Fragment** shaders. If you're coming from OpenGL background, looking at this simplified pipeline diagram you will quickly notice that WebGL does not support Geometry shaders.

Geometry shaders are simply missing from the WebGL pipeline by design. But that's not so bad, because everything Geometry shaders can do can be accomplished in some other way. Not a big loss.

The coordinates are calculated in vertex shader and the color of each pixel is interpolated across the triangle surface in fragment shader based on the information received from vertex shader.

Vertex shader is always executed first and only then the results are passed on to the Fragment shader. This order is important, the shaders are not executed simultaneously.

You can think of them as chained together to produce the final result on the HTML canvas which ends up being the final rasterized image that will be rendered to the frame buffer.

In WebGL Browser Takes Care of Double Buffering

To create real time animation the frame buffer is "flipped" (copied) onto the canvas much like traditional "notepad animation" where one sheet of paper quickly replaces the one lying underneath it. The image will then instantly appear on the screen.

This is done this way to fix the refresh rate gap between the memory writes and screen refresh rate. If you guided the GPU driver to write directly to the video memory on the screen, you would see a noticeable "tear" effect. But writing first to an off-screen buffer and waiting until that process is completed first eliminates that side effect.

In animated computer graphics in general, this process is referred to as double-buffering or off-screen buffering. In OpenGL it had to be done by the programmer or with the help of another library already written by someone else. This is because desktop applications are responsible for creating their own window and manually control all kinds of its aspects.

In desktop OpenGL applications you would have to manually "flip" the buffer by issuing a GL command just as the last execution call after your frame has been completely rendered to the offscreen buffer. Even after that takes place, it takes time to complete this operation as the data is passed on to the fragment processing mechanism which usually tends to be the slowest process in the entire pipeline.

This is why in OpenGL has a function SwapBuffers which flips the two surfaces after waiting to ensure the operations have finished rendering to the surface first.

However, WebGL hands this control over to the browser. Buffer swapping is not something you have to worry about when dealing with WebGL. It's done automatically by the browser.

Drawing Basic Primitives

What kind of geometry can we draw using the WebGL pipeline? Dots, lines and triangles for the most part is what you will be rendering on the screen. The actual pixel data is calculated in the shader process and finally sent to the screen.

WebGL lets us choose how the rendering mechanism should treat our vertex sets. They can either be rendered as filled in (textured) triangles, as lines connected between the vertices or as single vertices which would just display the 3D model as dots on the screen.

We'll see how this is done later in the book. For now, just note that the vertex shader only understands 3D vertex and color coordinates and isn't concerned with actually drawing anything on the screen. And the fragment shader takes care of the actual pixel (referred to as fragment) to be drawn on the screen.

Both OpenGL and WebGL refer to pixels as fragments because they are much more than regular 2D pixels. They are part of an entire process dealing with sets of data. However, the actual name is a little mysterious.

The term fragment is thought of to be referred to as a manageable part of the rendering process. In Tom Duff's "Compositing 3-D Rendered Images" (1985) the author uses "fragment" to refer to partial segments of a pixel.

However, Karl Sims in "Particle animation and rendering using data parallel computation" (1990) discusses "dicing" particles into "pixel-sized fragments" for parallel processing by "fragment processors". This is really all that I was able to find out about fragments.

Sometimes, they are interchangeably thought of as pixels tossed around by the shaders loaded into the GPU. The discussion of why pixels are called pixels is outside of the scope of this book:-)
We have just discussed the WebGL pipeline in its most basic form. But actually, in reality it looks a lot closer to something like shown on the diagram below.

You will see here the new additions are **Varyings** and **Uniforms**. Uniforms are sent into the shaders. And varyings are sent out.

These are the two data types specific to shader programming. You've already heard of ints and floats before from standard programming supported by pretty much almost every language you can think of, but these new keywords are unique to GPU programming. They are provided by the GLSL language.

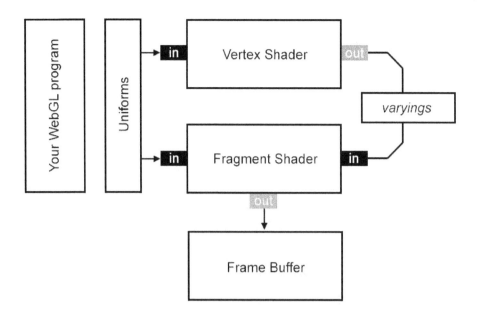

Varyings are simply variables declared within each individual shader. They can be used as helper flags or shader configuration utilities that determine different aspects of your shader functionality.

Light intensity, or distance for example. Just like any regular variable they can change throughout the lifecycle of your shader program usually written in GLSL language.

In OpenGL and WebGL we're often dealing with vertex and other information packed into data buffers. These data sets allocate memory space for blocks of data that does not change. This data is used for performance optimization.

In fact UBO's (Uniform Buffer Objects) are memory buffers allocated for sending data to the GPU from the host application (your WebGL program.)

The whole purpose of using uniform buffers is that they can be shared across multiple shaders (for example vertex and fragment shaders) without having to pass it to the GPU multiple times for each shader separately. This limits uniforms to being read-only data sets.

In contrast, varyings are usually defined in the first shader (vertex shader) and are passed on to the next shader for processing (fragment shader) and their value can and is often changed during the process.

To make use of uniforms they must first be bound to the shader inlet mechanism, which is accomplished using WebGL functions we'll take a look when we get to the source code.

Varyings do not need to be bound to anything. They are defined within the shader themselves.

The vertex and fragment shaders both have two virtual places for input and output of the data. The vertices are literally passed into the vertex shader through an inlet and come out on the other end through an outlet into the inlet of fragment shader.

This is a literal representation of how the data flow between shaders should be thought of. For this reason, when writing WebGL shaders (we're coming to that shortly in the following sections of the book) you will often see the in and out keyword.

Let's take a look at an actual GLSL program describing a simple vertex shader. We'll go in much more detail later. Note that we're still missing the fragment shader code that vertex shaders are paired with but eventually we'll get there. This is just an example to show what GLSL looks like.

And Then There Were Attributes

So we have varyings and uniforms keywords. But in our next shader example I'll throw in an additional type of a variable called attribute. I just didn't want to overwhelm you too soon with yet another variable type.

An attribute is for using in the vertex shader only. It's just another type of a variable.

An attribute is a variable that accompanies read-only vertex data. For example color or texture coordinates.

In comparison varying variables can be altered by the vertex shader, but not by the fragment shader. The idea is simply to pass information down the pipeline.

But let's take a look at these variables from another angle to get some perspective (no pun intended.)

What Exactly Is Varying?

You have to understand the principle of varying variables in order to gain a deeper understanding of WebGL shader programming.

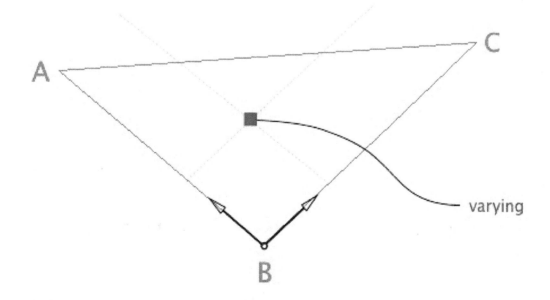

When vertex data is sent to the shader it will process one pixel at a time at that location. However the shader itself will apply its calculation to all pixels in a given rendered primitive.

The data is interpolated across vertices. As in diagram below, for example between vertex B-A and B-C. The pixel location is calculated internally on the GPU. We're not concerned with that. But the shader receives information about that pixel. One at a time.

And that's what a varying is. It's an interpolated pixel. The GLSL shader program's algorithm you will write will "close in" on that pixel. But rendering will apply to entire primitive.

Uniforms, Attributes and Varying

Looks like we've come full circle. We've taken a look at different types of variables used in shaders. Let's draw a quick outline and wrap up our discussion by adding a little more depth:

uniform
per primitive
Constant during entire draw call.
Like a const. Do not vary.

attribute
per vertex
Typically: positions, colors, normals, UVs …
May or may not change between calls.

varying
per pixel
Vary from pixel to pixel
Always changing on per-fragment operations in shader.

A uniform can be a texture map, for example. It does not change during the entire draw call.

Because attribute variables contain vertex data they are usually associated with an array. Of course that's because vertices are defined by at least 3 coordinates on the 3 axis. But keep in mind that most common 3D matrices pack into 4x4 space. And to comply with that standard, often each vertex is represented by an array consisting of 4 values, where the 4th coordinate is empty or represents some opportunistic value you want to pass to the shader.

From OpenGL to WebGL

I can't stress how many programmers come to WebGL from programming in OpenGL on desktop computers. In OpenGL we're also using the GLSL language to write our shaders. But there may exist differences across different versions of GLSL which can slightly differ in syntax or even miss features (casting from one type to another, for example). As an OpenGL programmer you may be familiar with following shader format:

layout (location = 0) in **vec3** position;
layout (location = 1) in **vec3** rgb_in;

out **vec3** rgb;

// Not actually used in this shader example
attribute **vec3** VertexNormal;

// Provided as example of "attribute" variable
attribute **vec2** TextureCoord;

uniform **mat4** Model;
uniform **mat4** View;

```
uniform mat4 Projection;

varying vec2 vTextCoord;
varying vec3 vLightPos;

void main() {
    gl_Position = Projection * View * Model * vec4(position, 1.0);
    rgb = rgb_in;
}
```

This is an example of a simple vertex shader written in GLSL
(Shading Language) demonstrating what the theory covered in this
chapter looks like in source code. Here you see that shaders have in
and out keywords to support common data flow between shaders and
your application.

Note however, that in WebGL we're using a slightly different version
of GLSL. Notice the areas highlighted in yellow. In other words: layout
(location = 0) and layout (location = 1) if you are reading this book on
a Kindle device in black and white. If you've seen these instructions in
OpenGL, chances are you won't in WebGL. I am only using them
here for reference. The rest of the WebGL shader code remains
primarily the same, depending on which version of GLSL is being
used. This may or may not always be true as shader standards
improve and continue to change. In this book, I am using only tested
WebGL shaders that actually work at least in Chrome browser. But
I've also tested the source code in others as well. The best bet is to
simply follow shader syntax shown later in this book as we move
forward. The "in" and "out" keywords are not actually used in WebGL,
they're shown here for transitioning from OpenGL.

The location parameters tells us which slot the buffers were packed in
before they are sent to this shader. They also tell us about the size of
the data. For example vec3 stands for a buffer containing 3 floating

point values which is enough to represent exactly one vertex coordinate set (x, y and z). These values are passed directly from your JavaScript program and will be shown later when we get to the examples that draw basic primitives.

Also notice that we take in variable called rgb_in and its "out" counterpart is reassigned to rgb. You can assign your own names here. For clarity, I added "_in" for data that is coming into the shader and I use just "rgb" for the data that is coming out. The logistics behind this come purely from a personal choice and I recommend using variable names that make the most sense to your own programming style.

Uniforms are like constant variables. In this case they are Model, View and Projection matrices (mat4 represents a 4x4 dimensional array) passed into the shader from our program.

These are multi-dimensional data sets that contain information about your camera position and the model vertices. They are shown in this basic example because they are the absolute minimum requirement to draw anything in 3D space - even if it's just points/dots.

Sometimes we also need to pass light source position matrix which is not shown in this example but the idea is the same. A light source is usually X,Y,Z center of the light. And an optional vertex indicating the direction which that light is pointing in (unless it's a global light source.)

Within the main() function of the shader is where you write your shader logic. It's a lot like a C program with additional keywords (vec2, vec3, mat3, mat4, const, attribute, uniform, etc.) I stripped this example down to its basic form but various GLSL versions (of which there are quite a few) vary in minor syntax differences. I skipped core version differences here. At this time, we're not concerned with that because I don't want to overcomplicate the book.

We've determined that vertices from our program are passed to the Vertex Shader. And from there, they are passed on to the Fragment Shader. Together vertex and fragment shader pair creates a representation of your rendered primitive in 3D space.

We'll continue our discussion about shaders, learn writing our own and even loading them from a web address on the local web hosting server (or localhost) in one of the following chapters. I briefly brought it up here so we can get familiar with them.

Gem 4 - Clearing the Screen

We've already initialized the 3D canvas and talked a bit about theory behind the WebGL pipeline. I think it's a good time to actually do something physical on the screen.

Let's use the very basic of GL commands on the newly created canvas. We won't do much in this section other than familiarize ourselves with a few basic WebGL functions. If you've ever programmed in OpenGL before, they have synonymous names. Except in WebGL they stem from the main context object (in this example it is called gl) as its methods.

This example assumes that jQuery library is included providing $ (document).ready function which executes at the time the page's DOM has finished downloading. But you can simply write this code at the bottom of your page just before closing </body> tag or execute these commands from <body onload = "here"> if you don't want to use jQuery.

jQuery is that kind of library that some programmers don't like because it adds an extra HTTP request to your page. And you won't be using most of its functions or methods. But it is exceptionally great for determining when DOM is loaded, without making a mess of your code.

For JavaScript Purists

Don't want to use jQuery? That's fine. You can use the following construct. Just rewrite the window's default onload function as follows. Remember that in JavaScript, thanks to a principle called hoisting functions don't have to be defined first in order to be used. And for this reason we can do something like this:

window.onload = InitializeWebGL;

function InitializeWebGL() { /* Write your WebGL init code here */ }

jQuery accomplishes this a single statement. It's up to you which one you will use.

Here is the jQuery example with actual WebGL initialization code:

```
// Execute this code only after DOM has finished loading completely
$(document).ready(function()
{
    var canvas = document.getElementById('gl');
    var gl = GetWebGLContext( canvas );

    if ( !gl ) {
        console.log('Failed to set up WebGL.');

    } else {
```

```
      // WebGL initialized!
      gl.clearColor(1.0, 0.0, 0.0, 1.0);
      gl.clear(gl.COLOR_BUFFER_BIT);
   }
});
```

If you supplied a buffer type that is not supported or does not exist, the result of your gl "clear" operation will produce the following error: INVALID_VALUE.

The function gl.clearColor accepts 4 parameters for the RGBA values. The RGB value in 0.0-1.0f format (where 0.0 = 0 and 1.0 = 255) for each one of the 3 color channels, followed by the fourth parameter specifying alpha value for translucency effect. In this case alpha was set to 255 to create a lush solid red color.

The color defined by clearColor is retained by the pipeline once it is set and you're not required to set it on every frame. It is changed only if clearColor function is used once again to reset it.

But it's the function gl.clear that is responsible for actually wiping the screen clean with the selected color. It takes gl.COLOR_BUFFER_BIT flag which says: clear the color component.

Basic Types of Memory Buffers

Color buffers are only one type of buffers in WebGL. And the flag COLOR_BUFFER_BIT represents simple [r, g, b] set. The other two flags are listed below.

COLOR_BUFFER_BIT
Only pixel color will be read / written

DEPTH_BUFFER_BIT
Operation will be performed on an off-screen depth buffer

STENCIL_BUFFER_BIT
Same as above, except for stencil buffer

Below is an example of how you would use functions that relate to setting the rest of the buffers. For example, note that clearDepth and clearStencil are used to specify Depth and Stencil buffers. These buffers must be first created, but we'll take a look at how that's done later in the book when it becomes necessary:

```
gl.clearColor( red, green, blue, alpha );
gl.clearDepth( depth );
gl.clearStencil( stencil );
```

The DEPTH_BUFFER_BIT represents the depth buffer and it is used for determining the distance between the 3D fragment and the camera / eye position. The depth buffer stores only the Z coordinate in 3D space for each pixel rendered on screen starting from the position of the camera in the world. The depth buffer does not store X and Y coordinates.

As we continue rendering polygons on the screen the data in the depth buffer is then compared with pixels drawn in the same physical location on the screen (if any.)

If there is a pixel "A" rendered in that same spot on the screen, the new incoming pixel "B" which happens to occupy the same space is tested for whether it is farther away or closer to the camera than pixel "A".

This process continues until all pixels in the scene are processed. The 2D depth buffer is built for each pixel on the 2D screen. Depth buffers are also often passed to shaders for aiding calculation for creating various effects that require knowing distance between the currently processed fragment and the camera.

Whichever pixel is closer to the camera takes precedence and is picked to be the one that will be actually drawn on the screen. All other pixels "behind it" are discarded.

This improves shader performance because we no longer need to render every single pixel that will appear at some [x= y=] position in screen space. Just ones that are the closest to the camera. This avoids performance loss from fragment overdraw.

Ideally, we would want to draw our 3D world and models in it using an algorithm that draws objects from back to front, imitating how an artist would paint on a physical sheet of canvas. The painter first draws the background scene and objects that are far away. On top of that, the artist then proceeds to draw objects that are closer, overdrawing background items.

However, that sounds good only until you realize that some polygons that are translated and rotated to occupy exactly the same volume of space cannot be always drawn using this technique without losing visual integrity. It makes sense because, which object would you choose to draw first if they shared the same pixel coordinates in 3D space?

In fact, if two objects are drawn in a way where their pixels will share exactly the same 3D location your program can experience something referred to as Z-buffer fighting.

This is when the shader is struggling to decide which pixel out of the two should be shown at that location. Often this creates a pixel flickering effect, or long jagged-edge stripes of pixels seemingly flipping on and off following a will unknown to us as shown in the diagram below:

 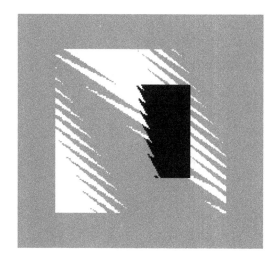

Image courtesy Department of Mathematics and Computer Science at Hobart and William Smith Colleges (http://math.hws.edu/graphicsbook/c3/s1.html)

This happens not due to the fault in the depth algorithm itself but because of the fact that floating-point operations on the CPU have limitations. Unfortunately, there is not much we can do in this case. Good news is that in most cases, we don't really need to.

To avoid this artifact we usually want to avoid drawing objects occupying exactly the same place altogether. But this depth buffer technique is still critical in being used for accurately rasterizing polygons that overlap each other when they do not occupy the same space.

If we avoid the depth buffer test, some of your polygons may appear to be rendered in random order and intersect each other, creating severe visual artifacts.

As long as large majority of fragments occupy a unique location in the world coordinates, the z-buffer technique is more than efficient to eliminate all issues with polygon ordering.

For example, consider this geometric object consisting of several rectangles.

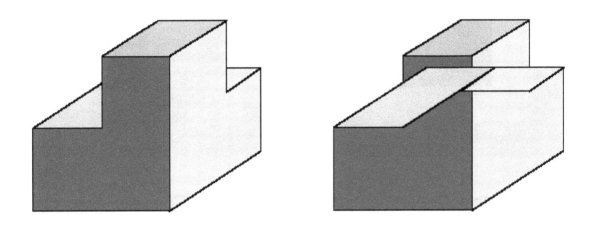

Image courtesy: "Glasnost" http://glasnost.itcarlow.ie/

When z-buffer ordering technique is applied, the object is rendered accurately (left hand side). Without it, the polygon rendering order is obscure, and the model is inaccurately drawn.

We'll deal with these cases in practice later on in the book. I just wanted to show you this now before we move on, in order to get an idea of how different types of off-screen buffers can be used in WebGL.

Gem 5 - Matrix Principles

So far we've had a great start. And I really don't want to get into matrices this early on in the book. We haven't even looked at a simple shader example! But, I am afraid that we have to talk about them at this point. Once we get them out of the way we'll move on with a solid foundation.

However in this chapter I will largely focus on principles behind matrix operations. Anyone could show pictures of a grid multiplied by another grid, which is what matrices appear to be at first sight. But what process do they actually simplify and more importantly why? Can we understand this conceptually before we move forward?

A bunch of mathematical formulas would only help those who are familiar with math in general. I don't want to make this sound shallow but in practice, those who want to learn WebGL are simply people who want to make games or cool 3D graphics.

While you don't have to understand the entire scope of mathematics, geometry and trigonometry at the very least you must understand the bare minimum of them. And that's the idea behind this chapter. It will help you get to know these areas of study so you can start using them as tools for manipulating some of the most common transformations in 3D: translation and rotation.

It's all tied together. If we avoid matrices now, we will not be able to fully understand shader programming either. And it'd definitely be a disservice to jump directly into the GLSL source code without any knowledge of matrices whatsoever. So let's start.

Introduction to Matrices

Vertex coordinates are defined by math behind your 3D camera representation. The camera can be represented by a 3D Matrix. Almost any important computational element of working with 3D models, cameras and views can be represented by a matrix. But what are they?

Matrices take a bit of time to study and delve into because they deal with mathematics and as a loose side effect with trigonometry. But ultimately once properly understood, they can be effectively used as tools for manipulating 3D data sets without having to write and rewrite vertex-specific equations for each 3D model separately. Matrices generalize common 3D computations which makes working with 3D math a little easier and more convenient.

Matrices can represent a wealth of mathematical data that ultimately can be helpful for achieving many CGI effects commonly seen in modern video games. Various matrix transformations, working together with shader logic are responsible for creating light scattering, refraction, shadow mapping and underwater effects to name just a few.

We'll deal with some of these advanced subjects later in the book. As a starting point, we need to determine some type of a building block. A place to start understanding matrices without having to deal with complex mathematical formulas. If this knowledge is skipped, it will be easy to detract from getting a truly deepened understanding of how they work. Which is useful.

I don't want you to think of matrices as something incredibly complex. In fact, only the opposite is true. Matrices help simplify complex operations. They only appear to be complex when we don't really understand why we are using them. Just like with most things in general.

When you drive a car, you don't really have to understand how the engine works. Just press pedals and shift gears. It's all intuitive. But when racing a sports car this knowledge will not get you ahead of your competitors. Even cutting a corner a certain way depends on your understanding of the vehicle you're driving, its torque and its limitations. In sports car racing even texture or temperature of your tires plays a role in creating a competitive strategy on the race track.

I guess you can either feel guilty about it and save time by simply using matrices without that type of in-depth knowledge. Or, you can learn to understand the basic principles behind them and get pretty good at programming 3D graphics.

Matrices are also used in setting up basic relationship between your 3D model (especially when it's being transferred from local to world coordinate system), the camera view and the projection so that the final result can be accurately rendered on the screen.

Let's take a look at one of the most commonly dealt matrix types first.

Common 3D Matrices

The Model matrix is self-explanatory. It deals with the 3D models loaded and displayed on the screen. It's the 3D data you're loading into your WebGL program to represent some kind of an object or in-game character.

The camera view is the position from which the model (and the rest of the 3D world) is being viewed from This view is mathematically defined by FOV (field of view) or the angle of view, the near clipping plane and the far clipping plane. You'll see seeing them a lot throughout this book.

And finally, the projection is the camera's cone size and dimensions that determine the final image on the screen for the currently rendered frame of animation in your game or 3D program. The projection is like a conglomerate of all the camera math combined. It produces a perspective-correct image on the screen. Or if you messed something up, a distorted one.

Some matrix operations will even be performed locally by the JavaScript software program you will be writing. For this, instead of reinventing the wheel we will use an existing matrix library later in the book. But still, it's nice to actually understand them.

Because of these basic principles that commonly apply to all 3D graphics, over the years graphics programmers have adopted 3 general-use matrices that will be used in pretty much most calculations that go inside your shader written in GLSL.

Model View Projection Matrix

Some of the common matrices are the Model matrix, the View matrix and Projection matrix. Together, they can be combined into what's known as MVP (The Model View Projection matrix) which is derived by simply multiplying them all together.

The cross-matrix multiplication to achieve the MVP matrix is a common operation because it deals with taking your model, calculating its position as seen from the current camera view, and figuring out how it will be projected onto the final 2D-rasterized image on canvas.

The MVP matrix is like the spinal cord of the whole system. Conceptually, it's what gives you control over the data sent to the GPU and puts the puzzle of the whole WebGL pipeline together. The rest of this chapter will make an attempt to accomplish that with simple explanations of each piece leading to gradual discovery of how it all works.

For the said reasons above you will see the MVP matrix used a lot. It's the basis for most shaders you'll ever write. It might appear difficult to grasp at first. But later as you practice, you'll see that it can be used as a tool to get things done within the world of geometric operations, without having to think about them mathematically. But even then, understanding them is still incredibly important if you want to create your own graphically impressive effects.

Gradual Discovery

This transition from the brute force math to a more intuitive approach can only happen by practicing, paying attention and memorizing the effect these calculations have. If you truly enjoy programming 3D graphics, eventually it'll sink in and become second nature.

Try drawing a scene on a piece of paper. Look at shaders already written by others. Experiment with your own WebGL code. Don't rush the process. Let it sink in. Eventually you will without a doubt grasp MVP which will be thoroughly explained later in this chapter.

But don't get discouraged if it doesn't make sense right away. These calculations have come from over a decade of research. It is only now it's put together into shader logic that is actually simplified. It's just been abstracted. And simpler abstract models always come from complexity. As we continue to learn more about 3D graphics one step at a time it will begin to make a lot more sense.

Birth of the Matrix

Matrices were used by the ancients way before computers or 3D graphics were even a thing. You may have not known this but in Latin the word matrix means womb. It kind of makes sense. It's like a grid-based basket for laying your eggs into. Where each egg is a number.

Matrices themselves are not 3D concepts. They just work miraculously well with 3D graphics.

Matrix Multiplication

So far we've only taken a very brief look at the tip of the iceberg and got familiar with a few basic matrix types. We will continue exploring this subject. But there is one more thing. There always is!

When writing WebGL shaders, we will be doing a lot of Matrix cross-multiplication operations. Each matrix multiplication pair produces a meaningful result. Matrices can be multiplied against each other. Sometimes a cross multiply between 3 matrices is required. And sometimes multiplication order matters.

For example, to transfer the coordinates of a 3D model into the camera view space we multiply the Model matrix (which contains coordinates of the model) by the View matrix. And finally to convert that into projection space we multiply it by the Projection matrix. The latter operation results in the physical pixel locations on the screen.

But if we mess up the order in which we multiplied these matrices, we will be in big trouble. Well, actually not so big. All we have to do is switch back to the correct order. But not knowing this principle, it is possible to spend hours trying to figure out why something is not working because the source code appears to "look right."

Multiplication Order

Multiplication order matters. If you multiply the 3 matrices in any other order than as shown on the diagram below, results will become unreliable. So keep in mind to ensure this order is used when building your own MVP matrices.

Projection × View × Model

This operation is used so often in shaders. In fact, you will see the following line a lot in almost any vertex shader you can possibly find:

```
uniform mat4 Model;
uniform mat4 View;
uniform mat4 Projection;

void main() {
    gl_Position = Projection * View * Model * vec4(position, 1.0);
}
```

This pattern can be found at the core of almost every vertex shader.

And likewise, sometimes the following pattern is just as common:

```
uniform mat4 MVP;

void main() {
    gl_Position = MVP * vec4(position, 1.0);
}
```

The difference is that in this case Projection * View * Model calculation was done locally in our JavaScript program (on the CPU) and only then passed on to the shader which as you know works directly on the GPU (your graphics card.)

There are many reasons as to why you would want to choose to do some calculations on the CPU and some on the GPU. This example demonstrates how to separate the two. But let's not stray from our primary subject. Matrix multiplication between either two or more matrices.

Here I have to mention that by multiplying View * Model together we get a type of matrix called ModelView matrix. And only then we multiply it with Projection matrix.

In fact, often when thinking about programming shaders the distinction is drawn between Projection and ModelView matrix. Not the 3 separate matrices (Model, View and Projection) as it might at first appear. But what's the difference between them? And why should we multiply Model matrix by View matrix in the first place?

Who Is Moving? Who Is Staying?

Remember that the Model matrix is the representation of the position of the 3D model being rendered in this shader pass. So a ModelView is simply a concatenation of the camera view and the model's position in the world.

Why are we doing it this way? I can explain this by drawing a simple analogy. In the semi-ancient times some people largely believed that the Sun rotated round the Earth. It was a natural conclusion to draw from observation.

The sunrise and sunset made it feel like it was true.

One time someone questioned that reality. And tried to prove that it is the Earth that's spinning around the Sun. Against the strong opposition of commonly accepted idea certain folks claimed it couldn't be true because of what it appears like.

In what I imagine to be a heated argument and against the claims for "obvious" evidence he who (accurately) claimed that Earth was spinning around the Sun posed a fundamental question:

"But what would it look like otherwise?"

The answer is obvious. You see, regardless of whether Earth spinned around the Sun or the Sun around the Earth, given certain conditions by the argument, the effect observed to the inhabitants of our earthly planet would still be exactly the same.

This reality also manifests itself into the world of GL camera system. Of course in WebGL we are only imitating reality. But it inherits similar properties. Compared to the example I've drawn our camera is a 3D object represented by the Earth that has its own orbit and path of movement. The Sun is also a 3D object in space.

Just like in reality where the Sun orbits the center of the galaxy, we have two moving objects. Looking at the Sun from the Earth (our camera) we are observing the Sun move. But it is only representative of the result of the Earth (camera) moving. Our "camera" just happened to be pointing at the Sun.

You can think about it in yet another way. When we are here on Earth, looking at the Sun, we are the ones who are actually rotating around the Sun. But to us it appears that the sunrise and sunset just "happen" separately from that fact. Unless pointed out, we are convinced that the Sun is moving toward or away from the horizon line. It's a beautiful illusion.

Similar principle is at work here.

Let's say the camera statically remained set in one place. Then the visible 3D model was moved to the left. Now imagine the same scenario, except the 3D model stays in place while the camera moves to the right. Visually on the screen exactly the same effect is observed regardless of whether the camera or the model moved. The only difference is that in first example the model moved left. In the alternative case the camera moved right.

And so, what happens then when we multiply Model and View matrices? A combinative matrix is formed that creates a conglomerate of mathematical equations encompassing both: the movement of the model and the camera movement in world space relative to each other.

It gets us a transformation of exactly what we need: a view achieved by current camera and model position and rotation angles. This data represents both at the same time. Multiplying it by the Projection matrix gives us the final result. A picture as it appears from the view of our camera. Note that Projection matrix is formed by the parameters describing the viewing cone of our camera projection.

From programmer's stand-point, to gain control over the camera's movement and ensure that the model is accurately displayed within that camera view regardless of its own movement, we create a ModelView matrix. They are simply both matrices combined and passed into the shader from our program as 4 dimensional arrays. We'll take a closer look at how this is done later in the book. You rarely have to use Model and View matrices alone by themselves. However, there are a few cases where they are useful in isolation.

In combination with other vertex data (such as location and direction of a global light source) this matrix data can also be used in implementing various camera transformations and shader effects. For example shadow casting. The details of that process are programmed via the fragment shader written in GLSL. When a fragment is determined to be in shaded area, we can simply color it black. While fragments that remain in the light are processed as usual. Which fragments lie within shadow and which ones remain lit is determine by an off-screen buffer technique also known as Z-buffering. It uses a 2D off-screen camera view, containing only Z values of a fragment, not its R, G, B color.

This technique retains the Z value (how far it is from the camera) of each fragment relative to the camera position. And if there are other objects present that "block" that fragment from light hitting it, that fragment will be shaded. When this process is done on the entire screen buffer, it creates an effect as though objects in the scene are casting shadows. Note, however, that this operation produces the same result regardless of camera view's position and angle. All with the help of ModelView matrix.

Another reason for existence of the ModelView matrix is that usually light operations (calculating light source data) are done after ModelView (final camera view) matrix and before the Projection matrix. It just gives us a flexible framework.

Shadow Casting

In this example I want to briefly introduce the kind of graphics effects that are possible to achieve with shaders. We won't be looking at actual implementation of the algorithm demonstrated on the screenshot below until later in the book. For now, let's take a look at this technique strictly from the point of view of abstract matrix logic.

In addition to fragment shader math, shadow-casting or "shadow mapping" technique relies on multiple matrix multiplications. Note that the shadow is cast independently of where the camera is. This technique uses the relative angle between the camera view and the light source to calculate which pixel should be in shadow and which one should be lit.

This whole effect is created by a tightly-packed GLSL shader algorithm which is usually just up to 10-15 lines of code combined (the main function of vertex and fragment shader) thanks to the efficiency of representing data using matrices, which feels almost symbolic. Here is a bit from the standard vertex shader that's used in most matrix calculations, including shadow casting:

```
gl_Position = Projection * View * Model * vec4(position, 1.0);
```

Imagine how long it would take us to actually write out each formula behind these matrices for each model? Or how about for each vertex? For each fragment? This symbolic, or rather abstract, mathematical representation simplifies a complex problem.

Another example from the shadow casting vertex shader looks as follows, where we are calculating the camera projection view as seen from the light source (not the screen camera).

```
vec3 FragPos = vec3(Model * vec4(position, 1.0));

LightSpacePosition =

    LightProjection * LightView * Model * vec4(FragPos, 1.0);
```

This code creates a mathematical representation of the camera view as if we are looking at the scene from the light source. If you want to get good at 3D programming, I suggest starting to get used to this type of logic. Looking at things from a light source is a common operation.

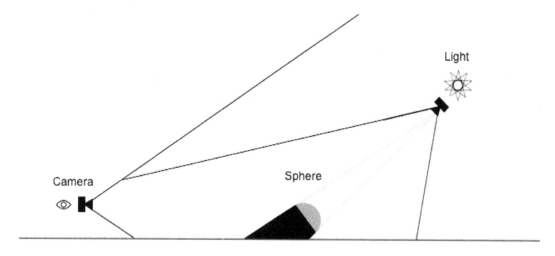

Later, down the WebGL pipeline in the fragment shader the shadow casting algorithm combines the model coordinates with two cameras to calculate the shadow effect for the currently rendered scene.

The Light camera creates its own view that we never have to see. (Although, by rendering our off-screen buffer on the screen we could!) It looks exactly as though we placed the camera at the location of the sun. It stores that image in a separate, hidden buffer. Of course we also have to create and prepare that buffer by allocating enough memory.

The shadow mapping algorithm is generally the same across many implementations, with a few tweaks here and there. All 3D books and tutorials describe the same formula. And yes you can copy and paste it from other places. But a huge part of it was understanding how it works.

If you can crack the idea behind of how the matrix multiplications were implemented, you will be able to expand your knowledge and gain creative power over bringing to life your own graphics effects without feeling lost.

We've gone on a bit of a tangent about shadow mapping here. But I just wanted to show you the possibilities by intentionally choosing a complex subject first. I've shown you the exciting things you can do with matrices. Otherwise we'd probably think the math is too boring to go on. But now we're going back to the beginning. Let's start our exploration of matrices from scratch.

Basic Representation

Understanding matrices is a common roadblock to programming 3D graphics in general. It's not that they are simply multi-dimensional arrays of vertex data. That's just how this data is organized to make it easy to work with. It's knowing the operations themselves that go on into matrix grids for manipulating that data. That, is the most commonly skipped subject from many books I've read on the subject. And, it is the inspiration behind this chapter.

Matrices are often misunderstood or not understood at all. I think that the modern game developer and the fact that tools like Unity and Unreal engine hide all of this functionality from our eyes doesn't make this task easier. Luckily, this book was written for the aspiring WebGL programmer who is curious enough to understand how these things actually work.

Let's take a look at one of the most simple matrices first. The 3x1 matrix, representing the 3D coordinate of just 1 vertex in space:

0 0 0

More commonly, we will see it appear in writing as, or 1x3 matrix:

0
0
0

This is very close to the bare minimum mental map for a Model matrix. The Model matrix is represented by a mere 3 items. But here, it doesn't have to be referring to a Model matrix specifically. Any 1x3 matrix looks this way.

Remember that the word matrix stands for womb in Latin? Why do these 0's actually look like eggs placed into a grid basket you often see at a supermarket store? Symbolic meaning is completely irrelevant here. But I feel like we're giving birth to understanding how they work.

A matrix is nothing more than a rectangular data set. A vertice contains X, Y and Z coordinates. So it is only natural that in JavaScript we will use an array to represent this data.

Matrices in general can come in a variety of dimensions. The reason for more complex matrices (multi-dimensional ones) is simple. It's just a way to represent our vertex data in a convenient pattern. It works visually and it is incredibly efficient from cross-calculation point of view.

Many 3D operations are derived from trigonometry where we're working with angles, PI and square root calculations to get distance or length of a vector between two points and so on.

This is obvious because in 3D computer graphics we will primarily be using sqrt, sin and cos operations to achieve vector length or rotation around a specific axis. Or around some other point in space.

There is no need to write all operations by hand, unless you really want to. There are existing matrix libraries that consist of all common operations already written for us. Operations such as scaling, rotating, translating and so on. But we'll take a look at them anyway.

Some matrix operations are still performed by your program and not the video card. Regardless of these facts, we still must understand how they work and what they do.

Translation and Rotation

No matter how much you study matrices when it comes to 3D graphics there are only two primary transformations: translation and rotation. They just manifest themselves in different ways or hidden behind layered interpretations. We'll take a look at them in the Starfield demo.

The Starfield demo will dissect these principles and show us internally exactly what most matrices help us do. Without actually using matrices themselves. This will provide the raw representation of mathematical principles behind matrices.

No, 3D matrix operations are not limited to just translation and rotation. So much more can be done with them, and often is. But these two operations are almost a fundamental side effect.

In the 1990's when 3D graphics were still maturing, we manually hard coded these formulas in software. Today, all these calculations and their optimizations are well known. They were moved over to the GPU or hidden in an existing matrix library. For this reason they are not well known.

Programmable shaders, you guessed it, work a lot with matrices. So while we don't have to understand the actual math behind calculating texture mapping coordinates, we still need to understand their practical use. Ironically, that'd be impossible without actually using that math.

It's almost as though you are assumed to already understand Model, View and Projection matrices before even starting writing any kind of shader code. And that is the purpose of our discussion up to this point.

Matrices take common mathematical equations and allow us cross-multiply, cross-divide, cross-subtract or cross-add entire sets of 3x3 or 4x4 data. A matrix can be of any dimension, for example: 2x2. But it's uncommon in 3D graphics. The smallest ones that you will see a lot of and often are 3x1 or 1x3 and 4x1 or 1x4.

Because each element in a matrix is basically the location of a vertex, if we multiply it by sin or cos functions (with an angle parameter) we can achieve rotation effect for one or all vertices in an object at the same time while hiding mathematical operations and symbolizing operation so it can be effectively used with practical abstraction.

Trigonometry functions help us rotate vertices. Adding values to a matrix, on the other hand, will move the model or the camera coordinates (or translate it) in world space. Translating and rotating are pretty much the most common operations matrices were made for.

Matrices are used a lot in calculating the final coordinates rendered on the screen. As I mentioned before, this is accomplished by multiplying the Model, View and Projection matrices together. Of course we can think that this process happens like magic. And oftentimes it seems just that way.

In fact we have taken math and represented it symbolically in an abstract way. After all, what does Model multiplied by View mean? What does actually happen when we multiply it all by Projection matrix?

It's questions like these that we really need to answer. If we can understand them, we can get away with not having to know the math behind them. But it is a bewildering truth that it is knowing what that math does in the first place, is what helps us understand them to the greatest extent possible.

Only if you have a lot of time on your hands, I recommend actually writing your own matrix library from scratch. If not, try to understand these principles as thorough as possible and then simply use a library written by someone else.

As pertaining to this book and examples in it, what I suggest is that we use an existing JavaScript matrix library. But I'll also give you an example of the type of logic that goes behind matrix calculations. So that we're not entirely lost on that part either.

Usually in 3D programming books many authors will display long mathematical equations of how matrix calculations were derived. And think they can get away with it. For historical purposes and just out of sheer fascination for the math workings behind matrices, that's okay.

But the irony is that often those same authors never actually explain what happens and what you as a WebGL programmed need to understand in order to start using them in practice, create your own shaders, and write meaningful algorithms by yourself (and not just copy and paste the MVP matrix formula.)

Let's fill the gap and take one solid look at the subject once and for all. From angles that matter.

In order to demonstrate the key purpose behind matrix operations and why they are required by shader programming, I'll break down the subject into 3 simple sub chapters listed below. They will help us gain a good grasp on how it all works before moving on to actually doing something useful in a 3D program.

Starfield Demo.
The inner workings of raw vertex-manipulation math calculations.

Common Matrix operations.
Matrices and their practical use in 3D graphics calculations.

Using a 3D Matrix library.
Source code with examples of common matrix operations.

This will give us a solid foundation and ability to move on to more advanced subjects without having to guess what matrices are, what they do and how to use them.

Starfield Demo

I'll use the starfield demo I made up to demonstrate what using matrices helps us accomplish at their practical level. What I mean by this is that even though matrices help us organize data when pertaining to 3D graphics they help us calculate actual 3D transforms.

I decided to do it this way because often matrices look plain weird when you put in sin, cos, tan, atan and other trigonometric formulas. They look like an Ankylosaurus, inspiring the question "What, now I have to learn something that looks like this?" This chapter distills that ancient logic. We're looking to understand these calculations for what they are. In simple form.

We'll approach the subject as if we're learning it from absolute scratch. This way there will be no misunderstandings later on when we actually start implementing Model, View and Perspective matrices in shaders.

These principles are fundamental to any 3D transformations and not just when dealing with WebGL. For this reason it almost doesn't matter what graphics outlet we implement here. I'll use regular 2D canvas and demonstrate how 3D points are projected onto a 2D screen.

Let's take a look at a diagram describing the matter at hand. We've initialized some star particles in 3D space far enough from the camera. Notice that in standard 3D coordinate systems by default the Z coordinate extends away from the camera in negative direction.

Standard Camera View Setup

Initialized Star Particles
Random area somewhere in space reasonably away from the camera on Z axis.

Star Movement
Increase Z of each star.
z += 0.001;
Move toward the camera.

Perspective Transformation
In 3D space we only change Z. But in 2D space on the screen, both their X and Y change. This is an after effect of perspective transformation.

What We'll Actually See On The Screen
Stars will appear moving in different directions toward the camera view. However, only star's Z coordinate is changed. This effect is defined by the mathematical representation of the **perspective** of our camera.

Once initialized at a random distant point we will move the stars toward the camera by decreasing only their Z coordinate. Their X and Y coordinates will not be touched. Once each individual star gets too close to the camera, we will reinitialize it by pushing it away from the camera again by subtracting a random value from its Z coordinate. This will create an infinite star field effect that appears to never end.

In this demo, I'll create everything from scratch. We won't even use WebGL to demonstrate this. We need to go into this territory to gain a deeper understanding of matrices.

I wrote a small star particle engine to demonstrate these principles on a 2D canvas. Of course when we will be working directly in WebGL then the GPU will crunch our matrix operations like a hungry dinosaur. But believe me, understanding the basics has tremendous repercussions in terms of getting better as a 3D graphics programmer. I think it's a road worth pursuing.

When watching stars move on the 2D screen to which the camera is projecting the final image we will notice something peculiar. Our stars are moving in X and Y direction. Even though in 3D coordinate system we're merely changing the Z coordinate of each star.

Even though the particles are rendered on a flat 2D screen movement of each star only appears to happen in 3D because it's how our brain and eyes process information. It's either that or it's because of how our camera projection transformation works. But then again, our camera projection imitates the original source of perception. Here we are faced with that "duality" of perception again. We won't go into the depth and logistics of this process. We can leave that for quantum physicists who are still struggling with the dynamics of this concept.

As far as 3D graphics go, here we are concerned with only one thing.

This transformation from 3D to 2D space is what Projection Matrix is responsible for.

And we can back track it all the way to our Model coordinates and the camera view.

But how does Model and View matrices fit in exactly? The Model matrix contains the X, Y, and Z coordinates of each star particle. Essentially it's the 1x3 matrix we've already seen at the beginning of this chapter. You can think of each star being represented by a single vertex. Or as a very simplified version of a 3D model. Hey, it's representative of just one vertex!

The View represent the position of our camera. Before I go into multi-dimensional matrix representations, which is how you should be thinking of matrices, and how you will naturally begin looking at them after the information in this chapter sinks in completely, I will show you a "bare bones" example using just the mathematical calculations.

Simple Particle Engine

To transfer our 3D coordinates to appear on a 2D screen we need to perform some basic calculations that create a camera projection transformation. Essentially this is what View matrix is for. But in this example we'll break down the calculations to their bare minimum.

To demonstrate this process, let's write a quick canvas demo with a basic star particle engine. I'll keep the code as short as possible. But we'll see exactly where 3D matrices take their origin when it comes to representing 3D data on a flat 2D display output.

Knowing these fundamental principles is important if you ever want to truly understand math behind most 3D operations. And really, most of them are just movement on 3 axis and rotation around one or more axis.

In the next sub chapter you will find the complete source code from starfield canvas program. There is also a web link to the working example. It's a basic program that displays stars moving toward the camera view creating the illusion of space travel.

The code is very basic here and the program itself is very short. It will fit on about two pages of this book. The purpose of this demo is to show that with just two types of vertex transformations (which are translation and rotation) we can create a foundation on which to build mathematical understanding of matrix functions.

The Star Class

First, we'll create a new Star class representing a single star using JavaScript's class keyword. It's not entirely similar to class keyword in languages such as C++ or Java, but it accomplishes a vaguely the same task.

This class will contain the X, Y and Z coordinates of the star particle. It will also have a constructor that will take care of initializing the default (and random on X and Y axis) position of any given star.

The class will contain functions reset for initializing a star, project which is the core 3D to 2D projection algorithm that demonstrates what matrices are actually trying to accomplish, and the draw function that will actually draw each star at its projected 2D coordinates.

Speaking of which, the Star class has two pairs of coordinates. One represents the actual placement of a star vertex in 3D world space using X, Y and Z coordinates.

But the class will also have x2d and y2d pair for separately storing the actual pixel coordinates when the star is rendered on the flat canvas view.

Finally, the class will also store the star's angle of rotation around Z axis to demonstrate the basic trigonometry operations you'll often see when dealing with 3D graphics.

Let's take a look at the source code:

```
var ScreenWidth  = 800;  // Output screen resolution
var ScreenHeight = 500;
var MAX_DEPTH    = 10;   // Maximum depth on -Z axis
```

```javascript
class Star {
  constructor() {        // Initialize the star object
    this.reset = function() {
      this.x = 1 - Math.random() * 2.0;
      this.y = 1 - Math.random() * 2.0;
      this.z = Math.random() * -MAX_DEPTH;
      this.x2d = 0;
      this.y2d = 0;
      this.angle = 0.001;
    }
    this.project = function() {

      var angle = this.angle;

      this.x = this.x * Math.cos(angle) - this.y * Math.sin(angle);
      this.y = this.y * Math.cos(angle) + this.x * Math.sin(angle);

      // Project the 3D star coordinates to the 2D screen
      this.x2d = ScreenWidth * this.x / this.z + (ScreenWidth / 2);
      this.y2d = ScreenHeight * this.y / this.z + (ScreenHeight / 2);

      // Adjust x coordinate by width/height ratio
      this.x2d *= ScreenHeight / ScreenWidth;

      this.z += 0.0025; // Move star toward the camera

      // Reset this star if it goes outside of the viewing area
      if (this.x2d <= 0 || this.x2d >= ScreenWidth ||
          this.y2d <= 0 || this.y2d >= ScreenHeight)
          this.reset();
    }
    this.draw = function() {
      var star_size = 3 - (-this.z / 2);
      var star_color = (MAX_DEPTH + this.z) / (MAX_DEPTH * 2);
```

```
            window.gfx.globalAlpha = star_color;
            window.gfx.fillStyle = 'white';
            window.gfx.fillRect(this.x2d, this.y2d, star_size, star_size);
            window.gfx.globalAlpha = 1;
        }
        this.reset(); // Reset (initialize) on object construction
    }
}
```

I chose the canvas size of 800 by 500 to simulate somewhat of an unorthodox wide screen format. Because I wanted to include aspect ratio adjustment, a necessary calculation in 3D graphics for screens whose width is greater or less than its height (or the other way around). Note that the width and height attributes of our canvas tag must also match these values.

The reset function provides default position values for the "starting point" of a star on the X and Y axis respectively:

```
    this.x = 1 - Math.random() * 2.0;
    this.y = 1 - Math.random() * 2.0;
```

These calculations will create random values between -1.0 and 1.0 for each of the axis.

To finish initializing our star we simply push the star away from the camera by a random value that falls somewhere between 0.0 and - MAX_DEPTH. After fiddling around with the parameters I've chosen MAX_DEPTH to be 10 units because visually it creates best results in this scenario.

```
    this.z = Math.random() * -MAX_DEPTH;
```

Note that the default z value is negative. This is normal. Remember that by default a 3D camera is facing toward the negative Z axis. It's something we're assuming here. This is the standard throughout OpenGL specification (which includes WebGL, of course). But here, we're imitating it in software. You could essentially reverse the Z axis if it were your preference. But we're trying to adhere to standard principles here.

The x2d and y2d are the final rasterized coordinates in 2D space. Are we not doing 3D graphics here? Yes, but the final pixel value is always rasterized to a flat 2 dimensional rectangle. That's the whole point of camera projection algorithm represented in the next method of the Star class called render. And in just a moment we'll see how it does that mathematically.

Apparently each star will also have an angle of rotation. Again, I am only including this to demonstrate a principle. In 3D graphics you will do a lot of rotation transformations. Here, in addition to moving stars toward the camera view, on each frame we will also rotate all of them in clockwise direction. This is achieved by simply incrementing the Z value of each star and also its angle of rotation.

```
var angle = this.angle;

this.x = this.x * Math.cos(angle) - this.y * Math.sin(angle);
this.y = this.y * Math.cos(angle) + this.x * Math.sin(angle);
```

The code above will rotate the star around its Z axis.

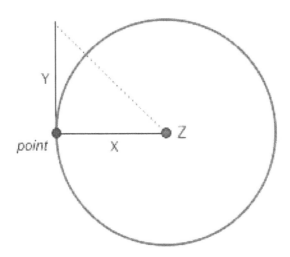

In order to rotate a point around Z axis we need to perform operations on X and Y axis. This is the standard trigonometric formula that can be applied for rotating any vertex around an axis.

For example, swapping y coordinate with z and plugging that into the formula above will rotate the point around Y axis. Swapping x coordinate with z will rotate the point around X axis. In other words, the point rotates around whichever axis is missing from the equation.

Changing the angle from positive to negative will rotate the point in an opposite direction. The general idea remains the same. Here is the pseudo code:

```
x = x * cos(angle) - y * sin(angle)
y = y * cos(angle) + x * sin(angle)
```

The angle here is the degree by which you wish the point to be rotated per animation frame. Whenever you're rotating a 3D object's vertex, you can be sure that behind all matrix operations this calculation is taking place in the raw. Perhaps, optimized by a look-up table.

In the star field demo we're rotating each star by 0.005 on each frame of animation. Note that the JavaScript Math.sin and Math.cos formulas take the angle in radians, not degrees.

Finally, we're going to project the star from its 3D coordinates to 2D on the screen.

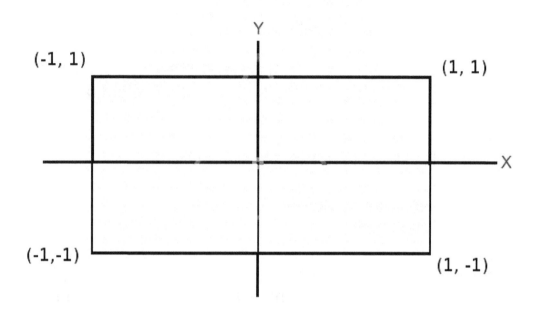

While we are still on a 2D canvas, the calculations below will transform the coordinate system to what's shown on the diagram above. In 3D graphics the camera by default is looking down negative Z. But what's more important, the X=0 and Y=0 are exactly at the center of the screen, regardless of the screen resolution.

It is for this reason that in 3D graphics we slice the screen into 4 quadrants. Whichever direction you go, whenever you hit one of the four bounds of the screen you will reach 1.0 which represents the maximum value in that direction.

And in our source code we have:

```
// Project the 3D star coordinates to the 2D screen
this.x2d = ScreenWidth * this.x / this.z + (ScreenWidth / 2);
this.y2d = ScreenHeight * this.y / this.z + (ScreenHeight / 2);
```

There is just one more thing. Remember that our screen is wider than it is taller. In other words, just this algorithm alone will produce a somewhat skewed effect unless both width and height of our canvas are the same. That's not the case here.

And for this reason we need to fix this weird effect by adjusting the X coordinate and multiplying it by the screen width / height ratio:

```
// Calculate screen ratio
var ScreenRatio = ScreenHeight / ScreenWidth;

// Adjust x coordinate by Screen Ratio factor
this.x2d *= ScreenRatio;
```

This is pretty much the equivalent of operations performed by Projection matrix. Except our matrix equivalent of this function will also include near and far clipping plane. We will talk about matrix structure and their basic function in just a moment.

By now in our source code we've projected the 3D star onto a 2D canvas view and rotated each star by 0.005 degrees (in Radians) on each animation frame.

Now let's move the star closer to the camera view by 0.0025 pixels per frame.

```
// Move star toward the camera
this.z += 0.0025;
```

I chose 0.0025 by trial and error. It just seemed to produce better visual results. But because the time animation function setInterval has no time limit in this particular demo (I set it to 0 wait time between frames) it may or may not appear exactly the same on your computer. The demo will be running as fast as is allowed by your system.

Have you ever wondered how our eyes see light? The particle (or wave?) enters through an opening in the pupil. But when these light particles land on the back of our eye and hit the retina the image is projected upside down. Our brain just has a magical way of reversing that information.

Come to think about this, our WebGL 3D camera is just a mathematical representation of this natural phenomenon. Who can tell? Jesus, I have no idea how it actually works. I really don't. But, in our little version of the eye mechanism since we have control over what happens here, we simply need to prevent vertices from falling outside of the viewing cone on the Z axis.

Clipping Planes

There is still one important part missing. When the star's Z coordinate reaches 0 and starts to increment in positive direction, our perspective formula will interpret it in reverse. In other words, stars that go >= 0 will start to appear as if they are moving away from us.

That's what happens when objects move past the threshold set by the near clipping plane. When objects move beyond it, the results are reversed. But this isn't what we need. In fact, we don't have to worry about any vertex data that breaks beyond that limit.

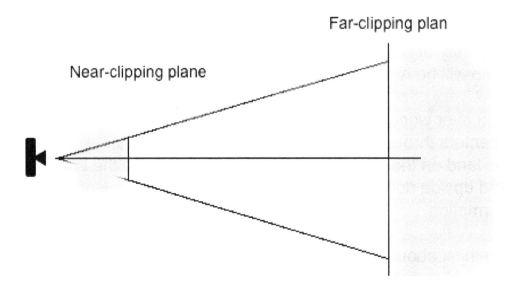

Far-clipping plan

Near-clipping plane

In our program it is important to set these boundaries. The starfield demo "cheats" a bit over this by eliminating all stars that go outside of the screen boundary in any direction, which only roughly coincides with them getting closer to the camera. And it also never draws any stars at all outside of the -10.0 boundary. It only creates an approximation of the clipping plane function.

A good way would be to simply exclude vertices based on their Z value. Your near clipping plane does not have to be at Z=0. It is usually a smaller value. For example -0.1 or -0.005.

But there is also a far clipping plane and it can extend out to 250, 500 and 1000 units or more. In our starfield demo it is only 10. It really depends on how far of the geometry you wish to be seen in your game world. And also on what a "unit" of space really means to your camera.

Generally a unit of space in most traditional 3D coordinate systems is simply 1.0. The rest depends on the relative scale of the models in your world. For example, in some games a house could be 1.0 by 1.0. In others 5.0 by 5.0. As long as objects are scaled proportionately relative to one another, they don't have to be a certain number of (or a fraction of) a unit. But in this example we don't have to worry about these things. Each star is simply a pixel.

Good news is that when we will be using a JavaScript matrix library later on, it'll take care of these issues. Nonetheless, a perspective projection is usually defined by two clipping planes. And we have to pass at least near and far clipping plane coordinates to the perspective-correct matrix projection creation function. These parameters are integrated into the camera projection matrix as required arguments.

I'm just glad we got these principles down now so it's easier to understand their implementation throughout the rest of the book.

Starfield Demo Results

The final effect achieved of our starfield demo so far will appear roughly as shown on the diagram below. Here I inverted the background color. In the actual demo the background is black. It looks better in a book this way and doesn't waste up black ink in print.

If you don't have access to a WebGL-enabled browser at this moment (reading this book on a Kindle device, for example) I wanted to include this diagram here to theoretically show you what we're trying to achieve.

Believe it or not, when I was a kid we had a ZX-Spectrum 48K computer. When building it my dad by mistake switched the wires before soldering them. This inverted the RGB spectrum. And a popular game "Elite" looked exactly just like this. With a white galactic space and black stars. It took a bit to get used to but never detracted from the joy from playing this brilliant 3D game.

Elite was made opportunistically on a 48K hardware. Did they use matrices then? Probably not, because matrices do have a memory imprint. And there is only so much you can do in 48K. But anyway, here is the diagram of our own "Elite" demo. At least the space traveling part.

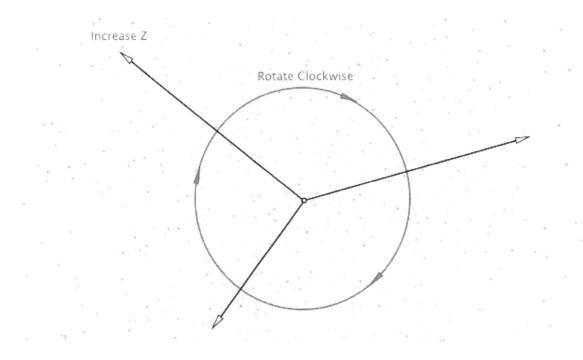

When executed in your browser these incredibly basic calculations we have discovered so far will create a hypnotic star travel effect. This screenshot barely represents actual immersion.

The remainder source code of the program to achieve this effect is located in the following example. It's really nothing more than an animation loop that initializes some stars from our Star class we created earlier.

In the "game loop" the Z of each star is increased. When projection transform is applied this will create the illusion that the stars are moving toward the camera. Or perhaps that we are traveling forward in space and stars remain in the same location in the space world.

This dual nature of 3D movement is not a coincidence. And we have already ran across this phenomenon when dealing with the 3D camera explanation earlier in this chapter. It's peculiar. But it's something you just have to get used to. Moving the world is the same as moving the camera in inverse direction. Visually the effect is indistinct.

We will talk a lot more about camera and learn how to control it with precision to do pretty much anything we could possibly need to in a 3D game, including mouse-controlled camera or creating a camera that's always following an object in the world.

But let's get back to our demo for a moment. We figured out the star transformations but need to finish writing the core program.

Here, each star is an individual particle. It is initialized by a for-loop as you will see in the source code shown below. In the demo I set the maximum number of stars to be 2000.

All of this is done by the remaining part of our JavaScript demo where we set some basic default parameters, initialize 2000 stars, and use JavaScripts timing function setInterval to execute a frame of animation without a time delay (as soon as possible.)

```
// Maximum 2000 star particles
var STARS_MAX = 2000;

// Create a large enough array to hold stars
var stars = new Array(STARS_MAX);
```

```javascript
// Initialize stars
for (let i = 0; i < STARS_MAX; i++)
    stars[i] = new Star();

// Create and initialize canvas
var canvas = document.getElementById("canvas");
var context = window.gfx = canvas.getContext('2d');

// Main animation loop
setInterval(function() {

    // Clear canvas screen with a solid color
    gfx.beginPath();
        gfx.fillStyle = 'black';
        gfx.rect(0, 0, 800, 500);
    gfx.fill();

    // Move and draw stars
    gfx.beginPath();
        gfx.fillStyle = 'white';
        for (let i = 0; i < STARS_MAX; i++) {
            stars[i].project();      // Do projection operations
            stars[i].draw();         // Draw the stars
        }
    gfx.fill();

}, 0); // 0 = no time delay between each frame
```

You can also launch this demo at my Tigris Games website in your browser:

http://www.tigrisgames.com/fx/starfield.php

Here you see in action the movement and rotation transformations that are very common to matrix operations. And we've already taken a look at their plain mathematical representation using basic trigonometry in the source code of this demo explained in this chapter.

We simply must understand these basics, whether we use matrix operations or not.

And although the only difference is in how matrices structure vertex data by packing it into 1x3, 3x3 or 4x4 arrays, under the veils they all perform the same exact math we just saw in the starfield demo.

The danger of studying matrices without knowing fundamental trigonometry and camera projection principles is that you will be required to think in these types of calculations when programming your own 3D software. Regardless of whether you use matrices or not.

Matrix Structure

We've taken a look at a brute force algorithm for projecting and moving vertex data around. Now let's continue our discussion on matrix structure. Let's pack all this math we've just discovered into a grid and call it a matrix!

A matrix is nothing more than data represented by a 2 dimensional grid where the number of columns and rows may vary.

Matrices come in different flavors. Mostly the difference is in the number of rows and columns. They can be defined by a grid containing different numbers of items for each of the vertical and horizontal rows.

Below on the left, one of the basic examples of a matrix could be represented by a grid fitting into a 3x2 box. And on the right hand side we see a common 1x3 matrix pattern representing vertex data containing just the x, y and z coordinates:

3x2 Matrix

```
a b c
d e f
```

Not used often in 3D calculations.

1x3 Matrix

```
x
y
z
```

1x3 matrix is often used as the Model view matrix.

I've rarely seen 3x2 matrix used to accomplish anything at all in 3D. This is just an example.

On the other hand the 1x3 (or sometimes 1x4 and you will shortly see why) is the Model view.

Then it is only natural that together with 1x3 (or even 1x4 sometimes) the other most common types of matrix grids we'll be working with in WebGL are shown below:

3x3 Matrix

```
a b c
d e f
g h i
```

ModelView or Projection Matrix
Non-homogeneous
Uncommon.

4x4 Matrix

```
a b c d
e f g h
i j k l
```

ModelView or Projection Matrix
Homogeneous.
Most Common 3D Matrix

This is due to the fact that most calculations contain vertices composed of X, Y and Z triplets. But occasionally (actually a lot of the time) there is data containing 4 values.

That's called homogeneous coordinates. You add one to the data set of 3 in order to fit into another 4x4 matrix by convention to pad calculations.

One good reason for the 4x4 format is because it falls neatly into computer memory. As you know all computer memory is usually organized by a power of 2 as the common denominator and it is not by accident 4x4 is 16.

Sequential Order

When it comes to 3D graphics it's as though matrices operate in different dimensions. And I am not only talking about the sequential order of the array they are represented by. There is also a diagonal pattern for data representation that we'll see in a moment.

First, let's take a look at the order of a simple 3x3 matrix represented by a JavaScript array. I am using semi-pseudo code here to demonstrate the principle.

There is a natural temptation to represent a matrix using a multidimensional array in JavaScript. It seems like this could be ideal for storing a matrix. For example, we could have used:

```
mat[0][0] = [ a ]
mat[0][1] = [ b ]
mat[0][2] = [ c ]

mat[1][0] = [ d ]
mat[1][1] = [ e ]
mat[1][2] = [ f ]

mat[2][0] = [ g ]
mat[2][1] = [ h ]
mat[2][2] = [ i ]
```

This might seem like a good idea at first. But computer memory in modern processors and GPUs is optimized for linear data. When dealing with thousands or even millions of vertex data sets - and this is not uncommon - we can run into performance issues.

Instead, let's represent our 3x3 matrix by a simple 1-dimensional array. The linear data without breaks will provide efficiency for dealing with large data sets.

```
var mat3 = [ a b c d e f g h i ]
```

And now let's organize it by simply visualizing a grid. This visually imitates multi-dimensional array structure without having to use one. And it's still something we can work with:

```
a b c
d e f
g h i
```

This is called the sequential order. Here, the matrix is represented by an array. Even though we see it as multi-dimensional data set, it's still just a linear array of data.

Even though the layout is linear 3D matrices separate each column to represent individual bits of information. In this case, the X, Y and Z coordinates of a vertex. Usually the data is represented following a diagonal pattern. Let's consider this example:

```
X 0 0
0 Y 0
0 0 Z
```

The values are represented diagonally for each column. This may not appear natural at first. Why not just pack X, Y and Z into the first 3 values and save memory? But remember that a matrix is by definition a multi-dimensional set of data formed this way to represent a homogeneous set (We'll talk about this in just a moment.)

Let's recall the sequential order for a moment.

In 3D graphics it is accepted as a convention to use the a, e and i indices for storing vertex coordinate values. This way when we cross-multiply matrices or apply other matrix operations on them we know exactly where each individual counterpart of the vertex data is stored.

```
a b c
d e f
g h i
```

In other words, the first column represents X, second Y and third Z. As we move forward to the next column from left to right the row is incremented by one as well. This creates a diagonal pattern.

In four-dimensional matrices, as we will briefly see in the next section we have a choice as to where the fourth value will be stored with regard to columns or rows. These two matrix formats are called row-major and column-major matrix notation.

Homogeneous Coordinates

What we've just discussed is called homogeneous representation of data. It's a great idea because basically we're using a common and unchanging format to represent different and complex datasets.

We've already talked that this is perfect for computer memory layout. And naturally homogeneous coordinate systems provide extra space for fitting into the same pattern. This is the reason we pad the matrix grid with 0's even though we're never using them.

```
X 0 0 0
0 Y 0 0
0 0 Z 0
0 0 1 0
```

Of course we can get away with not using matrices at all. We can just do raw calculations on the vertex or color data, similar to what we've done in the starfield demo earlier. But it's how GPUs have evolved and they expect to be fed matrices. It's just another reason why it's important to understand them.

Row-Major and Column-Major Matrix Notations

A lot of the time when it comes to GL (whether it is WebGL or OpenGL) you'll see matrices of two different types. It's really just a small quirk. Because we're packing padded 3x3 data into essentially a 4x4 matrix, we have an entire right column and bottom row empty.

These specific locations are often used for alpha (in addition to the r,g,b) value when the matrix carries color information. Or it is simply used to "pad" the data with value such as 0 or 1. Since multiplying by 1 or dividing by 1 produces the original result.

```
X 0 0 0        X 0 0 0
0 Y 0 0        0 Y 0 0
0 0 Z 0        0 0 Z 1
0 0 1 0        0 0 0 0
```

These are the most commonly used matrix layouts. They're nothing more than logistical preference. Sometimes, different software programs, matrix libraries and APIs differ in the assumed matrix format.

For example, OpenGL uses Column-Major Notation. Whereas Row-Major is the default layout in C language. Each API or language adopt a default layout.

These layouts have a long history that has to do with programming languages, their so-called evolution, APIs, preferences and generally accepted standards. It is possible to go on long tangents as to why they are the way they are. And we only have so much space in this book.

However, one thing I do have to mention that sheds a little more light on the issue. Being aware of memory optimizations is crucial for programming 3D graphics efficiently. So let's take a look at this one other thing before we move forward.

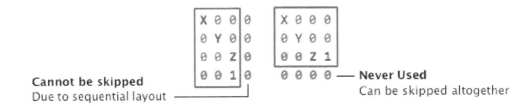

As seen on the left hand side representing Column-Major notation, we can't just jump over items in a sequential layout without additional calculations. However, the last 4 entries of a 3x4 matrix represented by Row-Major notation can be shaved off at the bottom. And this layout, although rarely used, can be packed into less space ultimately saving 4 bytes per vertex entry.

This is a major (no pun intended) reason for why in WebGL shaders we use uniform variable type to represent our matrices.

Default Camera Position

In the diagrams above, as well as the starfield source code the camera is placed at its standard location. Right in the center of the world coordinate system (x=0, y=0, z=0.) Cameras usually have a view vector. In this case, the vector is simply pointing toward the negative Z direction.

But this assumption is made by pretty much skipping the code altogether. At this point, while we're still exploring common math operations behind matrices, we're not concerned with actually having control over the direction of the camera.

Even though all camera coordinates are practically 0 including the rotation angle, we still need a way of representing it using a matrix. It would look something like this:

var view_matrix_4x4 =

```
[ x,  0,  0,  0,
  0,  y,  0,  0,
  0,  0,  z,  0,
  0,  0,  1,  0 ];
```

The camera direction vector is usually specified separately. Here we're using Column-Major notation and the trailing 1 is used opportunistically. But we cannot understand its purpose until we delve into actual cross-calculations between matrices. Let's take a look.

Efficient Cross-Matrix Calculations

At first, an array that stores 16 values instead of 3 might seem like a recipe for bloated data representation. But remember that the goal is to fall within the 3x3 (or sometimes 4x4) data pattern. The whole point of a matrix is to represent data in a multi-dimensional way. This is done to organize data calculations. Imagine having to cross-calculate every vertex by every other vertex in another data set and pick each X, Y, Z, etc coordinate by hand. This would result in complicated code.

Yes, we're using more data than we have to. But the overhead is small compared to the benefits of increased ease working with the vertex data in this format. Also, the GPUs are already optimized for crunching data represented by these layouts by assuming them.

Common Cross-Matrix Operations

We've talked a lot about the physical layout of matrix data. Now it's time to take a look at the actual operations we'll be implementing to achieve various results.

Cross-operations require that both matrices share the same dimension. Whether it is 2x2, 3x2, 3x3 or 4x4 doesn't matter as long as they are the same for both matrices used by the operation.

Perhaps one of the most common matrix operations is the cross-matrix multiplication. We'll start with it to demonstrate basic principles.

Multiplication

When we multiply a matrix, we cross-multiply each entry in one matrix by an entry in another matrix in consecutive order:

```
a b c           j k l
d e f     x     m n o
g h i           p q r
```

The result of any cross-matrix operation is a new matrix sharing the same dimension. In this example, the resulting matrix would consist of the following calculations:

```
a*j   b*k   c*l
d*m   e*n   f*o
g*p   h*q   i*r
```

That's the common idea. Simply multiply all items at the same location in each matrix. The result is a new 3x3 matrix containing cross-multiplied values.

Matrices are often multiplied by a single vertex. But the principle stays the same, we just have less operations to perform. Let's try this out with an actual data set that we'll come across in a real-world scenario, where we're multiplying an identity matrix by some 3D vertex containing only 3 values (it's x, y and z coordinate):

```
1 0 0          x    =    1*x    =    x
0 1 0    x     y    =    1*y    =    y
0 0 1          z    =    1*z    =    z
```

On the left hand side we have what is known as the identity matrix. You may have heard of it from working with OpenGL. The identity matrix consists of all 1's. After performing multiplication with the identity matrix we retain the original value.

On the right hand side we have our Model matrix representing the 3D object's X, Y and Z coordinates. Note that in most cases this operation occurs on an entire 3D model. And this is why matrices are efficient. This multiplication will happen for each vertex on the model regardless of how many vertices a model consists of.

Now that was just the identity matrix. It's pretty boring. It doesn't do anything.

Just for the purpose of practicing let's make our own matrix. First, let's recall that the projection matrix can be represented by the math we used for the starfield demo in the previous section of this chapter:

this.x2d = ScreenWidth * this.x / this.z + (ScreenWidth / 2);
this.y2d = ScreenHeight * this.y / this.z + (ScreenHeight / 2);

Now, our matrix representation of this formula will be a little different. We can't just plug in these values and have a projection matrix. This is due to the fact that the actual camera projection in determined by a slightly more complex set of trigonometric functions.

In fact, when we created the starfield, we cheated a lot by skipping worrying about near and far clipping planes, field of view angle (or the angle of view) and camera scaling factor.

Also recall that we had to divide the x coordinate by screen ratio (height / width) to make the objects in the view proportional to the screen without an odd skewing effect. This effect was created by the fact that our screen is not square. Had it been, we could avoid this calculation altogether.

Tangent Metamorphosis Into Camera's View Matrix

We will now, for the first time, factor in the FOV (field of view) into our camera projection calculation. We are not changing anything. We're looking at the same thing from a different angle. The tangent angle.

In order to do this we need to introduce the tangent formula into equation. This is just a trigonometrical way of rewriting our starfield projection calculation.

Tangents work with triangles that have a 90 degree angle. But our camera viewing angle can be anything we want. How do we deal with this problem?

By simply dividing any angle by 2 we can ensure that it will be part of a 90-degree triangle. Still don't believe me? Take a look at this diagram I created (see illustration on next page.)

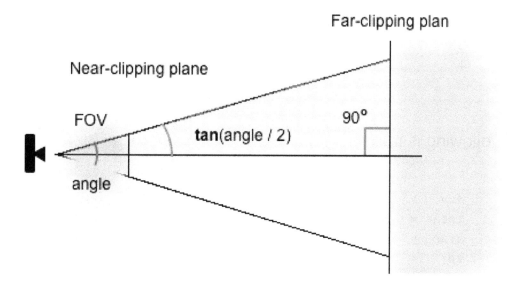

Defining our camera perspective using the tangent is important because instead of taking a wild guess, we can now choose the viewing angle of our camera lens. In normal circumstance it can range from 45 to 90 degrees.

Instead of relying on the screen width and height we will now rely on the camera's viewing angle or FOV. It's just an intuitive way to base our camera projection on.

Having said this, introducing the camera lens matrix calculation or camera's View matrix:

$$1 / tan(fov/ 2)$$

Literally coming from this point of view we can construct the following 4x4 projection matrix:

```
(1/tan(fov/2))/a    0               0              0
0                   1/tan(fov/2)    0              0
0                   0               -zp/zm         -(2*zfar*znear)/zm
0                   0               -1             0
```

Where following is true:

```
fov   =   camera's viewing angle or "field of view"
znear =   distance from camera lens to near clipping plane
zfar  =   distance from camera lens to far clipping plane
zp    =   zfar + znear
zm    =   zfar - znear
```

And of course… there is "one more thing" that went into this calculation that we haven't talked about yet. The aspect ratio. Perspective projection construction functions usually require the following parameters to be supplied in order to create a unique camera view:

Aspect Ratio:
The width / height of the screen represented by a single number.

Field of View:
The field of view angle. Common examples: 45, 90.

Near Clipping Plane:
Distance from camera lens to near clipping plane.

Far Clipping Plane:
Distance from camera lens to far clipping plane.

This way we are no longer tied to the limitation of our simplified Starfield demo earlier in the book. This is a solid representation of our

3D camera that gives us various levels of control over its field of view and aspect ratio.

And finally, here is what our camera model looks like from above looking down the Y axis.

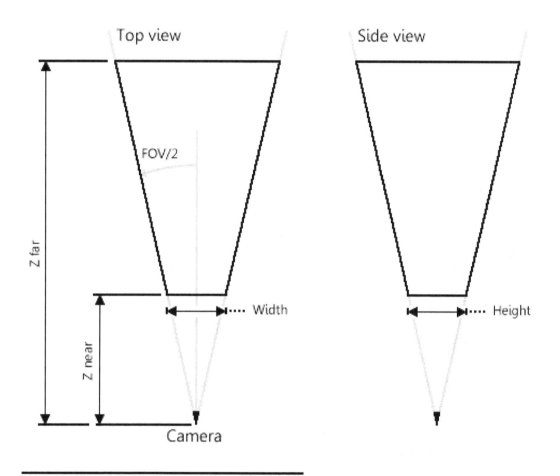

- By default width and height have a range of [-1, 1]
    - Using an Aspect Ratio will changes these ranges
- Setting a bigger Field Of View will make the end of the frustum larger
- Anything before the Z near and after the Z far value will get discarded as well

Diagram courtesy of wiki.lwjgl.org

I hope that preceding explanations have cleared that fog and provided enough material to start experimenting with being a cameraman in games or applications written by yourself.

As we continue moving forward, in further examples presented in this book we will take a look at how this knowledge can be used in practice to do some interesting things.

In fact, the principles and math behind them are so simple. It's just a matter of focusing on the right thing. If our patience is tested by them, then how much more impatient would we be when we study advanced subjects that require far more mental endurance than this?

Other Common Matrix Operations

Although I tried my best to explain the gritty details of matrix calculations and their use in 3D computer graphics, I've purposely included a complicated matrix operation first. But I don't want you to run scared thinking all matrix operations include crazy trigonometry and tangent math.

In fact, to conclude our discussion let's take a look at these other common, yet simple matrix operations. We've already seen what matrices do. Adding simple examples now we can solidify our knowledge of how they are used in general so we can finally put an end on the subject.

We've spoken of this earlier in the book. Other than the projection view matrix the two other common operations are translation and rotation. Yet, another is a scale operation. It's used when you want your camera to imitate the zoom effect often seen in film. We'll take a look at all three in a moment.

Local and World Coordinate System

Before we move on I briefly have to mention here that matrix operations are independent of the coordinate system in which they are used. This will be demonstrated in our first example where we will translate and rotate a sphere around its own local coordinate system.

When translating a model in local coordinate system you are pushing it off center. When you are translating a model in world coordinate system it remains "mounted" to its own center, but movement occurs only in world space.

Again we see this relative duality between operations in 3D space and the models within it. However, in this case, it's something to be mindful of. Local and world coordinate transforms do not produce the same results when combined with rotation. Because of one important detail.

I'll start with rotation for one simple reason. When thinking about transforming 3D coordinates in local space of a model, you must train yourself to usually think about performing rotation first before translation. Here order matters because changing it will produce significantly varied results.

Demonstration of the importance of transformation order.
Sphere on the left ends up being in a different place than sphere on the right.
All because two transformations (exactly the same ones) were done in a different order.

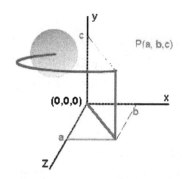

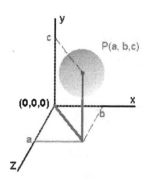

First move (indicated in red lines)
then rotate around Y (blue curve)

First rotate (no visual effect on sphere)
then move to a position (red line)

Importance of transformation order in WebGL, represented using a visual diagram. How order of moving or rotating the model first affects the final result. Part of model transformation tutorial diagram.

Assuming that the sphere is originally located at (x=0,y=0,z=0) in local space, if we first translate it (in local space) and then rotate (in local space) the sphere will end up at a location shown in the diagram, off its own center.

This is exactly the problem with translating and only then rotating, when animating a model. Notice also that both translation and rotation here take place in model's local space. Of course, we could move the model in world space, and then rotate it in local space without problem but this example is shown to demonstrate that there is a difference when both operations take place in space local to the model itself (the coordinate system which was used while construction of the model when it was created in Blender around x=0, y=0 and z=0 point).

However, rotating the sphere around its own center first and only then moving it produces accurate results. Still, this is ambiguous. In other words it's relative to what you wish to accomplish with your transformations.It's just something to be mindful of.

Rotation Matrix

The rotation matrix consists of 3 separate matrices. Each axis has its own rotation matrix. But scaling and translation of any object are performed only using one matrix per operation inclusive of all axis at the same time.

This means, every time you rotate an object you have to choose which axis it will be rotated around first. Here order of operations also matters and will produce different results if rotations are performed in a specific sequence around each axis.

It might come as a surprise that if you've read all the way up to this point in the book, you have already implemented (or seen implementation of) the rotation matrix around Z axis. We performed that operation using raw math in Starfield demo when we made the incoming star particles rotate around Z.

Let us recall the actual formula:

var angle = this.angle;

this.x = this.x * Math.cos(angle) - this.y * Math.sin(angle);
this.y = this.y * Math.cos(angle) + this.x * Math.sin(angle);

Provided angle stored in variable angle we can calculate the position of a given vertex on a particular axis. In the Starfield demo we rotated around Z. But to "switch axis" we simply have to switch either X, Y or Z with one another. There are only 3 possible combinations.

We're already familiar with that fact that a rotation matrix uses the common trigonometry formulas cos and sin, the formulas we've already seen implemented in Starfield example. Now let's make another metamorphosis. This time from our basic math to matrix implementation.

Rotation Around Z-axis

```
cos(angle)  -sin(angle)  0          0
sin(angle)   cos(angle)  0          0
0            0           1          0
0            0           0          1
```

Rotation Around X-axis

```
1          0              0            0
0          cos(angle)    -sin(angle)   0
0          sin(angle)     cos(angle)   0
0          0              0            1
```

Rotation Around Y-axis

```
cos(angle)   0          sin(angle)   0
0            1          0            0
-sin(angle)  0          cos(angle)   0
0            0          0            1
```

Similarly, the scale and translation matrices are shown below:

Translation Matrix

```
1     0     0     X
0     1     0     Y
0     0     1     Z
0     0     0     1
```

Scale Matrix

```
X     0     0     0
0     Y     0     0
0     0     Z     0
0     0     0     1
```

That's what translation, scale and 3 rotation matrices look like.

At this point we've taken a look at calculations behind some of the most common 3D transformations. We've represented them by simple mathematical equations. And we've also taken a look at their equivalent form in matrix format.

We will be using these matrices throughout the book to accomplish transformations.

Using a 3D Matrix JavaScript Library

You could definitely write your own matrix library containing all of these operations. Matrices could be made up of linear arrays treated as multidimensional in principle. And while it's a fun exercise that will help you solidify your knowledge it also takes time.

However, I wouldn't want to write out every single matrix operation in this book to help save space. The purpose of this section is to demonstrate how we can use our new knowledge of matrices in practice using an existing matrix library.

This will help us with examples later in this book to actually get something done in our WebGL JavaScript program as we're slowly parsing through the theory and coming closer to that point.

Matrix Libraries And Where To Get One

There are quite a few JavaScript matrix libraries out there. Not all of them produce optimal performance. Khronos Group, the creators of OpenGL and WebGL recommend CanvasMatrix and not without a good reason. CanvasMatrix is one of the fastest matrix libraries for

JavaScript. And that's what we will use. It also has simple syntax. Exactly what we need to match the style of tutorials in this book.

To check out other matrix libraries and their benchmark calculations visit the following link:

http://stepheneb.github.io/webgl-matrix-benchmarks/
matrix_benchmark.html

Matrix Library Examples

Simply download CanvasMatrix from its GitHub location and included it in your webpage using SCRIPT tags. And we're ready to start using it.

We will pass matrices generated by CanvasMatrix directly into our shader. The shader will modify the viewing angle of the camera, or rotation and position of the model based on the transformations we specified in these matrices.

Matrices are also used to represent the camera view cone dimensions. We'll talk about this in more detail when we get to the camera chapters. For now, let's take a look at the most common matrix operations and how they are constructed using CanvasMatrix library.

First include CanvasMatrix in your page:

```
<script src = 'http://www.tigrisgames.com/fx/matrix.js'></script>
```

The original file name of the library was CanvasMatrix.js but I renamed it to matrix.js

Let's create some matrices representing various things that games use a lot for moving objects around. It's just a simple example. We will be creating matrices within our rendering loop on the go and passing them into our currently selected shader.

The matrix class in CanvasMatrix library is called CanvasMatrix4. This means we will be instantiating new objects from this class whenever we need to create a new matrix. But we want to do this outside of the main rendering loop, so we don't end up recreating it in memory more than once.

Inside the rendering loop, however, we are free to modify the matrix and send it dynamically into the shader. This gives us control over translation and rotation of the model.

```
// Use our standard shader program for rendering this triangle
gl.useProgram( Shader.textureMapProgram );

// Create storage for our matrices
var Projection = new CanvasMatrix4();
var ModelView = new CanvasMatrix4();

var model_Y_angle = 0;

// Start main drawing loop
var T = setInterval(function() {

    if (!gl)
        return;

    model_Y_angle += 1.1;

    // Create WebGL canvas
    gl.clearColor(0.0, 0.0, 0.0, 1.0);
```

```
gl.clear(gl.COLOR_BUFFER_BIT);

// Set active texture to pass into the shader
gl.activeTexture(gl.TEXTURE0);
gl.bindTexture(gl.TEXTURE_2D, road.texture);

gl.uniform1i(gl.getUniformLocation(
      Shader.textureMapProgram, 'image'),0);

// Size of our canvas
var width = 800;
var height = 500;

// Create camera perspective matrix
Projection.makeIdentity();
Projection.perspective(45, width / height, 0.05, 1000);

gl.uniformMatrix4fv(
    gl.getUniformLocation(Shader.textureMapProgram, "Projection"),
    false,
    Projection.getAsFloat32Array());

// Generate model-view matrix
var x = 0
var y = 0;
var z =-5;

var scale = 1.0;

ModelView.makeIdentity();
ModelView.scale(scale, scale, scale);
ModelView.rotate(model_Y_angle, 0, 1, 0);
ModelView.translate(x, y, z);
```

```
gl.uniformMatrix4fv(
    gl.getUniformLocation(
        Shader.textureMapProgram, "ModelView"),
    false,
    ModelView.getAsFloat32Array());

// Draw the model
gl.drawElements(gl.TRIANGLES,
    indices.length, gl.UNSIGNED_SHORT, 0);
});
```

This is an update to the main drawing loop, which will also be explained a bit later in the book.

It assumes Shader.textureMapProgram is loaded into our main Shader object. Shaders are explained in detail later in the book as well. So, if you don't understand parts of this code, you will stumble across them in the next section on shaders. I just had to show some kind of a practical example. But shaders and matrices always work together, so I had no choice but to demonstrate it ahead of time.

Just refer to this example for now whenever the time is right to start translating your model in 3D space or rotate it around one of its 3 axis.

The code is self-explanatory. First, we created Projection and ModelView matrices. The theory behind them has been explained throughout this whole chapter in great detail.

Then, we used CanvasMatrix to set scale, rotation and translation 3D transforms to modify final appearance of the model. In particular, we didn't do anything other than rotate it around its Y axis by a value that changes by 1.0 degree on each animation frame. This rotates the model around its Y axis. But you can include other axis as well to create a wobbly effect.

Conclusion

As we have just seen Matrix operations help us "close in" on the calculation itself without thinking about each vertex individually. Matrices help us accomplish so much without worrying about the details.

We've learned that there is a set of predetermined matrices common to 3D graphics which are the View, Model and Projection matrices. The structure of these matrices will never change. And we often don't need to invent m(any) other matrices ourselves.

But there are also matrices for rotation, translation and scaling that are of equal importance. These are responsible for object animation in 3D space. Even complex frame-based animation, or 3D "bone" based animation are all using these principles.

We've also taken a brief look at a JavaScript matrix library. Why rewrite a library that already exists? We've done our dues actually understanding the principles behind matrices. You could still write one but chances are it'll look exactly or nearly the same as what's already done.

From now on we will use matrix operations as tools to gain control over rendering and animating our 3D world. Sort of like using a remote control to manipulate the model knowing it is already pre-made and tailored to be used for achieving a particular transformation effect in 3D space.

Not surprisingly, the same exact principle is at work in shader programming. Where we operate on each fragment individually, writing the GLSL program once, which will be executed on every fragment in a 3D primitive. And consequently on the primitives that make up the rest of our 3D model consisting of however many fragments.

Together, matrix operations and our shader program form a fundamental building block of rendering and animating 3D graphics on the screen in a projection view that matches the size of the screen no matter what it is without distortion, using aspect ratio correction.

Now that we have a pretty decent grasp on matrices we're ready to do an investigation of GLSL shaders. It will bring us even closer to our goal of ultimately creating a simple game using WebGL toward the end of the book. Even though we're still far from getting half way through.

Gem 6 - Simple Shader Example

We've briefly taken a look at shaders in the past chapters. Based on how this book is organized, now is the right time to learn how to use them.

Let's consider one of the absolutely most basic vertex and fragment shader pair, listed below:

We always start with the vertex shader. Recall from previous chapters that values that appear in "out" variables will actually be intercepted by the fragment shader and picked up as "in" values on the other end in the pipeline.

Simple Vertex Shader

```
layout (location = 0) in vec3 position;
layout (location = 1) in vec3 rgb_in;

out vec3 rgb;

uniform mat4 Model;
uniform mat4 View;
uniform mat4 Projection;

void main() {
    gl_Position = Projection * View * Model * vec4(position, 1.0);
    rgb = rgb_in;
}
```

Notice that main does not have a return value. It only takes specifying a variable using the out keyword to ensure that it will be passed along to the fragment shader once main() function finishes executing. Then, simply assign the value from within the main function and you're done.

For this reason, the out values are usually calculated as the last step in the function. As long as the variable name is defined using the out keyword you can be sure that it will be passed on to the next step in the pipeline.

Simple Fragment Shader

Surprisingly the fragment shader is even simpler than the vertex shader. That's because all we do here is receive the fragment color passed from rgb variable from the vertex shader.

```
in vec3 rgb;

out vec4 color;

void main()
{
    color = vec4(rgb.r, rgb.g, rgb.b,  1.0);
}
```

Here you will see that we're once again using an "out" variable color. But this time the fragment shader sends it out to the actual drawing buffer, usually created and bound in our WebGL JavaScript application. This will be shown in the next chapter when we learn how to load shaders from files.

Notice that **vec3** value rgb that was received from vertex shader contains 3 properties representing the color triplet: r, g, b. We can use them individually and even perform mathematical operations on them to somehow distort or change the original color. And this is how the fragment shader gains control over the pixel data of each individual fragment. But you could have use your own colors here, regardless of what crossed over from the vertex shader in out variable.

What's important to understand here is that the fragment shader singles out each individual pixel. In other words, the actual looping mechanism for the whole area of the screen is outside of our control. It takes a bit of time to get used to this, but the brilliance of fragment shader is in its limitation. It singles out only what's important. Surprisingly, this provides enough horsepower to achieve pretty much any effect we can think of without hindering creativity.

For now, let's consider this simple example of using this shader pair to actually draw something on the screen. In this case, we'll simply draw a single point and later on use the same shader pair to draw more complex shapes like lines and polygons.

Shaders In a String

Before we move forward, I need to mention one peculiar thing about JavaScript language and the way it defines string literals. Ideally, shader programs should be located in separate files, for example myshader.vs and myshader.frag for the vertex and fragment pair respectively. And then we would naturally load them into our program as string variables. But loading shaders isn't until next chapter of the book. Until then we will use regular string variables to store the GLSL source code for each shader in the pair.

In EcmaScript 5 specification of JavaScript language, which has been available since the dawn of time, we have to add strings up with the + sign as follows:

```
// Entire source code on one line
var shader = "void main() { int a = 1; int b = 2; }";
```

```
// Same source code with linebreaks for added clarity
var shader = "void main() {\n" +
"    int a = 1;\n" +
"    int b = 2;\n" +
"}";
```

Notice in second example we're also using the cumbersome \n to indicate line breaks within our GLSL program, in addition to the " and + characters. This is optional. But, it looks a lot more complicated than it can be.

We can conclude that since we are writing GLSL code inside a string, things can get a little quirky. As of 2017 most browsers should support latest version of JavaScript called EcmaScript 6 which actually provides a simpler way to handle this situation using backtick quotes:

```
// Use backticking for maximum clarity when it comes
// to JavaScript string literals
var shader = `
void main() {
    int a = 1;
    int b = 2;
}`;
```

If you ever worked with long multi-line strings in JavaScript using the + and " megalomania you will know that backticking is a heavenly way of writing GLSL in JavaScript. If your browser supports EcmaScript 6, then you should definitely adopt this style instead.

But there is yet another way of specifying shaders in a JavaScript application. Traditional script tags can be used with x-fragment and x-vertex types made specifically for this purpose.

```
<script id = "shader-vs" type = "x-shader/x-fragment">
    // Your vertex shader source goes here
</script>

<script id = "shader-fs" type = "x-shader/x-vertex">
    // Your fragment shader source
</script>
```

You can simply read the contents of each tag by ID that was assigned to it and use that as the source string for your shader.

Initializing Shader Program

Writing shader source code and putting it into a string isn't enough. We must also initialize our shaders. And then we must create a shader program which combines the vertex and fragment pair. This program must then be linked and selected.

Selecting the linked program that contains our compiled shaders (which we've done in a previous step) will make it current default program that will be passed to the drawing function. Once selected, it is assumed to remain selected until another shader program is chosen. For simple examples like the one you will see in this chapter, you don't have to select the shader program on every animation frame, just once during initialization.

Multiple Shader Programs

Only one shader program can be selected at a time. Switching shader programs during the same animation frame has the potential of slowing down performance of your application. For this reason switching shader programs should be carefully considered. Each shader set normally represents a material.

Your 3D application should be planned in such way so that the shader program switching is led to a minimum. The shading program should switch between materials, not type (player, enemy, world). This leads to ordering your model rendering process by material rather than type.

For example, first you would switch on the shader program responsible for drawing all metallic materials across all models. After that you would switch on the glass shader and render elements in all models that are made out of glass. Finally you might want to switch on the tree bark shader to render the forest and so on.

Drawing a Point

For each material type you should have a separate shader. Later on we'll take a look at how to create more striking 3D models. In this simple example we're going to be using a very simple shader capable of rendering points on the screen and determining their size.

Let's do that right now by creating a new function InitializeShader that takes 3 parameters:

1. The **gl** context object
2. Source code string for the vertex shader
3. Source code string for the fragment shader

```
function InitializeShader(gl, source_vs, source_frag)
{
    // Create shader objects
    var shader_vs = gl.createShader(gl.VERTEX_SHADER);
    var shader_frag = gl.createShader(gl.FRAGMENT_SHADER);

    // Link created shaders to source code
    gl.shaderSource(shader_vs, source_vs);
    gl.shaderSource(shader_frag, source_frag);

    // Compile our shader pair
    gl.compileShader(shader_vs);
    gl.compileShader(shader_frag);

    // Check compilation status of vertex shader
    if (!gl.getShaderParameter(shader_vs, gl.COMPILE_STATUS)) {
```

```
        alert("An error occurred compiling the vertex shader: " +
            gl.getShaderInfoLog(shader_vs));
        return false;
    }

    // Check compilation status of fragment shader
    if (!gl.getShaderParameter(shader_frag, gl.COMPILE_STATUS)
    {
        alert("An error occurred compiling the shaders: " +
            gl.getShaderInfoLog(shader_frag));
        return false;
    }

    // Create shader program consisting of shader pair
    var program = gl.createProgram();

    // Attach shaders to the program
    gl.attachShader(program, shader_vs);
    gl.attachShader(program, shader_frag);

    // Link the program
    gl.linkProgram(program);

    // Return the linked program object
    return program;
}
```

Let's see what's going on here.

gl.createShader - First we have to actually create the shader object in memory. At this point, it's just a memory placeholder. This operation is done for both shaders passed into the InitializeShaders function.

gl.shaderSource - Now that we have allocated some memory space for our shaders, we need to populate it with actual source code. We're simply using the shader strings from our earlier discussion here for each one of the shaders.

gl.compileShader - The source code that was linked to the shader object now needs to be compiled. And if there are no source code errors, this function will succeed.

gl.getShaderParameter - This function is used to ensure that the shader has been successfully compiled. This is critical for finalizing our shader objects. Unless we receive the green light from this function, we cannot proceed further to creating actual shader program.

gl.createProgram - We'll create one singular shader program out of the vertex and fragment pair that was just compiled in the previous step. This makes it easy to switch this program on and off in the future.

If only one shader program is present it should be switched on at least once during the application initialization process. Which is what we're accomplishing in InitializeShader function which always enables the last shader you passed to it as the default shader program. So if you have multiple shaders keep this in mind, and pay attention to which shader program is currently enabled.

gl.attachShader - This function helps us attach the precompiled shader pair to the actual program. Whenever the program is switched on, it will engage the shader source code you've passed on to InitializeShader function.

gl.linkProgram - We now link the program containing our shaders. This is a required step. If you have more than one shader, each one must be initialized and linked individually. This is what finalizes creation of your shader program and stores it in memory for later use.

Below I'm presenting a working JavaScript application that uses what we now know about shaders to render a single point on the screen.

It's a simple program that demonstrates everything we have learned thus far.

```
// Create global canvas and gl objects
var canvas = document.getElementById('gl');
var gl = GetWebGLContext(canvas);

if (!gl) {
    console.log('Failed to set up WebGL.');
} else {

    // WebGL is initialized - Let's make our shader pair
    var vertex_shader = `
      void main() {
          gl_Position = vec4(0.0, 0.0, 0.0, 1);
          gl_PointSize = 10.0;
      }`;

    var fragment_shader = `
      void main() {
          gl_FragColor = vec4(1.0, 0.0, 0.0, 1.0); // Red
      }`;

      // The shader pair above is designed to draw
      // a single red point at [x=0, y=0, z=0] 10 pixels in size
      // which will appear right in the middle of the canvas

      var program = null;
```

```
program = InitializeShader(
    gl, vertex_shader, fragment_shader );

// Initialize shader program
if ( !program )

    alert('Failed to initialize shaders.');

else {

    // The program must be selected
    gl.useProgram( program );

    // Clear screen with a dark gray color
    gl.clearColor(0.1, 0.1, 0.1, 1.0);
    gl.clear(gl.COLOR_BUFFER_BIT);

        // Draw the point using currently selected shader program
        gl.drawArrays(gl.POINTS, 0, 1);
    }
}
```

Note the addition of the vertex and fragment shaders and the initialization process using the new InitializeShader function. If the program is valid WebGL shader object, we passed the final initialization test and ready to draw the vertex data. In this case it's just a point.

gl.useProgram - Finally, we must tell WebGL that we are going to select or "use" this program we just created and initialized. Only one shader program can be in use at a time.

Drawing in WebGL is accomplished using the gl.drawArrays function. It assumes that currently selected shader program will be used. So our shader program currently set to be in use will be automatically executed for rendering vertex data during this call. You don't have to pass the shader program itself to drawArrays function.

The function takes the type of primitive to be rendered as. In this case our shader supports a static point in the middle of the screen using hard-coded coordinates [x=0, y=0, z=0]. This is also why we are passing gl.POINTS rendering type to gl.drawArrays.

Other flags can be used to choose the type of primitive to draw from the vertex data set:

POINTS
Draw points

LINES
Draw lines

LINE_STRIP
Line strips are vertices connected by lines

LINE_LOOP
A self-closing line sequence

TRIANGLES
Draws a triangle from a set of 3 vertices

TRIANGLE_STRIP
Can draw two triangles from a set of 4 vertices as a strip

TRIANGLE_FAN
Draws a triangle fan where first vertice is always the center

Each flag responds to the number of vertices passed into the vertex shader. Each one assumes a minimum number of vertices. Ideally, the number of all vertices supplied should be divisible by that number. In this example we don't have to worry about that because we're drawing a point.

However in other cases for example, if you only pass two vertices to the shader and try to render it with TRIANGLES flag, nothing will be displayed on the screen because a triangle primitive requires 3 vertices.

Contrary to this, if you switch the flag to LINES, a line will be drawn between the two passed vertices. Depending on the flag type you can produce different representations of your vertex data. We'll discuss how to pass multiple vertices to our shader shortly.

But first, I think it's a good time to create a better and more convenient way for managing multiple shaders. Eventually, we will need to use more than one, and you simply don't want to hardcode them without having some kind of a management system.

The next chapter is all about keeping shaders organized so they're easy to create, access, and select during the animation frame of your program. Examples that will be shown in the next chapter are not the only ways for managing shaders in JavaScript. But our focus is not on choosing which JavaScript data structures are best for this purpose. Instead, we'll focus on the fact that at this point we simply need some kind of basic means to keep things organized.

Gem 7 - Organizing Shaders

In the previous chapter we've talked about creating and initializing shaders from vertex and fragment pairs. But doing this every time we want to draw a 3D model can create overhead. We really don't want to write out shaders in string format before each call to gl.drawArrays function.

In this section we'll take a look at how we can organize our shader programs a bit better. Once your WebGL application gets complex enough you will want to implement some sort of a way to manage your shader programs. This way it's easy to turn them on and off on demand before performing the drawing operations. For example, for switching between drawing different material types in your rendering loop.

Switching shaders per animation frame comes at a price. We should try to limit shader-switching operations using the gl.useProgram command to a minimum, if and where possible.

But there is one trick you can use. You can always write a shader program that changes its rendering operation (using an if-statement inside its main() function) based on a flag you pass to it as an attribute variable.

This sometimes can be advantageous, because you can make one shader program that can create different effects based on what type of flags are passed to it, effectively eliminating an unnecessary shader switch operation within the render frame function itself.

But you have to be careful here because there are special cases where this isn't always going to create massive performance gains. This will depend on what you are trying to do, the number of materials contained by your model composition and various other factors determined by the design of your engine.

Creating Shader Program Manager

Let us create a JavaScript object that will contain a handle for each shading program that will be available throughout our WebGL application. This way we can always access the main Shader manager class, and pull the program object out whenever we need to use one.

By doing this, we are eliminating the rudimentary shader pair creation process from our main loop. It will be moved out to the initialization stage of our program where it righteously belongs.

First, let's create the ShaderProgramManager class. In EcmaScript 6 specification of JavaScript which is now supported by most browsers we have a new keyword class. It works similar to a class you would create in C++.

```
// Globally available shader programs
class ShaderProgramManager {

  constructor() {

    // Draw static point in the middle
    this.standardProgram = null;

    // Draw point defined by global parameters
    this.globalDrawingProgram = null;

    // Add your own here...
    this.myOwnProgram = null;
```

```
    }
}
```

// Create our global shader program manager "Shader"
var Shader = new ShaderProgramManager();

That's the constructor of the ShaderProgramManager class. In the spirit of the simple drawing example from the previous chapter, I added two shading programs to it as follows:

The standardProgram shader is the one from previous example where we drew a point at x=0,y=0 (in the middle of the canvas.)

The globalDrawingProgram is the shader responsible for drawing a point at a specific X and Y location on the canvas. We will implement it in one of the following chapters to demonstrate how our shader program manager works that takes arbitrary X, Y and Z coordinates.

In the future, if you wish to add more shaders to your program or game, simply add a new handle to the constructor here and the ShaderProgramManager object which was initialized using the new keyword will contain all of your shaders in one place, ready to be passed to gl.useProgram function whenever you need them. Example is shown below:

// Let's switch on our first shader
gl.useProgram(Shader.standardProgram);

// Some code goes here that renders vertices using
Shader.standardProgram

// To use another shader, switch it again:
gl.useProgram(Shader.globalDrawingProgram);

```
// Now draw with Shader.globalDrawingProgram
```

But this is not all. We now need some kind of a mechanism that initializes all of our shaders in one place so they are easier to manage in the future as we continue adding more.

I created a function CreateShaderPrograms to accomplish that. It's listed below:

```
function CreateShaderPrograms( gl ) {

    // Shader 1 - standardProgram
    // Draw point at x = 0, y = 0, z = 0
    var v = `void main() {
        gl_Position = vec4(0.0, 0.0, 0.0, 1); gl_PointSize = 10.0;}`;
    var f = `void main() {
        gl_FragColor = vec4(1.0, 0.0, 0.0, 1.0); }`; // Red

    Shader.standardProgram = InitializeShader(gl, v, f);

    // Shader 2 - standardProgram
    // Draw a point at an arbitrary location,
    // which is determined globally by the JavaScript application
    // This is done via "a_Position" attribute
    v = `attribute vec4 a_Position;
        void main() {
            gl_Position = a_Position; gl_PointSize = 10.0; }`;
    f = `void main() {
            gl_FragColor = vec4(0.0, 1.0, 0.0, 1.0); }`; // Green

    Shader.globalDrawingProgram = InitializeShader(gl, v, f);
}
```

This function takes global WebGL context as gl parameter passed to it. It assumes it is already created and initialized.

Notice that first shader will draw a red point. The second one a green one. This way we can make a distinction when seeing them being drawn on canvas. This is included in the source code demos that comes with this book and fully tested in Chrome browser.

Here we are creating two shaders using vertex and fragment pairs as usual. You will also spot the familiar InitializeShader function each time we need to initialize our shaders. It returns a created shader program based on the source code we pass to it via v and f arguments. If you want to add even more of your own shaders, this is the function to add them to.

Gem 8 - Loading Shaders From <script> Files

Or...initializing WebGL Shaders From <script> Files

I intentionally kept this subject until now. In the earlier chapters we learned that shaders are stored in string format. Most tutorials you would find on the internet load them from the script tag. This avoids having to write your own file loading routines which gives you more time to focus on WebGL programming.

Loading shaders from script tags has also the advantage of avoiding the obscure string concatenation formats provided by JavaScript where the backtick is not available. For example, earlier implementations of JavaScript. Or maybe you simply don't want to store shaders in strings.

In the following example let's create our shader using script tags. All you have to do is open two separate script tags and type in the source code for both vertex and fragment shaders.

I intentionally waited for this subject until now. We've just looked at how to load shaders from strings. First, let's make our vertex shader:

```html
<!-- Standard vertex shader //-->
<script type = "glsl" id = "standard-vs">void main() {
    gl_Position = vec4(0.0, 0.0, 0.0, 1);
    gl_PointSize = 10.0;
  }
</script>
```

And now, our fragment shader:

```html
<!-- Fragment vertex shader //-->
<script type = "glsl" id = "standard-frag">void main() {
    gl_FragColor = vec4(1.0, 0.0, 0.0, 1.0);
  }
</script>
```

As you can see this makes writing shader code a little easier. Just type them in without using + or quote characters at the end of each line.

To actually read the string data from script tags we have to use JavaScript's innerHTML function. I am using the already-familiar example from previous chapters. However, here I highlighted the lines that actually read the shader source code and initialize it.

```javascript
var canvas = null;
var gl = null;
```

```javascript
$( document ).ready(function() {

    var canvas = document.getElementById('gl');

    gl = GetWebGLContext( canvas );

    if (!gl)
        console.log('Failed to set up WebGL.');

    else { // Load a shader from script tags

        var vs = document.getElementById("standard-vs").innerHTML;
        var fs = document.getElementById("standard-frag").innerHTML;

        Shader.standardProgram = InitializeShader(gl, vs, fs);

        gl.useProgram( Shader.standardProgram );
        gl.drawArrays(gl.POINTS, 0, 1);
    }

});
```

And I guess that's really all to it.

In the next chapter we'll take a look at how to create an even more sophisticated shader initialization routine by loading shaders from separate files on a web server.

Gem 9 - Loading Shaders From Files

Remember that up until now we wrote shaders using backtick strings or script tags. We've written them directly into our application, essentially hard-coding the shader source code.

But your WebGL application by design operates within the realm of the web. Loading shaders from a URL location will be essential for creating a flexible system. In this chapter we will discover how this can be accomplished.

JavaScript itself is a front-end language and has little to do with back-end operation of your program. However, we can create an HTTP request to a local file on the web server. But there is a small problem. Different browsers handle HTTP requests in different ways. Making writing a cross-browser HTTP request somewhat of a hassle to write.

However, one good alternative of achieving this with cross-browser operation in mind, is to add the jQuery library to your JavaScript project and use it's ajax request method. This ensures that no matter what system someone is viewing your WebGL program, the HTTP request will always succeed, provided there is a live Internet connection.

First, head over to www.jquery.com and download the latest distribution of the library. Save the library file to something like jquery.js (I'm intentionally keeping it simple here) and we're ready to make an Ajax call to the file system on the server.

This is an isolated example explaining how we would do this:

```
<!-- Somewhere in the head tag of your JavaScript application //-->
<head>
    <script src = "jquery.js" type = "text/javascript" />
    <script type = "text/javascript">

        // Load a file "shader.txt" from the web server
        $.ajax( {
            url : "http://localhost/webgl/shader.txt",
```

```
        type : "POST",
      success : function( msg ) {
         // Here, "msg" will contain the source code of shader.txt
      }
  });
  </script>
</head>
```

After running this code we have just downloaded shader.txt file into our application and its source code is now available via the msg variable if our ajax call succeeds.

But how do we actually assign a shader pair to our globally instantiated Shader object that we created in an earlier chapter for better managing our shader programs?

To solve this problem we can chain two Ajax requests one after the other. Let's create a function that loads a pair of shaders into our Shader object:

```
function LoadShader(gl,       // WebGL context object
                    program,  // Shader program
                    vs,       // vertex shader filename
                    fs) {     // fragment shader filename

   // The directory where shaders are
   var ShaderDirectory = "http://localhost/webgl/shaders/";
   var filename_vs = ShaderDirectory + vs;
   var filename_fs = ShaderDirectory + fs;

   // Placeholders for the shader pair
   var v = "";
   var f = "";
```

```javascript
    // Load vertex shader
    $.ajax( {

        url : filename_vs, type : "POST",
        success : function( msg ) {

            v = msg;

            console.log("Vertex shader '" + vs + "' loaded.");

            // Load fragment shader
            $.ajax( {
                url : filename_fs,  type : "POST",
                success : function( msg ) {

                    f = msg;

                    console.log("Fragment shader '" + fs + "' loaded.");

                    // We have a pair, link it into a shader program
                    program = InitializeShader(gl, v, f);
                }
            });
        }
    });
}
```

This function assumes an initialized WebGL context and instantiated
Shader object (our shader manager.) As long as we have them
initialized, we're ready to load our shaders.

Let's upgrade our shader initialization function
CreateShaderPrograms from previous examples to support loading

shaders from a file location on the web (usually our own local web server):

function CreateShaderPrograms(gl) {

  // Shader 1 - standardProgram
  LoadShader(gl, Shader.standardProgram, "v1.txt", "f1.txt");

  // Shader 2 - globalDrawingProgram
  LoadShader(gl, Shader.globalDrawingProgram, "v2.txt", "f2.txt");

}

Now this looks a lot more clean! Our shaders are moved out of our source code and are located at a unique location on our web server where they can be edited separately.

Here you have to pair your shaders by some kind of enumeration system. For example vertex and fragment shaders from the same program can be called v1.txt and f1.txt respectively.

Shaders don't have to be stored in files with extension *.txt

A pair of shaders for rendering water surface could be called water.vs and water.frag

Loading Shaders Asynchronously

Things get a little more complicated when we're reminded that Ajax calls are asynchronous. Unlike loading shaders in a C++ desktop application where source code is available immediately after file reading function returns, the Ajax call takes time to complete, even after the function has been called.

Moreover, Ajax calls that are executed simultaneously are not guaranteed to complete in the order they were executed. This depends on the delays when making an HTTP request.

This adds a not-so convenient assumption to our current WebGL engine build. Right now our main drawing loop assumes that the shaders have finished loading. Which can be sometimes a dangerous thing to assume.

Waiting for Shaders to Load

In the remainder of this chapter, we will write additional code that prevents execution of the main animation loop until we are 100% sure that the shader programs are fully downloaded and initialized.

Dealing with these types of issues is the focus of this source code provided below. Resource loader routines can take a small book in themselves to write about. So I've written a compact piece of code that accomplishes just what we need.

To get started we'll need to achieve the functionality described in following tasks:

    1. Create a function that loads shader pair using Ajax.
    2. Create an event that executes when all shader resources are finished loading.
    3. Do not initialize main animation loop until shader programs are loaded and initialized.

Let's create a "shader" folder in our project in the root directory and prepare our shaders. I saved them to shader.vs and shader.frag filenames that compose one shader program from a Vertex and Fragment shader source code:

shaders
    global.frag
    global.vs
    standard.frag
    standard.vs

Here we have 2 shader programs represented by 4 files. You can add your own.

We can probably write a PHP script that reads all files from the shader directory and builds an array of filenames that represent each. But in this example, we'll simple store them in a custom Array as shown in the following example.

```
// Enumerate shader filenames
var shaders = [
   "standard",        // standard.vs, standard.frag
   "global"           // global.vs, global.frag
];

// Enumerate shader program names
var shader_name = [
   "standardProgram",
   "globalDrawingProgram"
];
```

Here I created shaders array containing "standard" and "global" strings representing file names of our shaders. This assumes that we have a pair of the .vs and .frag files existing in shaders folder with the names listed in shaders array.

The standard.vs and global.vs are the separate files containing vertex shader source code written in GLSL from our previous examples. Same goes for their .frag counterparts. We're simply storing them in files now.

The shader_name array represents the names of the properties in Shader manager object we've also already constructed earlier in this chapter.

Updating LoadShader

We now have to update our LoadShader function. I won't copy it again here to save space. Instead, I'll only show you the parts I modified. In addition, you can get the complete source code from all examples in the book at the URL address mentioned in the intro chapter.

I highlighted in red the parts that were added:

```
function LoadShader(gl,          // WebGL context object
          shaderName            // program name Shader.shaderName
          program,              // Shader program
          vs,                   // vertex shader filename
          fs,                   // fragment shader filename
          index) {              // index
```

Here shaderName is the Shader.shaderName of our shader program we're loading.

In previous examples we've created shaders standardProgram and globalDrawingProgram, they are just properties of the global Shader object containing them. But this function receives them in string format.

There is a reason why we are doing it this way. In JavaScript we cannot pass an object to a function by reference. So instead, we're passing in the string representation of the shader program. Good news is that JavaScript allows us to access object's properties by string name when we're using square brackets as shown in the example below:

```
var a = Shader.standardProgram;      // by property name
var b = Shader["standardProgram"];   // by string name
```

Both a and b variables will link to the same shader program object represented as a property of the global Shader object. It's just a different way to refer to the same thing. But the significance here is that by using the string we can simulate "pass by reference" to a JavaScript function.

Otherwise, if we simply passed Shader.standardProgram to a JavaScript function as an argument, a copy of the object would be created. This isn't what we need. In our case, this means our global Shader.standardProgram would still remain null.

The rest of the mechanism that deals with preventing these errors is explained below (or rather on the next page):

(Have you ever tried editing a book? The diagrams are unpredictably jumpy and you have to figure out how to integrate them into the text without breaking page flow.)

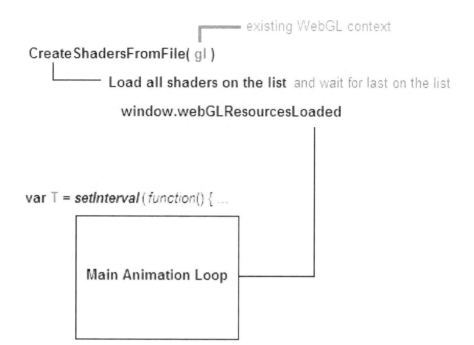

existing WebGL context

CreateShadersFromFile(gl)

Load all shaders on the list and wait for last on the list

window.webGLResourcesLoaded

var T = *setInterval* (*function()* { ...

Main Animation Loop

CreateShadersFromFile - This is our new function that reads shaders from a location on the web. It will utilize our global shader filename (shaders in example above) and shader program name (shader_name array containing program names in string format so we can pass them by reference to our updated LoadShader function) arrays.

Below I'm listing its source code:

```
// Scroll through the list, loading shader pairs
function CreateShadersFromFile( gl ) {
    for (i in shaders)
        LoadShader(gl, shader_name[i],
                shaders[i] + ".vs",
                shaders[i] + ".frag",
            i // pass in the index of the currently loading shader,
```

```
        // this way we can determine when last shader
        // has finished loading
    );
}
```

The function is pretty straightforward. We take our array of shaders and scroll through them, while loading each one using LoadShader function we discussed previously.

But there are a few new updates to the LoadShader function that were added. Let's take a look at them now.

Do you remember how in our original LoadShader function, within the second nested Ajax call, responsible for loading the fragment shader we executed the following command:

```
    // We have a pair, link it into a shader program
    program = InitializeShader(gl, v, f);
```

Well, in our new version, we will switch program variable with the shader program that was passed to the function by name as a string. The only thing we're changing in LoadShaders is that line. Now let's take a look at what code we will replace that line with:

```
Shader[shaderName] = InitializeShader(gl, v, f);

// Is this the last shader in the queue?
// If so, execute "all shaders loaded" event
if (index == shaders.length - 1)
    window.webGLResourcesLoaded();
```

Notice here access by string name via Shader[shaderName].

shaderName - is the argument passed to LoadShaders function.

Finally, we check whether the shader program index that was passed is the index of the last shader on the list.

Because JavaScript arrays store length property automatically using non-0 index (length of 1 actually means there is exactly 1 item stored in the array) we can access it and verify whether this is the last shader by subtracting 1 from index value, which in this case is 0-index based.

If the last shader has finished loading, we invoke a "all shaders loaded" event, which is also a function I wrote. The source code is displayed below:

```
// An event that fires when all shader resources finish loading,
// In this case it's called from CreateShadersFromFile function:
window.webGLResourcesLoaded = function() {

    console.log("webGLResourcesLoaded():" +
            "All webGL shaders have finished loading!");

    // Start main drawing loop
    var T = setInterval(function() {

        if (!gl)
            return;

        // Create WebGL canvas
        gl.clearColor(0.0, 0.0, 0.0, 1.0);
        gl.clear(gl.COLOR_BUFFER_BIT);

        // Draw a point in the middle of the canvas
        DrawPoint( gl );
```

```
        // Draw 100 random points
        for (var i = 0; i < 100; i++)
            DrawPointUsingGlobalParameters( gl,
                -Math.random() + Math.random(),
                -Math.random() + Math.random(), 0.0 );
    });
}
```

Notice that this function is attached to the global window object. This gives us the ability to call it from any callback function. A callback function is one that is called after a process or an event has finished executing.

I am not going to list the entire JavaScript application here. That would create too much clutter in the book. This example is provided in the working source code that comes with this book. Just make sure that you create a "shader" folder in your project and have all the shaders stored there that match the names listed in shaders array.

In this example, you've noticed a new function **DrawPointUsingGlobalParameters**. This function draws using a shader that takes arbitrary location to draw a WebGL primitive of type POINT. But we haven't seen this function before. All of this time we've simply been drawing a single point in the middle of the screen at x=0, y=0, z=0.

That function is taken from a future chapter. However, in the next chapter we will look at the internal mechanics of drawing primitives by passing arbitrary location coordinates. We could do better than drawing a single point in the center of canvas!

This next function we will take a look at that will explain not only that, but also how to map mouse coordinates to the WebGL coordinate system. You see, they are not the same. On a WebGL canvas, the x=0, y=0, z=0 falls right in the middle of the canvas.

In JavaScript 2D canvas, and in general, x=0, y=0 is always in the upper left corner of an HTML element. The function DrawPointAtMousePosition from next chapter will explain how to tackle this situation. Head to the next chapter to learn how to do this!

Cache Busting

In JavaScript we often deal with URLs when loading files asynchronously. If you've never programmed in JavaScript before or never dealt with loading files sometimes you will be faced with a problem that might take up some time to figure out.

Let's say you updated your shader GLSL source code. You reload your program, you even try CTRL-F5. Still you're not seeing the results change. It looks and feels as though your previous version of the shader is still at work. You might be right. The browser saved the last version in cache and is still feeding it to you, even if the source code of the original file has changed.

This will often happen when modifying shader source code. To fight the problem, let's bust the cache. All we have to do is add a version name to the file being loaded. Adding a ?v=1 to any file name will signal the browser to grab a new version rather than looking in the cache.

The problem is if you've used shader.vs?v=1 already then that name will too be stored in cache for future time. How do we solve this? The trick is to change the v=1 to a unique number each time the file is loaded. In JavaScript we can grab UNIX time from built-in Date object by dividing the results of getTime method by 1000.

This is a perfect way to bust cache. Because we are guaranteed a unique version number each time shader loader is invoked. Let's update CreateShadersFromFile function to ensure we always get the latest version of the shader.

```
// Scroll through the list, loading shader pairs
function CreateShadersFromFile( gl ) {
    // generate unique version #
    var cache_Bust = Date.getTime()/100010;
    for (i in shaders)
        LoadShader(gl,
                shader_name[i],
                shaders[i] + ".vs?v=" + cache_Bust,
                shaders[i] + ".frag?v=" + cache_Bust,
            i // pass in the index of the currently loading shader,
                // this way we can determine when last shader
                // has finished loading
        );
}
```

I highlighted the new parts. Notice the creation and inclusion of the new cache_Bust variable.

By the way this technique is the same for loading texture images. I am sure you can figure out how to add this functionality to our current image loader as well by replicating the logic shown in this example.

Conclusion

It looks like in this chapter we have just figured out how to load our shaders from either strings or from separate files stored on the web server. We've also taken a look at how to load the latest version of the source code by busting browser's cache system.

From this point on all future chapters and source code will assume that we understand how that works and use these functions in following examples and tutorials.

Having said this, let's do something interesting. Let's see how with our newly loaded and initialized shader programs we can draw points at arbitrary location on canvas. In particular, let's create a program that draws a point on canvas that follows the mouse cursor.

We will move on to triangles and polygons in a bit. But drawing a point with a WebGL shader will isolate the problem to shader mechanics so we can understand them first, before moving on to more complex primitives.

Gem 10 - Drawing in Space

In this example, to demonstrate specifying vertices with arbitrary values (as opposed to drawing points in the middle of the screen) we will draw a point on canvas located at mouse coordinates in real time.

Determining mouse coordinates is going to be essential to any serious WebGL application anyway and I think it's important to mention it here, even though it is not directly related to writing WebGL applications.

We can create JavaScript events using standard JavaScript function set. However, to ensure cross-browser capabilities we'll use jQuery library once again. It also simplifies the syntax and this can be generally helpful for avoiding unnecessary clutter in the source code.

```
// Draw points at mouse move position
$('#gl').on("mousemove", function( e )
{
    // Clear GL canvas with a solid color
    gl.clearColor(0.0, 0.0, 0.0, 1.0);
    gl.clear(gl.COLOR_BUFFER_BIT);

    // Draw the point at mouse coordinates,
    // intercepted from "e" event object
    DrawPointAtMousePosition( canvas, gl, e );
});
```

Remember once again that <canvas id = "gl"> is our canvas tag. Here we are using jQuery to select the canvas tag by its id "gl" and attach the mousemove event to its JavaScript object.

This means that every time the mouse is found moving over the canvas surface, it will generate an event and the anonymous function(e) will be called each time that is the case.

Here, the "e" parameter is the mouse event object. Consequently it is passed into the new function I wrote called **DrawPointAtMousePosition**, which assumes a globally accessible canvas object, an initialized WebGL context gl.

Let's take a look at the DrawPointAtMousePosition function. Provided that our Shader object is already instantiated and shaders are loaded, it makes its internals incredibly basic and as easy to read as some ancient wisdom or proverb (I just care a lot about source code clarity.)

```
function DrawPointAtMousePosition(canvas, // Our canvas object
                      gl,      // WebGL context
                      e)       // Mouse event object
{
```

```javascript
// Use the program
gl.useProgram( Shader.globalDrawingProgram );

// Get mouse position coordinates from click event object
var x = e.clientX;
var y = e.clientY;
var z = 0;

// Output the coordinates to console
console.log("Mouse x=" + x + ", y=" + y);

// Get a pointer to a_Position attribute within the vertex shader
// Note, variable doesn't have to be called 'a_Position'
var a_Position = gl.getAttribLocation(
        Shader.globalDrawingProgram, 'a_Position');

if (a_Position < 0)
    console.log("Failed to get attribute pointer a_Position.");
else {

    // Translate mouse coordinates to WebGL coordinate system
    var r = e.target.getBoundingClientRect();

    x = ((x - r.left) - canvas.width / 2) / (canvas.width / 2);
    y = (canvas.height / 2 - (y - r.top)) / (canvas.height / 2);

    // Pass point coordinates using global
    // attribute a_Position from our JavaScript program
    gl.vertexAttrib3f(a_Position, x, y, z);

    gl.drawArrays(gl.POINTS, 0, 1);
}
}
```

Because WebGL canvas, like OpenGL has a Cartesian coordinate system and by default the 3D camera view is looking down the -Z axis, points we draw at [0,0,0] position will appear in the middle of the canvas.

In both OpenGL and WebGL software it's not uncommon for values to be represented as ranges between 0.0f - 1.0f. Starting from the middle of the screen, the canvas, no matter what size, is represented as follows:

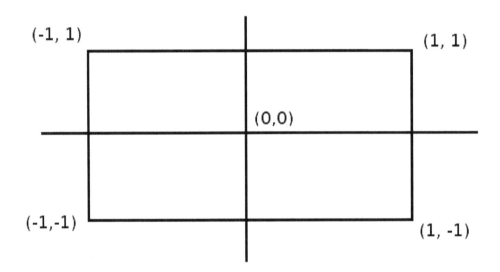

This inherently WebGL coordinate system must be mapped to our canvas from standard HTML element coordinates. The equation for that is shown below:

var newx = ((x - r.left) - canvas.width / 2) / (canvas.width / 2);
var newy = (canvas.height / 2 - (y - r.top)) / (canvas.height / 2);

Here x and y are mouse coordinates on the canvas element. And newx and newy pair are mapped to WebGL. The only thing left is to actually send the coordinates to our vertex shader.

To pass coordinates to a shader we're using a custom a_Position variable here. In order to make this happen, we must receive the attribute memory location from the shader program we created. And then bind an x, y, z location to that memory address.

Binding data to an attribute is done native WebGL function called gl.vertexAttrib3f that stems from the main gl context object. Many WebGL function follow a similar function naming convention. Let's take a brief look at the explanation of why this function is called this way and what it means.

vertexAttrib3f - Here vertex means that we're going to be passing vertex data. Attrib is an abbreviation of the word "attribute". And 3f means that this function requires 3 arguments. In this case it's the x, y and z axis coordinates in floating-point format which is what f in 3f stands for.

These 3 floating point values will be the ones we'll be passing to our new shader program. For simplicity sake I called this shader program globalDrawingProgram. It draws a point at an arbitrary location that was passed to the shader via its attribute a_Position, defined within the vertex shader itself. Its source code is displayed in its entirety below:

The vertex shader of globalDrawingProgram shader:

attribute **vec4** a_Position;

```
void main() {
   gl_Position = a_Position;
   gl_PointSize = 10.0;
}
```

The fragment shader is listed below:

```
void main() {
   gl_FragColor = vec4(0.0, 1.0, 0.0, 1.0);
}
```

The fragment shader requires a 4f value (vec4) and here it's filled out with static green color represented by RGB color as (0.0, 1.0, 0.0) and extra placeholder so that the value won't have to be cast from another type when it enters the shader. (Most common operations in GLSL shaders use vec4 values.)

This is why a_Position within the vertex shader must be defined using vec4 (not vec3, to match 3f coming in from vertexAttrib3f function.)

This way we're only concerned with passing XYZ values (3 variables) into the shader from our JavaScript program. Within the shader it is then automatically cast to a vec4 value which contains 4 values, because it's just the value the shader takes by default.

Changing vec4 a_Position to vec3 a_Position will result in the following shader compilation error:

An error occurred compiling the shaders: ERROR: 0:5 'assign': cannot convert from 'attribute highp 3-component vector of float' to 'Position highp 4-component vector of float'

This is because by default our shader expects a vec4 value. It will convert vec3 to vec4 when needed. Primarily this is because many data structures that make up color (another frequently used data set for passing into shaders) are usually defined using 4 floating point values for R, G, B and A. Where the fourth value A stands for alpha (transparency or strength) of the color.

However, position in 3D space is defined using only 3 coordinates X, Y and Z. The fourth value needs to be padded with pretty much nothing, if you're passing a vertex location to the shader. When we get to matrices later in the book you will see that most matrix operations in WebGL are usually done on 4x4 matrices (rather than 3x3) even for values whose 4th parameter is 0.

This is just standard convention that has been traditionally kept from early days of OpenGL (And even Direct3D) programming. The 4x4 arrays also conveniently represent 16 data parts, which is great news for GPU processors whose machine instructions are designed to operate on data divisible by8.

Gem 11 - 3D Transformations

Transformations are the necessary evil of learning 3D graphics. I know we've already spent a lot of time explaining just how to load shaders in all the different ways. But to draw anything interesting on the screen we need some kind of a basic understanding of how to operate within the coordinate system of a 3D world.

We've gone through a lot so far and things didn't even start to look very exciting yet. This is why I think this is a good place to cover transformation and object movement in 3D space. This will help us to finally draw our first triangle on the screen and prepare us for the following chapters where 3D camera movement, rendering triangles, texture mapping, lighting and shading techniques (such as shadow mapping) will be discussed.

Even lighting and shadows do not always look very impressive on static objects. So before we venture into that territory let's get a good grasp of 3D transformations. There really only a few and they are not burdensome or difficult to understand.

The material in this chapter will help us later when we'll learn how to move objects in 3D space and then add some light to make those objects' shadows move, depending on where our light source is. This will of course create something more realistic than a static colored triangle, which we haven't got to yet!

I want to write about some fundamentals first and then will go into technical stuff like Transformations and Matrices. You don't really need to know the math behind them. I remember learning about transformations from other books and thinking that I don't really understand the complex math behind them, presented in long formulas. If you're someone who loves math, they will probably be fun to delve into. But, we simply want to understand the principles behind them.

What you do need to understand is how they work and to understand the transformation pipeline. That is the order in which transformations are performed which is essential to understanding concepts behind moving the view, the world itself and the objects in the world. Lets see what can possibly be done to an object to change its position in 3D space first.

Translating

An object can be moved (we will use the term translating from now on because this term is more common among 3D programmers) on all 3 axis (X Y and Z) in either negative or positive direction.

An object can also be rotated around the 3 axis. The axis an object can be rotated about are different from the axis it is translated on. An object is usually rotated around its local coordinates and translated along the world coordinates. But it can also be rotated in world coordinates in certain cases. The two types of rotation (local vs world) are often mistaken for one another which results in inaccurate object rotation results.

Scaling

One of other types of 3D transformations is called scaling. Scaling is simply achieved by multiplying all vertices of an object by the amount you want to reduce or increase the size of that object. Just think about this, if a 3D object is built around the x=0, y=0, z=0 local coordinate system, multiplying its vertices should naturally produce a larger object. Scaling can also be used in horizontal only or vertical only dimension to achieve stretching or "shrinking" of the object.

To build more complex objects than just a polygon we would need to have some utility software because it's a huge pain to do it manually by hard coding all vertices manually and highly undesirable.

For this reason and for simplicity's sake in this chapter translation and rotation will be demonstrated on a single triangle. Just think of it as an object. The same rules apply.

Objects after all are made of triangles too, there are just more than one triangle enclosing them. Also I should mention Object (or Model) Composition is a different topic and will be covered in future chapters just before we go into WebGL light model and how light works in general; that way we will be able to see lit, rotating objects rather than just plain boring polygons.

But let's get back to the basic principle at hand. If you can understand this you will easily understand most other transformations. You'll see that transformations that appear complex are simply rotating and moving (on either local or world coordinate system) done in a certain order.

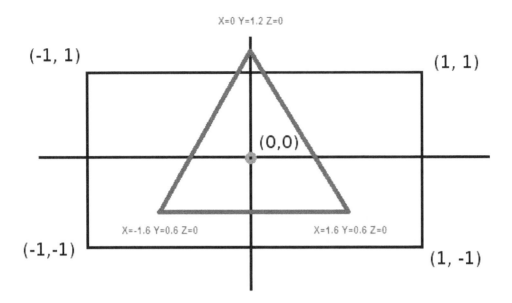

If you're learning 3D graphics for the first time you've been probably just thinking of rendering random triangles anywhere on the screen by suggesting its coordinates. But what makes this triangle different is that it has a center. This is of course, an imaginary center. But it demonstrates the idea that 3D objects are usually constructed around the center of their local coordinate system. This is why when you open Blender, 3DS Max, Maya, Z-Brush, 3D Coat, or other similar software, new objects appear exactly in the middle of the coordinate system.

You see, when you build unique individual 3D models you have to always make sure you build them around the logical center which is located at X=0, Y=0, Z=0 in the object's local coordinate system. If you don't follow this simple rule, your object will not rotate evenly. In addition, later this can introduce a plentitude of other problems.

Here's another example of how an object or a Half-Life 1 model, in this case, is built around its center. I know Half Life 1 is a pretty old game. But I simply love this image because it so clearly represents the idea. Notice the 3 colored lines underneath the monster in the 3D model view. Those lines spread out from the center along the x y and z planes.

As you can see the body of the monster is built around the center. And it's "standing" exactly at the point where all X, Y and Z coordinates equal 0. That's because this is the imaginary point that will be used for collision detection against the ground in the game. This is the general rule behind building models and/or objects.

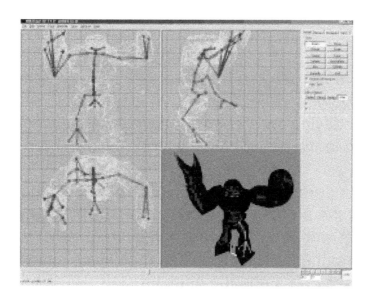

Moving and rotating objects is not the only thing involved in 3D graphics transformations. As I mentioned before you're always viewing the 3D world from your eyes. This is usually referred to as the camera view. The camera can also be rotated and translated so that it would be possible to change your viewpoint. Transformations (moving, rotating, scaling) to your object are done in local coordinate space. But in order to view them on the screen, the camera view matrix is multiplied by the model matrix. We'll get to this a bit later in this book.

Remember that initially, after WebGL perspective is initialized, the camera is located at the origin of the coordinate system, looking down the negative Z space by default. When we think of drawing primitive, we think about drawing them a little further into the screen (maybe about -4.0f on Z axis or so?) so that it would be possible to see them from the camera.

But what if the camera wasn't placed at the origin? What if we moved it to a new location, and gave it a new viewing angle? That leads us to conclusion that our 3D objects will be drawn with respect to the camera position. Which creates another level of complexity for view calculations.

When you move the camera (and this step should always be first, before you move your objects or do any other transformations) you are actually modifying the view by applying the Viewing Transformation to the coordinate system.

It is crucial to understand that when you are moving the camera, what happens is not the actual movement of camera in space. In fact, both the camera movement and the model movement are tied together into the same mathematical formula that gives us simultaneous control over the camera and the object(s).

In both cases, you are in fact modifying the coordinate systems by applying transformations on them. What matters is the end result which makes us think the objects move and the view is moving the way we want them.

So all movement in 3D is based on these theoretical transformations. There are rules to these transformations. Specifically, concerning which transformation should be performed after which in order to produce accurate results. In the following examples I will explain all types of transformations and we'll take a look at when they should be applied!

As complex as transformations can be, WebGL makes your life a lot easier by giving you specific functions to perform movement in 3D space. They are described below. In general you don't even need to know anything about how everything works from the mathematical standpoint as long as you pay close attention to the principles. For this reason this demands additional explanations, which is what follows next.

3D Transformations

3D Transformations are achieved when transformations are applied to the coordinate system in which your camera or model resides. For example when you want to change the camera view, the Viewing Transformation is applied to the camera location and position in 3D space. Camera and other objects are usually placed within what's called the "world coordinate system". This is the global space in which all of your 3D world is rendered. In addition "local coordinate system" pertains to the space in which the 3D model itself resides in.

After a transformation is performed, any time you draw a new object, it is drawn according to the new position which was just modified by that transformation. That's what makes the objects appear to be moving or looked at from a different vantage point in the camera view. The purpose of transformations is to imitate movement of objects or the camera.

There are 4 types of main transformations we will be concerned with. You can even create your own by modifying some of the matrices. The standard transformations have their respective matrix layouts. We shouldn't concern ourselves with them or what they are at this point. In the past, working with OpenGL in "Immediate Mode" has taken care of these operations for us. Later, when VBO-based programming came out, you had to either write your own or use an existing Matrix library, usually written in C or C++.

The Four Transformations

The 4 transformations I will talk about are VIEWING, MODELING, PROJECTION and VIEWPORT transformations. There is a 5th transformation called MODELVIEW but it is really a combination of VIEWING and MODELING transformations which are actually the same as you will see. You just have to multiply them together in the correct order.

Understanding transformations is crucial to writing 3D applications in any environment, including WebGL. But it isn't until later that you will start to use them as your second nature like tools that get certain things done. However, it might take a little time to sink in.

Viewport Transformation

The VIEWPORT transformation is performed to scale the result into the window, it's the least difficult transformation to understand, because WebGL does this automatically for us. It simply stretches the 3D camera of the final view over the <canvas> tag.

If you're familiar with OpenGL Immediate Mode (which is the dinosauric way of programming 3D graphics by now) you will remember having a function for specifying the current matrix which was called glMatrixMode.

It takes a single parameter mode which can be one of the following: GL_MODELVIEW, GL_PROJECTION or GL_TEXTURE. However, in WebGL and most modern OpenGL implementations, we need to supply our own matrix data into the shader.

We've somewhat already done that in the shader chapters, but things get a little more complex as we move forward. But we're not quite there yet.

The Viewing Transformation

The Viewing Transformation specifies location of the viewer or the camera. This transformation should be performed first before any other transformations. All consequent transformations will be based with respect to the vertex manipulation in this step.

Think of it as the main transformation that moves the view (camera) to a certain viewpoint. If you skip this step the camera will remain at the origin looking down the negative Z coordinate because it is transformed to the origin by default, which is its "reset" state.

The Modeling Transformation

The Modeling Transformation is used to modify the position, rotation angle and size of your object (or parts of it) in a scene. Scaling is a type of modeling transformation if you apply it to your object. And if you do, that object will either appear smaller or bigger (depending on the scaling factor) in the view.

Any movement applied to the objects, for instance if you move your monster model from one point to another, is achieved through the modeling transformation; and combined with say, walking animation (which has nothing to do with transformations) will result in a walking monster! Both animation and modeling transformation put together makes a monster appear to be walking.

Frame-based or bone-based animations are advanced subjects and are not the topics of this chapter. Because that is where entire topology of a model is animated using internal levers or "bones" over a timeframe length. However, there is another type of animation in 3D graphics that can be easily achieved by simply rotating an object around one of its axis. Rotating the blades of your helicopter model, for example, can be considered a modeling transformation.

The Modelview Transformation

As a combination of the two, the MODELVIEW transformation requires a little more explanation. The Viewing and the Modeling transformations are really the same in terms of technicality. You see, there is really no difference between moving the view forward in the direction of the objects or moving all the objects backward in the direction of the camera.

The resulting effect is identical. The term modelview indicates that there is no distinction between the modeling and the viewing transformations and the principle behind which transformation it really is, is left to the programmer. So the Modelview Transformation can be used as both viewing or modeling transformation, depending on how it is used.

In a way, one is the reverse-mirror transformation of the other.

The Projection Transformation

As a final step the Projection Transformation is performed. This transformation finalizes what you will see on the screen by establishing the 2D view (based on 3D coordinates of desirably all visible objects' vertices and the camera position) as seen from the current camera view.

The Viewport Transformation

This is by far the easiest concept to understand. Once we have the 2D view of our 3D scene. The Viewport Transformation stretches that view into the OpenGL window.

Once you modified the coordinate system you can place objects on it and they will appear as if they were transformed by whatever operations were originally performed. You can even save the current state of the coordinate system and then retrieve it later on after more transformations are applied and then to use it as a starting point for consequent transformations.

By using this technique you will see that you will be able to place objects at any position and angle you want and you will even be able to draw objects that rotate around other objects that also rotate (simulating orbiting planets for example) around some other objects.

3D Transformation Order

All transformations are consequent. It is up to the programmer to come up with the right order of transformations to achieve a wanted effect. For example, consider a Modeling Transformation of an object. Let's say you have a sphere object built around the center of its local coordinates. The order you perform your Modeling Transformation on the sphere is very important.

Imagine that you first move the sphere left and then rotate it around the Y axis. The outcome is that the sphere will be rotating around an imaginary origin (located at [0, 0, 0]) as if it's a planet rotating around the sun and not around its center because you first displaced the sphere from its center and only then rotated it. Keep in mind that rotation is performed around the center of the given coordinate system.

Now, imagine the same set of actions performed in a different order - first rotation and then movement to the left hand side. The sphere will appear to be rotating around its center at a distance from the center on the coordinate system (because you dislocated it left a little).

Demonstration of the importance of transformation order.
Sphere on the left ends up being in a different place than sphere on the right.
All because two transformations (exactly the same ones) were done in a different order.

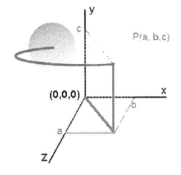

First move (indicated in red lines)
then rotate around Y (blue curve)

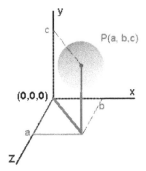

First rotate (no visual effect on sphere)
then move to a position (red line)

Importance of transformation order in OpenGL, represented using a visual diagram. How order of moving or rotating the model first affects the final result. Part of model transformation tutorial diagram.

The functionality of transformations in WebGL is really not that hard to understand even if you're a beginner. And it gets better the more you practice them.

On the other hand, anyone could just learn a function and remember that "that function" rotates an object and "this function" moves an object. That is also acceptable but you don't really learn anything substantial about 3D graphics with that.

That's the reason I included these theoretical explanations here in this chapter.

And now that we know how transformations work, we're ready to start putting them into action. Let's write some code that demonstrates principles covered in this chapter.

Gem 12 - Draw Triangle

I think we've accumulated enough knowledge up to this point to start doing something interesting on the screen. Let's construct a basic primitive out of vertex coordinates. Triangle is the building block of a 3-dimensional model. Let's see what it takes to create and render one on the canvas screen. We will use initialization and shader functions from previous chapters.

Recall how in Gem 8 we found out how to wait for shaders to load before starting the render loop. We used a function we created attached to the root window object called webGLResourcesLoaded.

In this section we will modify the contents of that function with triangle-rendering code. We'll take a look at the process one step at a time given that our shaders are already loaded from either SCRIPT tags or a URL location.

Let's enter the webGLResourcesLoaded function:

```
// An event that fires when all shader resources
// finish loading in CreateShadersFromFile
window.webGLResourcesLoaded = function()
{
```

```
// First, we need to specify actual vertices of the triangle. In WebGL
// we will need two arrays to orchestrate this. The actual vertex array
// vertices and the array indices.
```

```
    console.log("webGLResourcesLoaded(): All webGL shaders have
finished loading!");
```

```
    // Specify triangle vertex data:
    var vertices = [
       -0.0,  0.5, 0.0, // Vertex A (x,y,z)
       -0.5, -0.5, 0.0, // Vertex B (x,y,z)
        0.5, -0.5, 0.0  // Vertex C (x,y,z)
    ];
```

```
    // One index per vertex coordinate
    var indices = [0, 1, 2];
```

The next step is creating buffers for storing both of our shaders. Each shader must be then bound to its respective array buffer gl.ARRAY_BUFFER and gl.ELEMENT_ARRAY_BUFFER flags help us accomplish this.

Once the buffers are bound, we now need to link it to the actual data stored in vertices and indices arrays. This is done by using gl.bufferData function.

Finally, the buffer is unbound. We have to detach the buffer because at this point we're done and we no longer need the buffer object. It was used temporarily only to link up our vertex and index array data to the buffer. Passing null as the second parameter to gl.bufferData will unbind it:

```
// Create buffer objects for storing triangle vertex and index data
var vertexbuffer = gl.createBuffer();
var indexbuffer = gl.createBuffer();

// Bind and create enough room for our data on respective buffers
// Bind it to ARRAY_BUFFER
gl.bindBuffer(gl.ARRAY_BUFFER, vertexbuffer);
// Send our vertex data to the buffer using floating point array
gl.bufferData(gl.ARRAY_BUFFER,
    new Float32Array(vertices), gl.STATIC_DRAW);
// We're done; now we have to unbind the buffer
gl.bindBuffer(gl.ARRAY_BUFFER, null);

// Bind it to ELEMENT_ARRAY_BUFFER
gl.bindBuffer(gl.ELEMENT_ARRAY_BUFFER, indexbuffer);
// Send index (indices) data to this buffer
gl.bufferData(gl.ELEMENT_ARRAY_BUFFER,
    new Uint16Array(indices), gl.STATIC_DRAW);
// We're done; unbind, we no longer need the buffer object
gl.bindBuffer(gl.ELEMENT_ARRAY_BUFFER, null);
```

But now we have to repeat the process for each buffer and rebind them to ARRAY_BUFFER and ELEMENT_ARARY_BUFFER:

```
// Associate shaders with the buffer objects we just created

// Bind our vertex and index buffers to their respective buffer types
gl.bindBuffer(gl.ARRAY_BUFFER, vertexbuffer);
```

```
gl.bindBuffer(gl.ELEMENT_ARRAY_BUFFER, indexbuffer);
```

Assuming Shader.standardProgram has already been loaded, compiled and linked, we will now select it as the default shader program. This way the triangle being rendered will be using the vertex and fragment pair we created in the earlier chapters.

```
// Use our standard shader program for rendering this triangle
gl.useProgram( Shader.standardProgram );
```

Vertex shaders have a value a_Position (although, you can name it anything) which stands for attribute position. This maps the memory location of the vertex arrays we're passing from JavaScript into the shader program.

We're now ready to draw the bridge between our vertex arrays and the shader. This will help us to pass data to the shader dynamically. If it changes in our JavaScript program, it will be automatically updated in the shader. This is accomplished by code that follows:

```
// Get attribute location
var coords = gl.getAttribLocation(
    Shader.standardProgram, "a_Position");

// Pointer to the currently bound VBO (vertex buffer object)
gl.vertexAttribPointer(coords, 3, gl.FLOAT, false, 0, 0);

// Enable it
gl.enableVertexAttribArray(coords);
```

We simply created the coords variable and stored the attribute location in it. Then we passed it to **vertexAttribPointer** function to establish a link between the two in memory.

Finally we must enable this vertex attribute array by calling **enableVertexAttribArray** by passing it our coords variable containing the association.

Congratulations, we have just finished the preliminary setup for rendering a triangle on canvas. I know it was a bit of a handful, but this code is necessary to get started. It would be nice to create separate functions for each process that could be reused later and make the code look cleaner but I kept the examples simple in purpose.

And now we are going to enter the main rendering loop:

```
// Start main drawing loop
var T = setInterval(function() {

   if (!gl)
      return;

   // Create WebGL canvas
   gl.clearColor(0.0, 0.0, 0.0, 1.0);

   gl.clear(gl.COLOR_BUFFER_BIT);

   // Draw triangle
   gl.drawElements(gl.TRIANGLES, indices.length,
gl.UNSIGNED_SHORT,0);

});
```

Here we clear the background with black color and execute gl.drawElements function that ultimately renders the results on the screen.

This is where our indices array is used because drawElements needs us to specify the number of vertices that are stored in vertex array we bound to the vertex array buffer earlier. Luckily JavaScript objects of type Array have a native length property for that.

} // End of window.webGLResourcesLoaded function.

The result of these operations is a white triangle on a black background:

Changing values in vertex array is the key to manipulating its location. Usually, vertex data isn't typed by hand but is loaded from a file in some sort of an object format such as OBJ or PLY. This type of a 3D model can be generated by free software such as Blender and many other popular 3D editing packages.

OBJ models do not contain vertex color data. That's their only downfall. That's okay if you're taking a completely modern approach and will be using "global illumination" for your entire game world rendering where vertex color isn't very meaningful and everything is accomplished within shader logic.

However, chances are your first WebGL game is probably not going to be Mario Kart 8. Instead you probably want ease into gradually building your engine up increasing quality along the way. In this sense, you will probably have to experiment with light using vertex colors.

All this means is that I recommend using PLY format for that. PLY is amazingly great for storing all possibly needed data for your 3D world from vertices, texture coordinates, normal coordinates, and yes… the r,g,b color for each vertex. PLY format can accomplish so much more than OBJ, and surprisingly even the PLY format loader code is simpler to write.

Most beginners however start with OBJ format. Thankfully, in this book we will cover both PLY and OBJ model loaders. But it's up to you which one you want to use in your own projects.

Gem 13 - Vector Class

I wish I could continue talking about the rest of the subjects without having to write any utility JavaScript code before we move forward. But in order to save space in this book by not going on random tangents about subjects that have little to do with WebGL, it appears that it's one of those times where we have to do exactly just that.

All of this is the necessary "peeling of the onion" or most commonly known among programmers as Yak shaving (I hope you have heard this phrase before) process common to programming complex modular systems. It means that we have to grasp a lot of seemingly small or even unrelated concepts in order to progress onto following subjects that depend on them. But by accomplishing one of the parts, we're that much closer to making the whole work as intended.

In this section I will not go into deep mathematical representations of each principle we need to understand at this point. That's simply not the purpose of this section. We'll create a JavaScript class Vector and go over its methods. Meanwhile, the key ideas behind why we even need to worry about this now will be explained.

This Vector class will later be used together with Segment class. Together they will form a library that will help us work with various vector data that's a little too common to both 3D graphics programming and game programming. Unfortunately, there isn't a way around this.

The good news is that it's always easier to learn 3D principles by reducing the problem to 2D. Besides, later in the book we will be making a 2D game in WebGL. And I will give you access to an entire 2D JavaScript library for working with objects in 2D space.

Even though in WebGL we are working with all 3 axis we can set up our camera in such way that would visually represent a 2D plane. And all standard 2D rules would still apply to it.

Again, this is in particular useful for making 2D games. And if you purchased this book in order to find out how to do that (which is a reasonable request because WebGL provides superior performance to the regular HTML5 canvas implementation) then you will be much interested in this library. It will also be included in the GitHub account for the book. Which you should already be able to access via:

https://github.com/gregsidelnikov

For the reason stated above this chapter will introduce you to the Vector library. Several principles covered by the methods of this class can be easily transferred to represent and calculate 3D values by simply adding an extra axis as one of the properties of the class and renaming the class to something like Vector3D. But it's the logic of the actual algorithms that matters.

Let's dive straight into the source code. And then I'll explain what's happening here.

Vector Class

A vector can be added to, subtracted from or multiplied by another vector. As simple as these operations are it's quite surprising how frequently they are used in both 2D and 3D programming.

Let's create a class that we can reuse later in all future examples.

Mathematically, most of the common operations are surprisingly simple.

```
// Vector class (2D only for now)
var Vector = function(_x, _y)
{
  // Vector is defined by two coordinates
  this.x = _x;
  this.y = _y;
```

```javascript
// Add to another vector
this.add = function( vector )
{
    return new Vector(this.x += vector.x, this.y += vector.y);
}


// Subtract another vector from this one
this.subtract = function( vector )
{
    return new Vector(this.x -= vector.x, this.y -= vector.y);
}


// Multiply two vectors
this.multiply = function ( multiplier )
{
    return new Vector(this.x *= multiplier, this.y *= multiplier);
}


// Calculate length of this vector
this.length = function()
{
    return Math.sqrt(this.x * this.x + this.y * this.y);
}


// Calculate the cross product
this.cross = function( vector ) {
    return this.x * vector.y - this.y * vector.x;
}


// Calculate the dot product
this.dot = function( vector ) {
    return this.x * vector.x + this.y * vector.y;
}
};
```

Of course, I didn't want to just dump this vector class on you as a stipped down version of a similar class that deals with 3D vertices. But to explain important principles that all game developers are commonly faced with a lot of the time.

Vector Representation

A vector can be represented by an origin and an end point. However, when programming we want to reduce the memory bandwidth and size if and where possible. For this reason, we will represent our vector by only two coordinates: it's stretch on x and y axis and assume that it is always located at the origin of the coordinate system.

We're not concerned with 3D operations. These same calculations can be performed on a 3D plane as well, just add or juggle around the coordinates.

But why is our 2D vertex determined only by two coordinates? This might appear odd at first. How then would we handle calculations between vectors that are located at arbitrary locations in space? Surprisingly, the origin of each vector is irrelevant in order to complete accurate calculations. That is, these operations are performed on two vectors after they are translated to the same origin. And that's what our class is already tailored for. So this step can be skipped altogether if we're doing it this way. Which, as you may have imagined, will save us a lot of time in the long run. Translating one vector to origin of another just to perform an operation (which more often than not assumes vectors share same origin) on both vectors can become tedious fast.

But we can make our life a bit easier.

This is due to the fact that because each vector is already stored using the assumed "default" positioning at x=0 y=0 coordinate system origin (just add z=0 if working in 3D vectors) translating vectors from those very arbitrary positions in space can be skipped altogether.

So not only do we gain advantages in memory storage but also in reducing complexity of the calculations themselves. When a particular vector operation is performed (addition, subtraction, multiplication, cross or dot product of two vectors) we simply translate the final result to the original location of the vector we started with.

These operations may at first appear meaningless. So what that we are adding vectors? But in reality they are useful when it comes to calculating velocities of objects. And that's just one practical use. Let's take a look at each operation separately.

Adding Vectors

Adding two vectors produces a combination of the two. Here all we are doing is adding x and y coordinates of one vector to another.

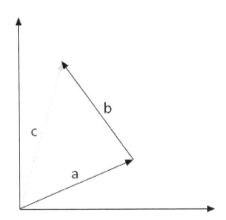

One interpretation of what happens when two vectors are added. Naturally adding one vector at the end of the tip of the first one.

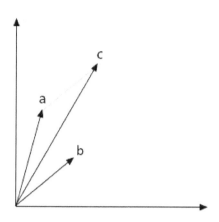

Another interpretation. The difference this time is that we choose to look at both vectors as starting at the origin of coordinate system.

The two examples add two different vectors in each case. So they are distinct from one another. Here, aside from using origin-based coordinates, they are both simply showing two random situations.

The result between adding vector a and vector b is a new vector c. Notice in the example on the right that the convenience lies in having all vectors being defined at the origin of x=0 and y=0. Choosing to interpret vector operations in this way we can store only the end point our JavaScript Vector class, saving memory.

Mathematically we can represent this operation roughly as follows:

```
var a_x = 6;
var a_y = 2;
var b_x = -4;
var b_y = 5;
```

```
var c_x = a_x - b_x;
var c_y = a_y - b_y;
```

The results, from mathematical stand-point, are exactly the same in both cases, regardless of whether we treat the vectors as starting from the origin of coordinate system or at the tip of one of the vectors. Each of the examples could have been calculated to the same end result in each case.

This is just a matter of whether you want to represent your vectors by translating them back to the origin of the coordinate system or not. This is one of the choices we have to make. If we are going to use vectors that start from the origin, we need to assume that this representation will match all vectors we will be working with.

Subtracting Vectors

Similar to addition, except we are subtracting coordinates. The principle is exactly the same:

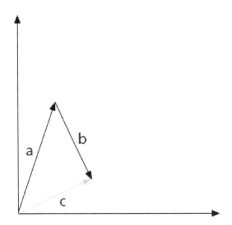

Again, you can think of each vector as starting at center of coordinate system or connected to each other. The result is the same anyway. The difference is that we have a different point of origin. You can convert between the two

Here we are subtracting vector b from vector a. The result is vector c.

Multiply Vectors

Multiplication of two vectors is a bit different because we're not multiplying a vector by another vector. That wouldn't make much sense. Instead, we multiply both vector's coordinates by a single value.

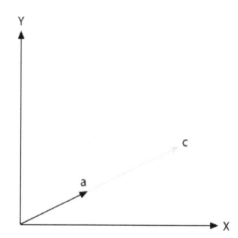

This is scalar multiplication. The resulting vector is one that points in exactly the same direction but becomes longer.

Division

Division of a vector shortens it. It's reverse of scalar multiplication.

Length

Square root is the common operation for determining the length of a vector.

Cross Product

Cross product is used for calculating a so called "normal" vector of another vector. A normal vector is simply a perpendicular line to a given vector. To demonstrate its importance in either 2D or 3D graphics, let's take a look at these diagrams:

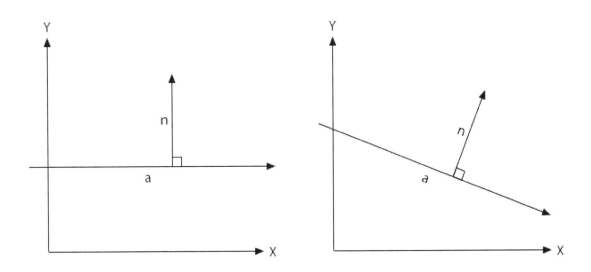

Left side. Starting out with vector a we can create a normal vector c.

Right side. Even after the original vector a is rotated, the normal still points away at a 90 degree angle..

Here, the direction of a vector is complimented by a 90 degree angle. Regardless of whether the original vector was rotated, the normal vector always points directly away from it. This is in particular useful for physics simulations where we need to calculate the angle of reflection when one object collides with another.

Dot Product

The Dot Product is a scalar value (not an angle) and it's calculated by determining the angle between two vectors. In particular, whether that angle is greater or less than 90 degrees. This technique is used to figure out whether two vectors are headed in roughly the same direction, or are pointing away from each other.

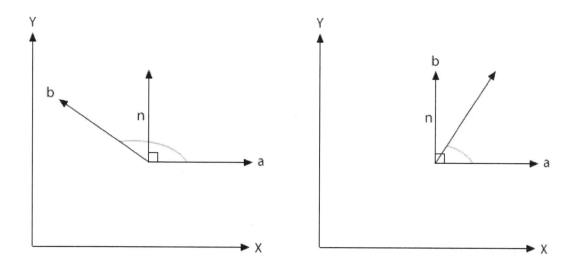

Left side. The degree between vector a and b is greater than 90. This means two vectors are pointing in two radically different directions or "away" from each other"

Right side. Less than 90 degrees between two vectors a and b. Two vectors are pointing in roughly the same direction. The surface of the polygons or segments they represent are facing the same side of a plane.

By using **Dot Product** WebGL can figure out whether the camera vector is pointing toward a polygon's face (surface) or away from it.

Dot Product is often used for determining relative direction of a side. Usually in 3D computer graphics all polygons have a front and a back face. Sometimes we need to clip away the invisible polygons. The ones that are facing away from the camera. Dot Product to the rescue!

If we know that a given polygon points away from the camera we can exclude it from our render list because it would be "facing away from the camera." Such polygons are usually clipped away and not rendered because they usually represent either the "inside" of a concealed object facing away or any other object. It's the area that we are guaranteed will never be visible to the camera.

When I was just starting to learn these principles they appeared to be overly complex for something as fun as what game development at first appeared. But they are all here to help us make some abstract decisions that can be easily formulated by thinking intuitively.

In general, there are not that many operations that require a deep knowledge of trigonometry when it comes to 3D graphics. You just have to thoroughly understand what they are and what they're used for. Eventually after a bit of practice it'll become like second nature.

Gem 14 - Vertex-Colored Triangle

In previous example we created a white triangle and rendered it on the screen. Traditionally to create colored or "smooth-shaded" surfaces (which are incredibly useful for imitating how light scatters across a surface) GPUs also enable us to work with color by creating new array bindings for data containing per-vertex color in RGBA format. The A stands for alpha channel.

The previous triangle only bound vertex coordinates and passed it to the GPU. Let's take that code and upgrade it so we can now draw colored triangles. This psychedelic-looking triangle will not accomplish much other than demonstrate how we can pass multiple array buffers representing various data about our geometry.

The purpose of doing this will become much more clear as we gradually move toward constructing entire 3D worlds that have more detail and where shading realism will be drastically increased.

Binding To a Secondary Buffer

You can bind as many buffers as you want representing vertex position (x,y,z), vertex colors (r,g,b), texture and normal coordinates (u, v, and s, t) and tangent space normals (on this a little bit later).

But the point is that WebGL allows us to bind multiple arrays representing various data about our primitive. In addition to vertex coordinates, to add vertex color data for each vertex we have to bind an additional data array to the memory buffer and pass it to the GPU.

The process is exactly the same as in previous chapter, with just a few slight modifications. WebGL as well as OpenGL retain "default" or "current" buffer while binding operations take place. This means that we can bind to one buffer at a time. So we will juggle around the code and end up with the source code listing shown below.

While reading other technical books I noticed that I would often get confused when source code was skipped and "..." was used instead to make sure that no unnecessary page space was used to repeat what was already said. I can definitely understand authors of those books. However, that has the drawback of page to page browsing that ultimately slows down the learning process. So I am going to copy the previous source code in its entirety here. However, I will highlight only what was changed so it's easier to process.

If you are viewing this on a non-color Kindle device or a printed book, the highlighted areas are the ones that appear darker than the rest and their comments start with the word "// New". Everything else is exactly the same.

Please note that I am doing something else to the vertex data now. I am initializing vertex and the new color array using native WebGL object Float32Array. These are just like regular JavaScript arrays. The convenience is that we can grab the byte size of each value via Float32Array.BYTES_PER_ELEMENT property, wheres prior to this we used gl.FLOAT.

var BYTESIZE = vertices.BYTES_PER_ELEMENT;

Here vertices is our array filled with vertex data.

This simply gives us the convenience to refer to the data size when specifying vertex attribute pointers using vertexAttribPointer function. The last two parameters of which are size of the data per vertex and stride.

In our new example size is BYTESIZE * 3 in each case because vertex coordinates are in XYZ format, and colors are in RGB format, each containing 3 unique variables.

And now we are going to demonstrate this with an actual example. After that we will modify our shader code so that we can pass newly bound color data via standard.vs and standard.frag to the GPU. And only then we can render a colored triangle.

Let's first revisit the webGLResourcesLoaded function:

```
// An event that fires when all shader resources
// finish loading in CreateShadersFromFile
window.webGLResourcesLoaded = function()
{
    console.log("webGLResourcesLoaded(): " +
            "All webGL shaders have finished loading!");

    // Specify triangle vertex data:
    var vertices = new Float32Array([
      -0.0,  0.5, 0.0, // Vertex A (x,y,z)
      -0.5, -0.5, 0.0, // Vertex B (x,y,z)
       0.5, -0.5, 0.0  // Vertex C (x,y,z)
    ]);

    // New: Specify colors for each vertex as well
    var colors = new Float32Array([
        1.0, 0.0, 0.0, // Vertex A (r,g,b)
        0.0, 1.0, 0.0, // Vertex B (r,g,b)
        0.0, 0.0, 1.0  // Vertex C (r,g,b)
    ]);

    var indices = [0, 1, 2]; // One index per vertex coordinate

    // Create buffer objects for storing triangle vertex and index data
    var vertexbuffer = gl.createBuffer();
    var colorbuffer = gl.createBuffer(); // New: also create color buffer
    var indexbuffer = gl.createBuffer();

    var BYTESIZE = vertices.BYTES_PER_ELEMENT;
```

```javascript
// Bind and create enough room for our data on respective buffers

// Bind vertexbuffer to ARRAY_BUFFER
gl.bindBuffer(gl.ARRAY_BUFFER, vertexbuffer);
// Send our vertex data to the buffer using floating point array
gl.bufferData(gl.ARRAY_BUFFER,
    new Float32Array(vertices), gl.STATIC_DRAW);
// Get attribute location
var coords = gl.getAttribLocation(Shader.vertexColorProgram,
                    "a_Position");
// Pointer to the currently bound VBO (vertex buffer object)
gl.vertexAttribPointer(coords, 3, gl.FLOAT, false, BYTESIZE*3, 0);
gl.enableVertexAttribArray(coords); // Enable it
// We're done; now we have to unbind the buffer
gl.bindBuffer(gl.ARRAY_BUFFER, null);


// Bind colorbuffer to ARRAY_BUFFER
gl.bindBuffer(gl.ARRAY_BUFFER, colorbuffer);
// Send our color data to the buffer using floating point array
gl.bufferData(gl.ARRAY_BUFFER, new Float32Array(colors),
        gl.STATIC_DRAW);
// Get attribute location
var colors = gl.getAttribLocation(Shader.vertexColorProgram,
                    "a_Color");
// Pointer to the currently bound VBO (vertex buffer object)
gl.vertexAttribPointer(colors, 3, gl.FLOAT, false, BYTESIZE*3, 0);
gl.enableVertexAttribArray(colors); // Enable it
// We're done; now we have to unbind the buffer
gl.bindBuffer(gl.ARRAY_BUFFER, null);


// Bind it to ELEMENT_ARRAY_BUFFER
gl.bindBuffer(gl.ELEMENT_ARRAY_BUFFER, indexbuffer);
// Send index (indices) data to this buffer
```

```
    gl.bufferData(gl.ELEMENT_ARRAY_BUFFER,
        new Uint16Array(indices), gl.STATIC_DRAW);

    // We're done; unbind, we no longer need the buffer object
    gl.bindBuffer(gl.ELEMENT_ARRAY_BUFFER, null);

    // Use our standard shader program for rendering this triangle
    gl.useProgram( Shader.vertexColorProgram );

    // Start main drawing loop
    var T = setInterval(function() {

    if (!gl)
        return;

    // Create WebGL canvas
    gl.clearColor(0.0, 0.0, 0.0, 1.0);
    gl.clear(gl.COLOR_BUFFER_BIT);

    // Draw triangle
    gl.drawElements(gl.TRIANGLES, indices.length,
        gl.UNSIGNED_SHORT,0);

});
```

Most notably we're using a new shader here. We can no longer use Shader.standardShader from previous example. It has been replaced with Shader.vertexColorProgram which will be discussed in a bit.

When we bind an array to ARRAY_BUFFER it becomes current. And we can use only one at a time. All functions after this operation will be performed on that buffer. For example, actually sending the data to the buffer using bufferData function. This is why we have to bind vertexbuffer first, attach our vertices array to it, and tie it to a_Position attribute that will be available from within the vertex shader.

Likewise, we will bind colorbuffer to ARRAY_BUFFER once again, and then tie it via a_Color attribute so we can access that data from within the new shader itself.

Once a buffer is bound and connected to our JavaScript array containing either vertices or color data, we now must enable it with gl.enableVertexAttribArray function. This process is repeated for both vertexbuffer and colorbuffer.

We will now modify our shaders. Note, that we need an entirely new shader here. Not our old standard.vs and standard.frag pair. We're building on them, but if we modify these shaders with new code to support vertex color, our previous demos will cease working. The code will break because they don't pass a_Color attribute and these shaders expect one.

So I created a new pair: vertex.vs and vertex.frag.

```
vertex.vs
attribute vec4 a_Position;
attribute vec4 a_Color;     // New: added vec4 attribute
varying vec4 color;    // New: this will be passed to fragment shader
void main() {
   gl_Position = a_Position;
   color = a_Color;    // New: pass it as varying color, not a_Color.
}
```

Just three new lines were added. a_Color is now passed together with a_Position. I also created varying vec4 color. It is also specified in the fragment shader:

```
vertex.frag
precision lowp float;      // New: specify floating-point precision
varying vec4 color;        // New: receive it from vertex shader
void main() {
   gl_FragColor = color;
}
```

We must specify floating point precision. If it is removed the shader will not compile. The precision directive tells the GPU about which type of floating point precision to use while calculating floating-point based operations.

Use highp for vertex positions, mediump for texture coordinates and lowp for colors.

And finally, putting this all together and running it in the browser will produce the following result:

Here, each tip of our triangle is nicely interpolated between the colors we specified in our colors array. Switch them to any color you'd like and you will see a smooth transition between them. This is done on the GPU by our fragment shader.

Binding One Buffer At A Time

Remember that our fragment shader works with one fragment at a time. However, the vertex coordinates we submitted with vertices array are pseudo-automatically interpolated by the GPU. If we lived in the 90's, you'd have to write procedures that computed these colors manually.

But graphics programming has grown up since then. Many common sub-operations like these are now done on the GPU, without taking away control of the important parts (setting the color to each vertex.)

Ideally, when we deal with real applications or games, we will not be shading our triangles using these psychedelic colors. Instead, they will be shaded across by colors that naturally appear in nature or illuminated by custom light sources. This example only demonstrates the bare polygon shading principle at work.

One More Thing

We're coming to a point where you're starting to add your own shaders to the project.

When you write your own demos using the base source code from this book, let's make sure we're not skipping another important detail when adding new shaders to our engine to avoid all kinds of JavaScript build errors.

Because we're adding an entirely new shader, let's see which code needs to be updated. Here I added new "vertex" string representing vertex.js and vertex.frag pair to the shaders array. We now have 3 shaders!

```
var shaders = [ // Enumerate shader filenames
    // This assumes "standard.vs" & "standard.frag"
      // are available in "shaders" directory
    "standard",
    "global",
    "vertex" // New: Added this new filename for the shader pair
];
```

Now let's give our new vertex color shader a name we can refer to by in our program.

```
var shader_name = [ // Enumerate shader program names
    "standardProgram",
    "globalDrawingProgram",
    "vertexColorProgram"     // New: added new shader name
];
```

I simply named it vertexColorProgram and from now on when we need to use it to draw anything with vertex colors we can issue the following gl command:

```
// Use our new vertex color shader program for rendering this triangle
gl.useProgram( Shader.vertexColorProgram );
```

And this is pretty much the entire process whenever you want to add a new shader and start using it. Let's quickly review it.

We switched to loading shaders from URLs. Because we are now automatically scanning the "shaders" directory in our project. All shaders found in it will be automatically loaded into our Shader object. We've also given them all a name so they're easy to select and use.

Just make sure that each time you add a new shader you specify its filename in shaders array, write the actual shadername.vs and shadername.frag pair and drop it into "shaders" folder and create a unique name you want to use by storing it in shader_name array. That's it!

Of course this process could be even further automated. And that's the setup for it. For example, you could further scan the "shaders" directory and automatically make the shaders list from scanning filenames without the extensions. I just don't want to complicate the process while teaching the subject.

You could even create your own shader names as the Shader's object properties algorithmically. Because alternatively to object.property_name = 1 assignment in JavaScript, you can assign properties to objects using object["property_name"] notation. This language feature is excellent at automatically loading data from a folder and storing it using variables that partially resemble those filenames. I'll briefly discuss it here and then we'll move on. For example:

```
var filename_vs = "texture.vs";
var propertyName = filename_vs.charAt(0).toUpperCase() +
filename;
```

```
object["program" + filename];
```

And now your shader will be available as:

Shader.programTexture and can be enabled by
Shader.use(Shader.programTexture);

And what does this give us? We will never have to bother with
creating shader arrays manually by hand just because we wrote a
new shader. You'd simply drop your shader pair into the "shader"
folder and it would be automatically read from there (you can write a
PHP reader that scans the shaders folder) and then the variable
names will become auto-magically available from the object itself as
in Shader.programShaderfilename. But this is the task I leave to you.
If you get this done perhaps you can venture into my GitHub (http://
www.github.com/gregsidelnikov) account fork it or submit a pull
request from my WebGLTutorials project and then push it back.

A bit later in the book, I will demonstrate how this is achieved, but for
another task: loading textures. This is such an important technique
that practically solves a lot of frustration. And while at first you might
think this is too complex and unnecessary, when you get to feel those
practical benefits actually improve your workflow you will fall in love
with this method and not want to go back.

You can further optimize your engine because at this point it is still
pretty simple and malleable. But even now already it's still a nice way
of creating, loading and using new shaders because writing them
inside <SCRIPT> tags all the time is a management nightmare.

And this is all we require at this point.

The shaders are automatically loaded from the URL using function
CreateShadersFromFile we wrote earlier. Let's recall it from a
previous chapter:

// Scroll through the list, loading shader pairs

```
function CreateShadersFromFile( gl ) {
  for (i in shaders)
    LoadShader(gl,
            Shader_name[i],
            shaders[i] + ".vs",
            shaders[i] + ".frag",
            i);
    // Pass in the index "i" of the currently loading shader,
    // this way we can determine when last shader
    // has finished loading
}
```

As you can see filenames are generated from our shaders array. We never have to specify the pair manually, just its common filename without the extension.

Thus, once our new shader is loaded at the last index [i] in the array, we're ready to continue initialization process and start rendering our object using it.

Gem 15 - Drawing Multiple Triangles

I won't spend much time and space talking about drawing multiple primitives. In this case, triangles. Our current code is already easy to expand to drawing multiple shapes. I'll only briefly show it here. This step is necessary so we can move forward to creating more advanced shapes in the next chapter.

```
// Specify triangle vertex data:
var vertices = new Float32Array([

// Triangle 1 vertices:
    0.0,  0.5, 0.0,      // Vertex A (x,y,z)
```

```
    -0.5, -0.5, 0.0,          // Vertex B (x,y,z)
     0.5, -0.5, 0.0,          // Vertex C (x,y,z)

// Triangle 2 vertices:
    0.05 + 0.0,  0.75, 0.0,  // Vertex A (x,y,z)
    0.75 - 0.5, -0.75, 0.0,  // Vertex B (x,y,z)
    0.15 + 0.5, -0.75, 0.0,  // Vertex C (x,y,z)
]);

var colors = new Float32Array([

// Triangle 1 vertex colors:
    1.0, 0.0, 0.0,          // Vertex A (r,g,b) -- red
    0.0, 1.0, 0.0,          // Vertex B (r,g,b) -- green
    0.0, 0.0, 1.0,          // Vertex C (r,g,b) -- blue

// Triangle 2 vertex colors:
    0.0, 0.0, 1.0,          // Vertex A (r,g,b) -- red
    0.0, 1.0, 0.0,          // Vertex B (r,g,b) -- green
    1.0, 0.0, 0.0           // Vertex C (r,g,b) -- blue
]);
```

Simply continue adding new values to each attribute array. The next set of vertices in vertices array will define location of the second triangle. Likewise, the colors array is also extended to provide vertex colors for it.

Finally, there is one more thing to do. We now have to let the indices array know that we have new data. Simply add new indices in consequent order:

```
var indices = [0, 1, 2, 3, 4, 5];
```

When **drawElements** function is executed, it automatically calculates the length of our indices array as demonstrated below. This way there are on changes to be made here. indices.length will automatically pass the number of vertices that will be associated with this new set of data.

```
// Draw triangle
gl.drawElements(gl.TRIANGLES, indices.length,
gl.UNSIGNED_SHORT, 0);
```

And I think we're ready to go!

This example produces two triangles as shown on the screenshot below:

Note that the vertex colors are also switched around on the second triangle.

This lesson was important. Because we can now take these principles and load an entire game world into our engine from an OBJ or PLY file.

Gem 16 - Controversial Texture Image Loader

Traditionally, it is not a good practice to store data in global variables. But JavaScript is the kind of a language that breaks that rule by design. All variables created in global scope are automatically attached to the browser's window object.

If we are careful enough, we can exploit this technique for something that is going to save us a lot of headache. In web-based applications, preloading images is important. We cannot initialize our textures if the images have not finished loading yet.

If we load images asynchronously there will always be a wait time associated with loading resources. But in web-based games this is a given mechanism. We simply have to implement it one way or another. It's very similar to what we have done for loading shaders earlier in the book.

So, what's so controversial about it? In this section we are going to implement an image loader probably unlike you have ever seen before. We are going to scan our "textures" directory, return the list of files located in it (usually .PNG) and automatically load them into our image buffers.

Yes, but what's so controversial about it? Okay. Here it is. Soon as the texture is loaded, we will save the loaded object in a variable matching the name of the image, minus the extension name. And attach it to window object. This way, it will become globally available. For example: images like wood.png will become an object window.wood and can be accessible throughout our WebGL application in global scope via a simple variable called wood. (without the optional and implicit window object.)

Why are we doing it this way?

1. **It improves our workflow.** Simply drop PNG images into "textures" folder.
2. You never have to worry about writing a single line of code loading new textures.
3. Seamlessly integrate this logic into our WebGL texture binder mechanism.

If you are still worried that some images, for example "class.png" or "var.png" (for example) will be dropped into "textures" folder and converted to window.class or window.var properties ("class" and "var" are reserved JavaScript keywords and cannot be used as variable identifier names) you can always programmatically append "img", or "img_" to them so they become window.img_class and window.img_var respectively and avoid clashing with reserved names. We'll take a risk throughout this book and not do that and manually avoid using these types of names. In return, we gain a wonderful ability of simply saving our textures into "textures" folder and never worry about loading any new textures by hand. This will speed up the learning process and simplify WebGL programming in general.

The entire loader can be thought of as part of two operations:

PHP script that returns a listing of all files in "textures" directory.

JavaScript or jQuery's Ajax call that goes through the list, loading each image one by one.

The PHP script looks as follows:

```php
<?php

    $dir = "textures/";

    $return_array = array();

    if (is_dir($dir)) {
        if ($dh = opendir($dir)) {
            while(($file = readdir($dh)) != false) {
                if ($file == "." or $file == "..") {
                    // Skip upper directories
                } else {
                    // Add the file to the array
                    $return_array[] = $file;
                }
            }
        }
        // Return list of files in JSON format
        echo json_encode($return_array);
    }
?>
```

An HTTP request to this script will grab a list of all images in the "textures" directory and create new Texture objects from them. But where will it store them? First, we have to create a new Texture object in JavaScript.

Surprisingly, it's incredibly trivial. But then again, we're not doing anything more than loading an image programmatically:

```javascript
window.ResourceId = 0;    // Index of currently loading image
window.TotalTextures = 0; // Number of textures in "textures" folder
window.Ltimer = null;      // Timer that waits for all textures

// Do not output sprite name, width & height to console -- if true.
var SilentLoad = false;

var Texture = function(fn)
{
   var that = this;
   var root = this;

   this.filename = fn;
   this.width    = 0;
   this.height   = 0;

   this.image    = null;                     // JavaScript image
   this.texture  = gl.createTexture();   // Create WebGL texture object

   this.load = function(filename) {       // Primary image loader function
      this.image = new Image();
      this.image.onload = function(event) {
         var file = fn.split("/");
         that.width = this.width;
         that.height = this.height;

         // A set of commands required by WebGL to bind
         // loaded image data to the texture buffer
         gl.bindTexture(gl.TEXTURE_2D, that.texture);
         gl.texImage2D(gl.TEXTURE_2D, 0, gl.RGBA, gl.RGBA,
                  gl.UNSIGNED_BYTE, that.image);
         gl.texParameteri(gl.TEXTURE_2D,
                   gl.TEXTURE_MAG_FILTER, gl.LINEAR);
```

```
        gl.texParameteri(gl.TEXTURE_2D,
                gl.TEXTURE_MIN_FILTER,
                gl.LINEAR_MIPMAP_NEAREST);
        gl.generateMipmap(gl.TEXTURE_2D);
        gl.bindTexture(gl.TEXTURE_2D, null);

        if (!SilentLoad) {
            console.log("Loaded sprite (" + that.width +
            "x" + that.height + ")" + fn);
        }
        window.ResourceId++;   // increase resource counter
    };
    this.image.src = filename; // Assign resource to "src"
    return this;               // Return a link to loaded object
};

// Using the function load() above...
// Load texture, if filename was supplied
if (fn != undefined && fn != "" && fn != null)
    this.load(fn);
else
    console.log("Unable to load sprite. Filename '" +
            fn + "' is undefined or null.");
}
```

There is a common process in both WebGL and OpenGL where you have to bind the loaded image data to the texture object. It follows the pattern shown below:

bindTexture - bind the texture variable to the texture object
texImage2D - set color format of the image
texParameteri - set mipmap options and texture filters
generateMipmap - actually create mipmap levels for this texture

bindTexture to **null** (we no longer need this object, it's used only for setting parameters)

In WebGL we "bind" data to buffers and then when all operations are finished we unbind again. This prepares the texture to be later used in our shaders. You can choose only one texture at time when rendering a model. The same is true for shaders. For this reason in modern graphics we have to organize our 3D models by texture and material type when rendering. Some 3D geometry may share the same shader or texture. In this case no switch is required. We have to be opportunistic here.

And finally, to put it all together, we will make an HTTP request and load all images asynchronously. Notice the usage of new Texture operation from above in both of the examples below.

You can do it with a plain JavaScript HTTP request, if you don't want to depend on outside libraries like jQuery:

```
var xmlhttp = new XMLHttpRequest();

// Make an HTTP request to load texture images
xmlhttp.onreadystatechange = function() {
    if (xmlhttp.readyState == XMLHttpRequest.DONE) {
        if (xmlhttp.status == 200) {
            var msg = xmlhttp.responseText;
            if (JSON.parse(msg) != undefined) {
                var json = JSON.parse(msg);

                // Memorize total number of resources
                // for progress bar calculation:
                var resourceNumber = json.length;

                for (var i = 0; i < json.length; i++) {
```

```
            var appropriateName = json[i].split(".")[0];
            window.LoadingFileName = json[i];
            window[appropriateName] = new Texture("http://
www.tigrisgames.com/fx/textures/" + window.LoadingFileName);
          }
        }
      }
    }
}
```

I am assuming the images are located under www.tigrisgames.com/
fx/textures/ folder. Of course you should change it to your own
domain name or localhost.

If you ever want to make a progress bar (which for most games you
will have to) you can use the resourceNumber variable taken from
length of the returned JSON object. This is the number of resources
equal to 100% progress bar length. You can take it from there.

Perhaps the most important part of the code is the line below. It
creates a new texture object on global window object using its
"appropriate name". Which is the filename without the extension.

```
window[appropriateName] =
    new Texture("textures/" + window.LoadingFileName);
```

Or you can do it with the aid of jQuery, which is exactly the same
except we are invoking jQuery's ($'s) ajax method. Some
programmers prefer it this way because it's cross-browser and the
code looks somewhat more readable:

```
// Load graphics resources
$.ajax({"url" : "getResourceList.php",
        type : "POST",
```

```
            success : function(msg) {

                if (JSON.parse(msg) != undefined) {

                    var json = JSON.parse(msg);

                    var resourceNumber = json.length;

                    for (var i = 0; i < json.length; i++) {
                        var appropriateName = json[i].split(".")[0];
                        window.LoadingFileName = json[i];
                        window[appropriateName] =
                            new Texture("textures/" + window.LoadingFileName);
                    }
                }
            }
        });
```

Either way you do it is just fine.

Note in this Ajax example I shortened the URL to a relative address of "textures/".

The end result? Let's say you dropped rocks.png texture into "textures" folder. That's all. From now on you can access it's image data via window.rocks. It will point to a Texture object.

In this texture object you will have a property specifying a link to the texture image in memory. To access it on a newly loaded texture refer to it as window.rock.image And that's what we will pass to WebGL as a target for the texture image. This texture image script simplifies a lot of things we would otherwise have to do by hand.

My challenge for you is to use this example and rebuild its mechanism to auto-magically load shaders as well and store them in the main Shader object.

Then, from that point on you will have both shaders and textures: two of the most important types of assets in 3D graphics (the other being, the 3D model's vertices) loading automatically. Which is a really heavenly feature for a 3D engine. I will show you how to load OBJ and PLY models later in the book so we can display some reasonably interesting geometry in our game world.

Appropriate Name

In the script above the variable appropriateName takes care of cutting off the extension "png" (or "tga" which is often used for its ability to easily store the alpha layer) from the loaded file and turning it into a variable name. Just make sure to never use texture images that contain odd characters like $ or _ or spaces and even periods themselves (just keep one at extension name of course) and so on. Keep the names clean, memorable and short if possible.

Textures In Global Scope

This may be controversial because we're storing texture images in global scope. But it's a trade off. And in my opinion, it makes sense. Remember, this is JavaScript, not C++. Taking care of auto-loading images this way, even using globals, is a lot easier to manage than having to load each texture individually by writing code. You'll spend a lot of time doing that. Over a period of several weeks this process of adding, removing and changing textures in your JavaScript program by hand can take away several hours of time that could be spent on other aspects of game production.

Discarding textures that are no longer required is simple too. Want to remove the texture from your engine and save memory? Simply remove it from the "textures" folder.

This JavaScript image loader can be implemented in a wide variety of situations. From now on, we will use it to load our WebGL texture images.

We will also wait until all images have finished loading. I'll update our code a bit to adapt to this new texture loader. In which case an additional function called TexturesLoaded will be executed just after the shaders have finished loading.

Once this function is executed we can initialize our VBOs and VAOs (Vertex Buffer and Arrays Objects) and pass our texture image data to WebGL functions to bind them to arrays and pass them into the shader itself via uniform sampler2D image. More on this in just a bit.

One More Thing

But there is one more thing. (There always is, isn't there?)

Before we can enter the main WebGL rendering loop, we first must ensure that not only textures but also all shaders have finished loading. We've already done this test, but only for shaders. Now that we have included asynchronous texture loader, we must rebuild that loader so it takes a look at both.

The source code below helps us accomplish that. I moved out the shader test from the shader loader (not shown here.) And I replaced that with a check for both the textures and shaders within the texture loader itself.

The reasoning behind this change is that chances are textures will take longer to load than shaders. In games we often have large lists of textures that are over usually 1024x1024 and greater. It's probably reasonable to believe that images will take longer to load from a URL than loading and compiling shaders.

Here is the updated LoadTextures function. It now creates a timer that ticks until all textures and shaders have loaded. Then the main WebGL loop is invoked. With 4 shader pairs and 1 1024x1024 texture, on my machine it takes 124-127 ticks for this process to complete. Which is something like 0.012 of a second. Of course this time will increase the more shaders and textures we supply into our engine.

I highlighted the changed code. Again, for latest version of the source code from this book, find WebGLTutorials repository on my GitHub account: https://www.github.com/gregsidelnikov

Here is the code. I highlighted the areas that were added

```
function LoadTextures() {

    console.log("LoadTextures(); -- Loading textures");

    // Create HTTP request object
    var xmlhttp = new XMLHttpRequest();

    // Make an HTTP request to load texture images
    xmlhttp.onreadystatechange = function() {
        if (xmlhttp.readyState == XMLHttpRequest.DONE) {
            if (xmlhttp.status == 200) {
                var msg = xmlhttp.responseText;
                console.log(msg);
```

```javascript
if (JSON.parse(msg) != undefined) {

    var json = JSON.parse(msg);
    // Memorize total number of resources --
    // for progress bar calculation:
    var resourceNumber =
        window.TotalTextures = json.length;

    console.log("window.TotalTextures = " +
            window.TotalTextures);

    // Check until all textures are loaded in memory;
    // And only then initialize WebGL

    // Start ticking only if there are textures to load
    if (window.Ltimer == null && window.TotalTextures != 0)
    {
        window.Ltimer = setInterval(function()
        {
            if (window.ResourceId >= window.TotalTextures)
            {
                var n = window.TotalTextures;

                console.log("All ("+n+") textures loaded");

                // Check if all shaders finished loading
                if (window.ShadersFinishedLoading)
                {
                    // Prevent this timer from ticking again
                    // after all textures are loaded
                    clearInterval(window.Ltimer);
                    window.Ltimer = null;

                    // All textures and all shaders
```

```
                // have finished loading;
                // Start main rendering loop
                window.webGLResourcesLoaded();
              }
            }
          }, 0);
        }
        for (var i = 0; i < json.length; i++) {
            console.log("Loading texture <" + json[i] + ">");
            var appropriateName = json[i].split(".")[0];
            window.LoadingFileName = json[i];
            window[appropriateName] = new Texture("http://
localhost/tigrisgames.com/fx/textures/" + window.LoadingFileName);
          }
        }
      } else console.log("*** unable to open <getTextures.php>");
    }
  }
  xmlhttp.open("GET", "getTextures.php", true);
  xmlhttp.send();
}
```

Of course you would replace the base directory of:

http://localhost/tigrisgames.com/fx/textures/

To your own project location.

Gem 17 - Texture-Mapped Triangle

All is well in vertex color kingdom. And vertex colors add a lot more
realism to our 3D objects. Texture mapping is a technique that lets us
stretch or "paste" a picture across the triangle. Much in the same way

as color was interpolated across the triangle's vertices, we're going to interpolate pixel values taken from an image, or a texture.

Textures are usually square images of 256x256, 512x512, 1024x1024, 2048x2048 and 4096x4096 in dimension. This is your texture map. They contain detailed polygon surface image data that can be picked up via texture coordinates. Assigning texture coordinates is similar to how we assigned vertex colors in an earlier chapter.

Texture mapping is what helps us achieve that realistic polygon surface look when rendering large outdoor scenes containing mountains, brick walls, car tire tread marks and so on.

Like many values in WebGL texture coordinates range between 0.0 and 1.0 regardless what the actual size of the texture map is in pixels. It might seem strange at first, but it's quite convenient because this is what allows us to interpolate texture data across an arbitrary 3D polygon.

Let's take our previous example and write a new shader that will incorporate vertex colors and texture coordinates. We'll use it from now on every time we need to draw texture-mapped surfaces.

Creating Shader for Texture Mapping

In this section we will extend our vertex color shader by adding a new attribute: a_Texture. You can name it anything you want. But in this tutorial we will stick to the a_ naming format for our attributes just to stay consistent and keep attributes organized.

Whereas a_Position was a vec4 attribute because it took the 3 vertex coordinates and 1 more for padding (see Row-Major and Column-

Major Matrix Notations we discussed previously) the texture coordinates are passed in vec2 format. This means that there is only a u and v coordinate per texture. They are both processed in floating point format. And when it comes to floating point numbers in processing data, there is always loss of precision. No computer process is capable of a true floating point number. There is always a limit after the decimal point somewhere. And because these numbers can pretty much go into infinity, there is always a margin of error.

However, when developing games, rendering geometry and light, these computational errors are not visible due to the fact that they are so small. Still, in WebGL we can control the precision factor of our calculations from within our shaders. This is achieved by the precision directive. Some shaders will not compile when it is avoided. Let's specify medium precision for our texture's floating point uv coordinate calculations.

The following shader pair will take additional texture coordinates from our JavaScript program. I called it texture.vs and texture.frag accordingly. I also added it to our shader manager program following the same process described in the section where we created the vertex color shader. In the shader manager our new shader will be called textureMapProgram. And we will enable it by calling Shader.use(Shader.textureMapProgram). But for now, here is its source code:

```
texture.vs
precision mediump float;
attribute vec4 a_Position;
attribute vec4 a_Color;
attribute vec2 a_Texture;      // New: added texture

varying vec4 color;
varying vec2 texture;
```

```
void main()
{
  gl_Position = a_Position;
  color = a_Color;
  texture = a_Texture;
}
```

texture.frag
precision **mediump** float;

uniform **sampler2D** image;

varying **vec4** color;
varying **vec2** texture;

```
void main() {
  gl_FragColor = texture2D(image, vec2(texture.s, texture.t));
}
```

We have just changed the value of gl_FragColor completely from color to texture.

But what if you want to combine both the vertex color and texture images? There is no problem doing that in a GLSL shader. The solution? Simply multiply the vertex color by texture coordinate.

Here is how this can be achieved:

```
gl_FragColor = color * texture2D(image, vec2(texture.s, texture.t));
```

That's how simple it is to combine data in GLSL. The colors are automatically calculated by the shader. Multiplying values is something you'll be doing a lot of for achieving various results. It's used in a variety of shaders.

Combining your vertex color with texture pixels is a neat way of making your scene appear even more realistic. You can imitate dungeon or racing circuit lights by highlighting certain areas of your geometry with brighter colors, while keeping the rest of vertices 25-30% gray or some other natural sun shade color. This technique has potential of adding tremendous level of realism to your game world scene.

Gem 18 - Test Cube & Other Specimina

Until now we have drawn a simple triangle. It's okay that it's a simple shape. All we were doing was learning how to draw the most basic primitive using a shader and binding vertex data to an array that was then passed onto the GPU.

Everything has a beginning. And our simple triangle shape was a provenance to something more complex and a bit more exciting.

Flat triangles won't be of much help when it comes to demonstrating the sheer power of WebGL. Especially not when it comes to rendering more sophisticated visual effects. For example, rendering texture maps, bump mapping, per-vertex and per-fragment simulation of light to showcase how realistic graphics can be achieved will require a more intriguing object. Or a few.

We will use the cube and other simple 3D shapes throughout the rest of the book to show off effects generated by shaders. But first we have to generate them. We haven't gotten to the point where we can load models from a file. So we will algorithmically create them here.

Because shaders affect the look of an object based on its angle, we will also create a function that will help us rotate the said object using mouse controls. We'll use this mechanic in all other demos in this book. But that's in next chapter after this.

Later you can learn how to create more sophisticated level design using software such as Blender, Maya, 3D coat and so on. But first, let's create some objects

Cube

Let's construct a cube. A cube is simply a 6-sided object comprising of 12 triangles. Its sides are equally facing in all 6 directions.

We're simply going to extend our previous example where we drew 2 triangles. Now, let's stitch together an entire cube following the same technique.

This time, just for fun, I will paint each side of the cube in a different color using our pre-made vertex color shader.

We will be building our 3D cube mesh around the center of the coordinate system. Because each side of the cube will be 1.0 in size, we'll take strides of 0.5 in each direction. The mesh vertex shown below is not the most straight-forward one. But this is what you come up with if you try to draw it out on a piece of paper and then plug the values in.

I also started a new JavaScript file primitives.js and this is where our vertex-building functions will reside from now on. If you want to grab a cube, simply call makeCube() function and it will return the vertices describing a cube. Other shapes can be added later.

```javascript
function makeCube() {
  return new Float32Array([
        1.0,-1.0, 1.0, // triangle 1 of face 1
        -1.0,-1.0, 1.0,
        -1.0,-1.0,-1.0,
        -1.0, 1.0,-1.0, // triangle 2 of face 1
        -1.0, 1.0, 1.0,
        1.0, 1.0, 1.0,
        // ... 30 other vertices not shown here to preserve space
    ]
  );
}

function makeCubeColors() {
  return new Float32Array([
        1.0, 0.0, 0.0,
        1.0, 0.0, 0.0,
        1.0, 1.0, 0.0,
        1.0, 0.0, 0.0,
        1.0, 1.0, 0.0,
        1.0, 0.0, 0.0,
        // ... 30 other colors not shown here to preserve space
    ]
  );
}

function makeCubeTextures() {
  return new Float32Array([
        1.0, 0.0,
        1.0, 1.0,
        0.0, 1.0,
        1.0, 1.0,
        0.0, 1.0,
        0.0, 0.0,
```

```
        // ... 30 other UV's not shown here to preserve space
    ]
  );
}
```

Primitives.js

This and other primitives will be described in primitives.js from now on. Just open that file to see the rest of the data. The data for each array contains 36 vertex, color and texture UV sets. Just enough to cover each of the 6 sides of a cube consisting of 12 triangles and 36 vertices total. The redundant data is purposely skipped in the example above to save page space.

We can now use this cube to demonstrate matrix transforms. This way we will work with a shape that is a bit more complex than just a triangle. In the future we will use this cube to demonstrate shaders in action.

Gem 19 - Loading Model Data from PLY

Blender can export your model data in both OBJ and PLY format. In this section we will take a look at the PLY model loader source code.

Until now we either created our geometry by typing vertex data directly into our JavaScript arrays and passing them to the VAO or by using pre-made geometry-creation function for the cube box.

This is great for testing shaders but this won't do us any good for loading more complex 3D worlds created in modeling software such as Blender. Blender can save models in OBJ and PLY formats. PLY is better because there isn't a reasonably simple way to store vertex color data in OBJ files.

The solution is to write a PLY file format loading function, parse the vertex, normal, texture and color data and rebuild it as Float32Array data sets so we can finally pass it into the VAO (Vertex Array Object) just like we did in previous examples.

This is great news because from now on we can load complex geometry like racing tracks, castles, vast terrains and landscapes and pretty much anything limited only by your imagination.

Before Moving Forward

Note: when saving files in PLY format from Blender you need to ensure the following is true:

The model must contain at least 1 vertex-colored vertex. If this is not done, Blender will skip all color data completely from your entire PLY file to preserve space. In some cases this is reasonable. But not in this one. However, if you do paint at least one vertex color of your model any color Blender will insert default value of 255 255 255 to all other vertices. This is a required step for the PLY function to accurately load the data.

The model must be triangulated. Do not save model in Blender consisting of basic primitives (cube, cone, sphere, etc.) To triangulate the model make sure you're in Edit Mode and all vertices are selected. Then press Ctrl-T. Only then export the PLY file. If this step is skipped, the PLY loader will not work.

Your model must have texture data. In order to texture map your model in Blender, pull out a second view pane and press Ctrl-F10 to show your Texture Map. Select the object in the original view (not in the texture map pane). Then go to Edit Mode, select all vertices by pressing A key, then press U to "unwrap" vertices to a texture map. Select an appropriate Unwrap option from the pop-up menu. Adjust texture map if needed. Resave the model.

If any of the rules above are not taken in consideration the LoadPLY function will not work as expected and your model might lose data. But usually it will not load at all. So make sure you have at least one vector contain color by using Vector Paint mode on your object and just briefly touching one of the edges of the model. Also make sure the model is unwrapped onto a texture (it can be any image, even empty one. Just unwrapping vertices is sufficient enough.)

The entire loading process of a PLY file is semi-complex but not complicated. We still need to define some counters and data arrays to get started. First we prepare some basic data storage variables and arrays.

```
// PLY object
function PLY() { this.object; }

// Path to the folder where models are stored
var ModelFolderPath = "http://localhost/tigrisgames.com/fx/model/";

// Number of vertices in PLY file
var PLY_Vertices = 0;

// Number of faces in PLY file
var PLY_Faces = 0;

// For skipping header
var ReadingPLYData = false;
```

```javascript
// 11 entries per vertex (x,y,z,nx,ny,nz,r,g,b,u,v)
var PLY_DataLenght = 11;

var VAO_VertexIndex = 0;

var FaceIndex = 0;

// PLY file vertex entry format
function PLY_Vertex(x, y, z, nx, ny, nz, u, v, r, g, b) {
    this.x = 0; // a_Position
    this.y = 0;
    this.z = 0;
    this.nx= 0; // a_Normal
    this.ny= 0;
    this.nz= 0;
    this.u = 0; // a_Texture
    this.v = 0;
    this.r = 0; // a_Color
    this.g = 0;
    this.b = 0;
}

// PLY file face consisting of 3 vertex indices for each face
function PLY_Face(a, b, c) {
    this.a = a;
    this.b = b;
    this.c = c;
}
```

We need to choose some sort of a folder where all of our PLY models will be stored.

http://localhost/tigrisgames.com/fx/model/

Yours of course would be different.

Notably, the source code includes PLY_Vertex and PLY_Face objects containing the two primary data types commonly found in PLY file format.

The PLY format stores two lists. First, it stores the vertex list containing every single edge point of your model. Then it provides a similar list for each face. The face list only contains indices to the vertices from the first list. This way if any vertices repeat, we don't have to store a copy of that data in the face array. Simply refer to its numeric index value which is just an integer.

I created a simple racing track in Blender just to demonstrate this function in action.

It was originally saved as racingtrack.blend and exported to racingtrack.ply. The model contains vertex, color, normals (not used for now) and texture data. And that's what we

The PLY file format header looks as follows:

```
ply
format ascii 1.0
comment Created by Blender 2.74 (sub 0) - www.blender.org, source
file: 'racingtrack.blend'
element vertex 3425
property float x
property float y
property float z
property float nx
property float ny
property float nz
property float s
```

property float t
property uchar red
property uchar green
property uchar blue
element face 1942
property list uchar uint vertex_indices
end_header
vertex data line 1
vertex data line 2
vertex data line 3
vertex data line N…
Face data line 1
Face data line 2
Face data line 3
Face data line N...

As you can see there is a whole lot more of vertex data (3425 lines) than face (only 1942 lines) of data. When it comes to reading the header I made the lines we are interested in bold.

First, we want to read the number of vertices and number of faces from the file. Once we reach end_header line we can start reading the rest of the data which comes just after that.

What follows are two large lists. One is vertex data that comes first. And faces list right below it.

PLY format is uncompressed. This means lots of raw data can be stored in one medium-size model. The data for each vertex property is stored in the format shown in the header. First we have our x, y and z coordinates for each vertex.

After x, y and z we have normal coordinates in same format (nx, ny, nz). We haven't talked about normals in the book yet. And they won't be used in the example in this chapter. But this data is automatically stored when the PLY model is saved in Blender. Normals are used for applying light to your model as well as several interesting shader effects such as water refraction, cube mapping, etc. We'll load this data but it will not be used in this example.

Normals are followed by s and t coordinates for texture mapping. In our PLY model loader function we will be referring to them as u and v.

Looks like we're ready to read the model data now.

Introducing the LoadPLY function. The core of our PLY loader:

```
// Load PLY function;
function LoadPLY(filename)
{
    var vertices = null;

    var xmlhttp = new XMLHttpRequest();

    xmlhttp.onreadystatechange = function() {

        if (xmlhttp.readyState == XMLHttpRequest.DONE) {

            if (xmlhttp.status == 200) {

                var data = xmlhttp.responseText;

                var lines = data.split("\n");

                var PLY_index = 0;

                var arrayVertex,
                    arrayNormal,
```

```javascript
        arrayTexture,
        arrayColor,
        arrayIndex;

    var vertices = null;

    var faces = null;

    console.log("PLY number of lines = " + lines.length);

    for (var i = 0; i < lines.length; i++)
    {
        if (ReadingPLYData)
        {
            var e = lines[i].split(" ");

            // Read vertices

            if (PLY_index < PLY_Vertices) {

                vertices[PLY_index] = new PLY_Vertex();
                vertices[PLY_index].x = e[0];
                vertices[PLY_index].y = e[1];
                vertices[PLY_index].z = e[2];
                vertices[PLY_index].nx = e[3];
                vertices[PLY_index].ny = e[4];
                vertices[PLY_index].nz = e[5];
                vertices[PLY_index].u = e[6];
                vertices[PLY_index].v = e[7];
                vertices[PLY_index].r = e[8];
                vertices[PLY_index].g = e[9];
                vertices[PLY_index].b = e[10];

                // Read faces
```

```javascript
} else {

    // Reset index for building VAOs
    if (PLY_index == PLY_Vertices) {
        console.log("Resetting Index...");
        FaceIndex = 0;
        VAO_VertexIndex = 0;
    }

    // Wire face data to appropriate vertices
    var n = e[0]; // unused, always 3;
            // assumes triangulated models only
    var a = e[1]; // face vertex A
    var b = e[2]; // face vertex B
    var c = e[3]; // face vertex C

    if (FaceIndex < PLY_Faces)
    {
        // We don't really have to *store* face data
        // faces[FaceIndex] = new PLY_Face(a, b, c);

        // vertices
        arrayVertex.push(vertices[a].x);
        arrayVertex.push(vertices[a].y);
        arrayVertex.push(vertices[a].z);
        arrayVertex.push(vertices[b].x);
        arrayVertex.push(vertices[b].y);
        arrayVertex.push(vertices[b].z);
        arrayVertex.push(vertices[c].x);
        arrayVertex.push(vertices[c].y);
        arrayVertex.push(vertices[c].z);
```

```javascript
// normals
arrayNormal.push(vertices[a].nx);
arrayNormal.push(vertices[a].ny);
arrayNormal.push(vertices[a].nz);
arrayNormal.push(vertices[b].nx);
arrayNormal.push(vertices[b].ny);
arrayNormal.push(vertices[b].nz);
arrayNormal.push(vertices[c].nx);
arrayNormal.push(vertices[c].ny);
arrayNormal.push(vertices[c].nz);

// colors
arrayColor.push(vertices[a].r);
arrayColor.push(vertices[a].g);
arrayColor.push(vertices[a].b);
arrayColor.push(vertices[b].r);
arrayColor.push(vertices[b].g);
arrayColor.push(vertices[b].b);
arrayColor.push(vertices[c].r);
arrayColor.push(vertices[c].g);
arrayColor.push(vertices[c].b);

// uv
arrayTexture.push(vertices[a].u);
arrayTexture.push(vertices[a].v);
arrayTexture.push(vertices[b].u);
arrayTexture.push(vertices[b].v);
arrayTexture.push(vertices[c].u);
arrayTexture.push(vertices[c].v);

// index
arrayIndex.push(FaceIndex);
}
```

```
            FaceIndex++;
        }

        PLY_index++;

    } else { // Still reading header...

        // Read number of vertices stored in the file
        if (lines[i].substr(0,"element vertex".length)
            == "element vertex")
            PLY_Vertices = lines[i].split(" ")[2];

        // Read number of faces stored in the file
        if (lines[i].substr(0, "element face".length)
            == "element face")
            PLY_Faces = lines[i].split(" ")[2];
    }

    // Finished reading header data,
    // prepare for reading vertex data
    if (lines[i] == "end_header") {

        // Allocate enough space for vertices
        vertices = new Array(PLY_Vertices);

        // Allocate enough space for faces
        faces = new Array(PLY_Faces);

        // Allocate memory for returned arrays (VAOs)
        arrayVertex  = new Array(); // PLY_Vertices * 3
        arrayNormal  = new Array(); // PLY_Vertices * 3
        arrayTexture = new Array(); // PLY_Vertices * 2
        arrayColor   = new Array(); // PLY_Vertices * 3
        arrayIndex   = new Array(); // PLY_Vertices * 1
```

```
            ReadingPLYData = true;
        }
    }

    console.log("PLY_Vertices = " + PLY_Vertices + " loaded");
    console.log("PLY_Faces = " + PLY_Faces + " loaded");
    console.log("arrayVertex length = " + arrayVertex.length);
    console.log("arrayNormal length = " + arrayNormal.length);
    console.log("arrayTexture length = " + arrayTexture.length);
    console.log("arrayColor length = " + arrayColor.length);
    console.log("arrayIndex length = " + arrayIndex.length);

    // We now have both complete vertex and face data loaded;
    // return everything we loaded as
    // Float32Array & Uint16Array for index
    return [
        new Float32Array(arrayVertex),
        new Float32Array(arrayNormal),
        new Float32Array(arrayTexture),
        new Float32Array(arrayColor),
        new Uint16Array(arrayIndex)
    ];
        }
    }
};

console.log("Loading Model <" + filename + ">...");

xmlhttp.open("GET", ModelFolderPath + filename, true);
xmlhttp.send();
}
```

You can read through entire function and understand exactly what it's doing.

But to put it more compactly, here is the pseudo code of what it actually helps us accomplish:

Pseudo Code

```
LoadPLY {

  if (Request file <racingtrack.ply>)
  {
    lines = ReadAll();

    while (lines)
    {
      if (HeaderIsRead)
      {
        ReadVertices();

        ReadFaces();

        WireVerticesToFaceIndices();

        // Pack VAO / VBO data
        PackVertexArray();
        PackNormalArray();
        PackColorArray();
        PackTextureArray();
        PackIndexArray();

      } else {

        ReadHeader();
```

```
        vertices = ReadVertexNumber();
        faces = ReadFaceNumber();
        InitializeStorageArrays();
      }
    }

    return [
        new Float32Array(arrayVertex),
        new Float32Array(arrayNormal),
        new Float32Array(arrayTexture),
        new Float32Array(arrayColor),
        new Uint16Array(arrayIndex)
    ];
  }
}
```

First we open the racingtrack.ply file and read the header. Then we collect the number of vertices and faces. We then initialize our storage arrays. These are the arrays that will be returned from the function. They contain vertex, texture, normal and color data.

Once header is read, we begin scanning the file for a list of all vertices. This is the longest list in the file. The list of faces which follows is a bit shorter. Once the vertex and face lists are read, we have to rewire the data.

As described in the PLY file header, the data on each line comes in the following format:

x y z nx ny nz u v r g b

The data is separated by " " space character. So when we read it, we use JavaScript's split method to create an array from this string. Each array entry will be readable at its proper index:

```
e[0] // x
e[1] // y
e[2] // z
e[3] // nx
e[4] // ny
e[5] // nz
e[6] // u
e[7] // v
e[8] // r
e[9] // g
e[10] // b
```

And so on.

When we're loading color r, g, b values from the PLY file a conversion is required. Blender saves RGB colors in format ranging from 0-255 per color channel. But WebGL requires 0.0f - 1.0f. In order to remedy this situation we need to divide the incoming values by 255.0f. This will clamp the value to 0-1 range we're looking for.

And now we have to figure out how to deal with face data.

The list of faces specifies only indices of the vertices. So we take the vertices from the list in the order they were read and count that as their index value. We then go into the face list where each entry contains a polygon face consisting of 3 vertices each (triangle.)

Face indices:

    e[0] // index of the vertex A of this polygon
    e[1] // index of the vertex B of this polygon
    e[2] // index of the vertex C of this polygon

So these index values 0, 1 and 2 represent a link to the vertex of that index. By using them we will reconstruct the entire model as it was saved from Blender. Usually the order of the first few polygons is the same as it appears on the vertex list. But not the same for the rest of them.

In fact, the values in the resulting file are seemingly juggled around at various intervals. We do not need to worry about this as long as we properly rewire the model according to the indices stored in face object we just read.

We will associate the indices stored in faces with the vertices of that index. (We cannot simply read all vertices in the order they appear in the file and construct a model out of that data. We have to associate them with their respective indices stored in the list of faces.)

Now that this is done, we begin to extract the rewired data that was read and start packing it into separate arrays. Each array represents vertex, normal, texture and color coordinates. They all except texture array contain 3 entries. The texture contains only 2: u and v coordinate per vertex.

Once the function finished its operation we simply return arrays that were read. Then we convert them to their WebGL representation using Float32Array and Uint16Array types. Yes, you guessed it. These arrays is what we will pass to the GPU just in the same way as we did this in all of our previous examples. This function successfully constructs the model for us.

A Word Of Caution

Loading OBJ or PLY formats is not the ideal way of loading 3D model data into your WebGL application. These formats are created inherently for working with 3D modeling software.

Ideally, you want to load your data into your application in binary format. Preferably, compressed. However doing that is not covered in this book (eventually it will be covered in a future edition of this book.)

For educational purposes loading PLY formats is sufficient enough. We're not trying to write a high performance model loader here. Only to demonstrate principles of model loading and what's involved. Keep that in mind. You don't want to publish your model data openly in PLY format together with your game distribution if you care about security. Compressed formats, or at least models stored in binary format (not in text) provide additional safety for storing original content when it comes to actually publishing your game.

While saving to and loading models from binary formats is not covered in this book as of yet, it shouldn't be difficult to figure out how to do that. The principles are the same. We read the data, rewire the indices/vertices and send the data to our array buffer for upload onto the GPU.

New Level Of Complexity

Congratulations. You can now load a much more complex world into your graphics engine. In fact, this is exactly what we will do in this section. I created a simple racing track over the weekend while writing this book just to test the loader.

Let's take a look at the results.

The process of loading the model is exactly the same as with our previous demos in the book. The only difference is that now the vertex data comes from our LoadPLY function. Which, I modified just for this example (but it should still be updated to adapt to loading multiple models asynchronously; at this time in the book it is not yet necessary).

Let's plug it into our initialization routine and wire it into the rendering loop.

I've modified our asset loader code and instead of checking for shaders and textures, I am also checking for models to have fully downloaded. Once all 3 types of assets are done initializing, we can enter webGLResourcesLoaded function to set up our vertices.

To accomplish that the only other thing that I updated was the way we get vertex, colors, texture uvs and normals coordinates (normals are intentionally commented out here for now):

```
// An event that fires when all resources finish loading:

window.webGLResourcesLoaded = function() {

  console.log("webGLResourcesLoaded():" +
          "All WebGL resources finished loading!");

  // Get vertex data from loaded model
  var vertices = window.RacingTrack[0];

  var colors = window.RacingTrack[1];
```

```
var uvs = window.RacingTrack[2];

// var normals = window.RacingTrack[3]; // unused for now

var indices = window.RacingTrack[4];

   ...
```

Now instead of getting these values from our own functions, or even worse, write them all out by hand like we did with the cube, here they were redirected to the RacingTrack object loaded from LoadPLY function now in model.js. I won't show here these details. Really, they would only clutter the page space.

But I did add another function to model.js file:

```
window.ModelsLoaded = false;
```

```
// Store our racing track model in this object
window.RacingTrack = null;
```

```
function LoadModels() {

   LoadPLY("racingtrack.ply");

}
```

Because we don't have a fully functioning multi-model loader (which is a task I am leaving up to you.) I cheated here a little and modified LoadPLY to work with a single model only.

```
// ...toward the end of LoadPLY function...
```

```
window.RacingTrack = [
```

```
    new Float32Array(arrayVertex),
    new Float32Array(arrayColor),
    new Float32Array(arrayTexture),
    new Float32Array(arrayNormal),
    new Uint16Array(arrayIndex)
];
```

I hardcoded window.RacingTrack to load the model into. This is not the best (or even good) practice to say the least. But I intentionally want to challenge you to complete the model loader on your own following the shader and texture loaders. I don't want to repeat the same (or very similar) code again.

To see the full source code of this example just take a look at how it is all put together at the following URL demonstrating it in action:

http://www.tigrisgames.com/fx/index10.php

Open up the source code for this URL and you will see all of the techniques we've implemented so far working together to render a Mario Kart-style racing track. Now this is a lot more interesting than just a cube.

And here are the results. This is racingtrack.ply in the flesh:

(Please refer to the images on the next page.)

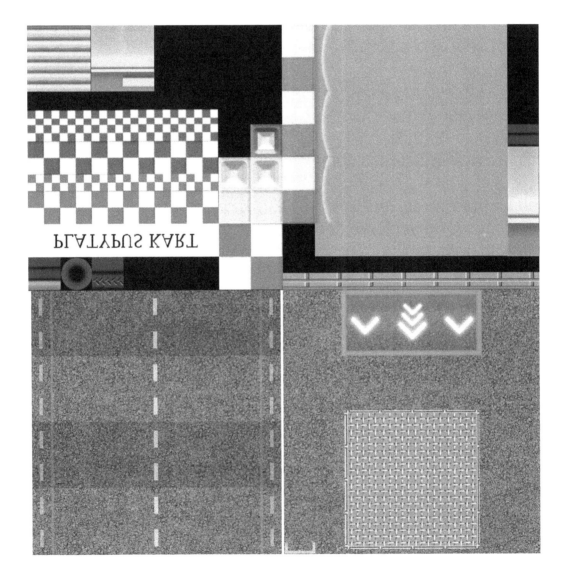

Above (on previous page) is the texture map that was used for the racing track. It resides in "textures" folder as road.png and is automatically downloaded. It becomes window.road variable in our code. Yes, that's all you have to do, is simply drop your textures into "textures" folder and refer to them as window.filename without the extension (such as PNG.)

Here you will notice that the PNG is really reversed. I did this after I finished working on the texture. WebGL loads PNGs up side down. You can probably write this into the texture loading code so you don't have to flip your PNGs every time you're done designing them.

I'm not trying to leave this out due to lack of explanations but to demonstrate principles and things you must be aware of when designing your own WebGL graphics engine. For example, if the PNG is not flipped (or you didn't know this could be an issue) you might become puzzled as to why the loaded level looks wonky and think that the problem is elsewhere.

Depth Test

It's probably worth mentioning that this is the first time in the book where we need to worry about the Z axis depth test. Without it, some of the polygons of the loaded model would "cut through" the others or simply not drawn in the correct order.

Internally WebGL decides which polygons to draw first. This depends on your WebGL driver. For this reason without the per-fragment depth test you can end up with some unpredictable results (just try disabling the depth test in this chapter's demo and move around the map using arrow keys.)

Thankfully, to battle the problem WebGL already takes care of this problem by providing gl.enable and gl.depthFunc methods. Let's use them to avoid inaccurately rendered polygons in the future.

```
// Enable depth test
gl.enable(gl.DEPTH_TEST);
gl.depthFunc(gl.LESS);

// Clear WebGL canvas
gl.clearColor(0.0, 0.0, 0.0, 1.0);

gl.clear(gl.COLOR_BUFFER_BIT);
gl.clear(gl.DEPTH_BUFFER_BIT);
```

Here we let WebGL know that we want to enable the depth test. Somewhere later in your rendering loop, we can call gl.clear command with either COLOR_BUFFER_BIT or DEPTH_BUFFER_BIT (or both.) This is because framebuffers can contain either color or Z buffer information at the same time. Either one can be cleared to a value specified by gl.clearColor or gl.clearDepth. Here we don't really have to set clearDepth color. While the depth test is enabled and now produces accurate polygon rendering clearDepth function is unnecessary here. It is usually used when we operate on the framebuffer's depth buffer directly from our shaders to achieve a particular effect. In this case we are not, so the function remains untouched.

Conclusion

Wow! What a progress we have made in this chapter. Loading large maps into your engine definitely gets you closer to making a complete game.

But loading large assets into the game world is just the first step. We can definitely create a racing game now which is limited to the car traveling on a flat surface. At this time there isn't a way to communicate the height of our map, even when the road starts leaning uphill. The car would simply "pass through" your level geometry.

Our game world can be populated by controllable characters capable of colliding with the geometry. If they are not aware of the vertex data we will not be able to add any reasonably fun game dynamics to the game. Thankfully our PLY model loader makes a copy of that data. And this is what we will use to cast a ray and collide with it.

Next chapter will be concerned with writing a collision detection function. This function will cast a ray from a particular location. For example, where your game character is at the time. This ray (or line segment, rather) will inevitably intersect one of the polygons we have just loaded from a PLY file. This means the data will not be used just for rendering the polygons by passing them into the GPU via shaders, but also for performing mathematical calculations on. When that happens, we can calculate the intersection point between the segment and the polygon and render a game character at a proper position in the world based on the terrain's height at that spot.

Once obtained we can align our 3D character model with that collision point. This way it will appear that when the character is moving it "walks" on the surface of the game map. This way you can create semi-realistic "kart" driving simulations or something as simple as a ball rolling down a hill.

Implementing collision detection together with an interesting level design layout gets you about 50-75% closer to making an actual game. From that point on most of your time would be spent designing the game level in Blender or similar software.

Gem 20 - Imitating 1st Person Walking Camera

Implementing a 3D camera that imitates first person view walking is best understood in context of two dimensions. Planar 360-degree freedom movement always depends on two axis. First, we identify the plane on which we want our character camera to "walk on". In majority of cases this plane is bound to X and Z coordinates. I'll explain what this means with an example.

In this chapter we will also create our own JavaScript Segment class for working with planar data. This class will not be particularly tailored to the problem we're trying to solve here. But it will be useful here. This way we can keep things organized instead of just working with random variable names.

Let's imagine for a moment that we're looking at our 3D world from some point above the ground and looking straight down some arbitrary angle. It doesn't matter which, our character can be facing any direction and be located anywhere on the ground plane.

Let's focus on the XZ plane because this way we can isolate the problem of movement in 3D and view it as a 2D problem first.

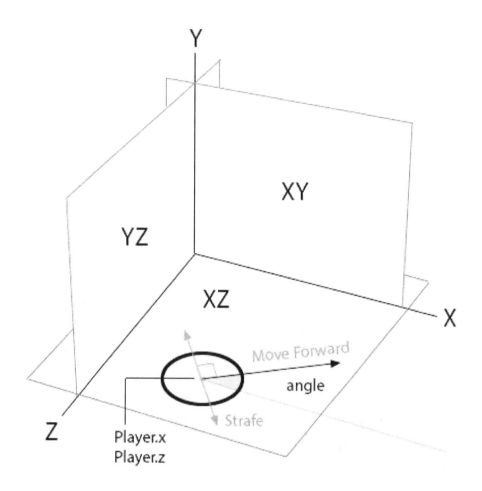

The ground plane XZ can be traversed in any direction by changing X and Z coordinates. However, the problem is complicated by the fact that our character can look in any particular direction while walking on this plane.

Therefore, we cannot achieve accurate results by simply adding or subtracting the same value from both Player.x and Player.z. The increment by which the player should move on either X and Z axis is calculated separately for each axis based on the direction angle.

This means that player's camera direction will be determined by the 360 angle on the plane toward which the game character will be walking when the player hits the UP arrow key or presses a joystick button bound to "move forward" action. If angle is <= 0 or >= 360, we will clamp it to be bound within those values to achieve seamless motion.

Strafing

Strafing is calculated by taking the current angle of direction and either subtracting or adding 90 degrees to it. It's simply moving the character in either left or right direction when the player is pressing LEFT or RIGHT arrow keys.

Default Direction

The code is relatively simple. We're going to use some trigonometry here to determine X and Z movement offset based on the angle.

We need to determine which axis is the default looking axis. In classic scenario it is looking straight down negative Z. But it really depends on your camera implementation. The matter of fact is that we simply have to make a choice and stick to it.

In order to minimize mental suffering we will reduce this problem to 2D.

Segment or Line?

This is the first chapter where we are actually working with 3D coordinate system to accomplish something practical. I'll use this opportunity to introduce several important principles that relate to many operations we will be doing throughout this book and during game development in general.

We've come to a point in the book where it may be reasonable start drawing a distinction between a Segment and a Line in 3D graphics.

This will help us not only to provide a reasonably organized way of making walking and strafing calculations, but will further simplify otherwise complex operations and help us abstract them into understandable and uncomplicated JavaScript code. As hard to believe as that might sound at first.

A Line is usually thought of as a span stretching into infinity in both directions. In other words, in 3D graphics lines are segments without ending points. They are represented by an angle. It's common to mistake a line for a segment because naturally we think of lines as having ending points. Not so in 3D graphics.

A Segment is a line with two ending points.

Our player is represented by an x and z position on the plane as well as a direction angle.

We could simply calculate these values and store them in variables to recreate illusion of walking on a 3D plane. However, in this chapter we will take this concept a bit further and create a JavaScript Segment class. This class will include basic segment-related utility functions.

We will then use these utility functions to simulate a first person view walking animation with keyboard controls and mouse look.

Introducing Segment Class

The Segment class is designed to work with 2D parameters. Thankfully as we just discussed we have reduced the problem to 2 axis and using this class is sufficient for our purpose.

Along the way, we will learn a few principles that I am sure will be reusable throughout your entire journey on the way to becoming a better game developer.

Again, this class for simplicity's sake will work only with 2-dimensional data. Which will also become incredibly helpful for mastering 2D games in WebGL. And it can be easily re-implemented for 3D data by simply adding an axis. However, in this case it is more than sufficient for the purpose at hand.

Let's take a look at the Segment class and a few utility functions now.

Note that some of the functions use a previously discussed Vector class in a few situations.

```
window.int_x = 0;
window.int_y = 0;

var DONT_INTERSECT = 0;
var COLLINEAR = 1;
var DO_INTERSECT = 2;

function same_sign(a, b) { return ( ( a * b ) >= 0 ); }

// Segment class; mostly for planar calculations
var Segment = function(x, y, vecx, vecy)
{
  this.x = x;   // A segment is represented by an origin and a vector
  this.y = y;
  this.vecx = vecx;
  this.vecy = vecy;

  // Calculate the length of this segment
  this.length = function() {
```

```javascript
    var dx = this.vecx;
    var dy = this.vecy;
    return Math.sqrt(dx * dx + dy * dy);
}

// Calculate normal vector
this.normal = function() {
    var x1 = this.y;
    var y1 = this.x + this.vecx;
    var y2 = this.x;
    var x2 = this.y + this.vecy;
    return new Segment(x1, y1, x2-x1, y2-y1);
}

// Calculate the center point of the segment
this.center = function() {
    var _x = this.x + this.x + this.vecx;
    var _y = this.y + this.y + this.vecy;
    _x /= 2;
    _y /= 2;
    return new Point(_x, _y);
}

// Calculate unit vector
this.unit = function() {
    return new Segment(0,
            0,
            this.vecx / this.length(),
            this.vecy / this.length());
}

// Multiply this vector by a multiplier value to affect its length
this.multiply = function(multiplier) { return new Segment(0, 0,
this.vecx*multiplier, this.vecy*multiplier);
```

```
}

// Project a vector from current one onto another segment
this.project = function( seg_onto )
{
    var vec = new Vector(this.vecx, this.vecy);
    var onto = new Vector(seg_onto.vecx, seg_onto.vecy);
    var d = onto.dot(onto);
    if (0 < d) {
        var dp = vec.dot(onto);
        var multiplier = dp / d;
        var rx = onto.x * multiplier;
        var ry = onto.y * multiplier;
        return new Point(rx, ry);
    }
    return new Point(0, 0);
}

// Planar 2D intersection algorithm between two segments
this.intersect = function( segment )
{
    // a
    var x1 = this.x;
    var y1 = this.y;
    var x2 = this.x + this.vecx;
    var y2 = this.y + this.vecy;

    // b
    var x3 = segment.x;
    var y3 = segment.y;
    var x4 = segment.x + segment.vecx;
    var y4 = segment.y + segment.vecy;

    var a1, a2, b1, b2, c1, c2;
```

```
var r1, r2 , r3, r4;
var denom, offset, num;

a1 = y2 - y1;
b1 = x1 - x2;
c1 = (x2 * y1) - (x1 * y2);

r3 = ((a1 * x3) + (b1 * y3) + c1);
r4 = ((a1 * x4) + (b1 * y4) + c1);

if ((r3 != 0) && (r4 != 0) && same_sign(r3, r4))
return DONT_INTERSECT;

a2 = y4 - y3; // Compute a2, b2, c2
b2 = x3 - x4;
c2 = (x4 * y3) - (x3 * y4);
r1 = (a2 * x1) + (b2 * y1) + c2; // Compute r1 and r2
r2 = (a2 * x2) + (b2 * y2) + c2;

if ((r1 != 0) && (r2 != 0) && (same_sign(r1, r2)))
return DONT_INTERSECT;

// Line segments intersect: compute intersection point.
denom = (a1 * b2) - (a2 * b1);

if (denom == 0)
return COLLINEAR;

if (denom < 0) offset = -denom / 2; else offset = denom / 2;

num = (b1 * c2) - (b2 * c1);
if (num < 0) window.int_x = (num - offset) / denom; else
window.int_x = (num + offset) / denom;
```

```
      num = (a2 * c1) - (a1 * c2);
      if (num < 0)  window.int_y = ( num - offset) / denom; else
window.int_y = (num + offset) / denom;
      return DO_INTERSECT;
  }
}


// Convert 2D vector coordinates to an angle in degrees
function vec2ang(x,y)
{
    angleInRadians = Math.atan2(y, x);
    angleInDegrees = (angleInRadians / Math.PI) * 180.0;
    return angleInDegrees;
}


// Convert an angle to vector coordinates
function ang2vec(angle)
{
    var radians = angle * (Math.PI / 180.0);
    var x = Math.cos(radians);
    var y = Math.sin(radians);

    var a = new Segment(0, 0, x, y);
    var u = a.normal().unit();

    return [u.vecx, u.vecy];
}
```

Let's briefly review this class. We will not only use it to create 360-degree movement in our game world, but also in many other situations.

Note that the Segment class has a dependency on the Vector class.

The Segment class contains these standard functions:

length calculates the length of a segment. This common operation returns the amount of space between two endpoints of a segment.

normal calculates the normal of a segment. A normal is a 90-degree vector stemming from the segment. They are incredibly useful for calculating direction or figuring out which surfaces face a certain direction or away from it.

center is simply the center point of this segment located right on the segment between its two endpoints.

unit vector is a normalized vector. Here, we should not mix a normalized vector with a segment's normal. A normalized vector is not its normal. The unit, or normalized vector, is the same exact vector that it was, except reduced to a smaller site: or its unit size. If we perform this operation on even the longest vectors, they will all be reduced to a size of 1.0 in length by performing this operation.

multiply is a function that will multiply the segment by a scalar value (not another vector/segment.) This is useful in making this vector/ segment longer or shorter.

project is a method that will "project" a vector onto another at a 90 degree angle. This function is often used in collision detection algorithms where you need to calculate whether a sphere (circle) collides with a line at the edges.

intersect is my favorite function in this class. It returns DO_INTERSECT, DONT_INTERSECT or COLLINEAR values between two segments. If two segments do intersect, it will also store the last intersection point in window.int_x and window.int_y global variables. This is a little quirky. But the other choice would be to store it in an array and returning an array. Some 3D applications and games require hundreds if not thousands (or even millions) of intersection points. This would not only bloat memory by multiplying array storage but also retrieving indices is probably more computationally expensive in a few cases.

vec2ang converts a vector (or a segment) to an angle.

ang2vec converts an angle back to vector coordinates.

The Segment class is a conglomerate of useful functionality. And each method, except the line intersection algorithm, can be easily extended into 3D versions. However, we will write a 3D collision detection function (3D segment vs 3D plane) a bit later in the book. Collision against a 3D plane is calculated in a slightly different manner and you can't easily transform it to 3D by simply adding a new axis to a similar function that was originally dealing with 2D coordinates only. But we haven't gotten to the point in the book where it will become necessary.

Walking in 3D Space

Finally, let's actually demonstrate realistic "walking" camera in our 3D world. We'll also control it with our JavaScript keyboard class we already covered elsewhere in this book. And we'll use camera view transformations that we already talked about as well. That is, if you've been following this book from the start :)

```
var velocity = 0.005;

var player_x = 0; // center player at the center of coordinate system
var player_z = 0;
var player_angle = 0; // direction angle, 0 by default
```

```
var dir = ang2vec(player_angle);
var dirx = dir.x;
var dirz = dir.y;

var x_vel = dirx * velocity;
var z_vel = dirz * velocity;
```

var dirz = dir.y is not a bug: **ang2vec** works in 2 dimensions and always returns x and y property. But our character camera is walking on the XZ plane. We simply rename the variable to match its appropriate axis.

This principle can be implemented in so many cases. An object often has an angle of direction and by calculating a planar directional vector we can use that information to move the object forward, backward or make it "strafe" (move left and right relative to its direction at 90 degrees; in other words move sideways.)

Gem 21 - Mouse Controls

In previous chapter we created a keyboard controls library. To supplement it with mouse controls we will yet create another class and add it to our project. This is probably the shortest chapter in the entire book. We simply need to get mouse controls going so we can quickly move on to continue exploring WebGL demos that require user interaction.

I will simply call the new class MouseControls. In the same way as what we've done for keyboard class - a global variable Mouse will be used to instantiate it.

In JavaScript to track position of the mouse on the screen we have to look at the event object returned from a mouse event such as onmousemove. In jQuery it is shortened to just mousemove. I created a file mouse.js that contains everything we need to detect current location of the mouse every time the event is intercepted.

mouse.js
```
// Global variable for tracking clicked state
window.clicked = false;

// Primary Mouse controls class
var MouseControls = function()
{

  // Last mouse coordinates
  this.x = 0;
  this.y = 0;

  // Memorize a link to this object
  var that = this;

  this.Initialize = function(element)
  {
    // Intercept mouse move event and extract position
    $(element).on("mousemove", function(event) {

      // Calculate mouse position relative to upper left screen corner
      that.x = event.pageX - $(element).offset().left;
      that.y = event.pageY - $(element).offset().top;
    });

    // Intercept single click event
    $(element).on("click", function(e) {
      if (!e) var e = event;
```

```javascript
    // Ignore native JavaScript event functionality
    e.preventDefault();

    // Determine coordinates in window space
    that.x = e.clientX - $(element).offset().left;
    that.y = e.clientY - $(element).offset().top;

    window.clicked = true;
  });
 }
}
```

And now we can put this code into action by instantiating the mouse controls object:

mouse.js (continued...)
```javascript
// Initialize global mouse object
var Mouse = new MouseControls();
```

Note the event.pageX in mousemove event and e.clientX coordinates are used to calculate accurate position of the mouse cursor on canvas. The canvas itself is not the entire drawing area on a web page. It is usually occupied by a custom-size rectangle. But the JavaScript mouse events return coordinates relative to the element the mouse is found it. So we need to do this conversion to ensure that our mouse coordinates are consistent and don't waver based on canvas element's position inside <body> tag.

Now that the global object Mouse is initialized we can safely look up mouse coordinates on any animation frame by looking at Mouse.x and Mouse.y.

```javascript
setInterval( function() {
```

```
    if (window.clicked)
    {
        // Where was the mouse clicked on the screen?
        var x = Mouse.x;
        var y = Mouse.y;
    }

}, 0);
```

I don't think the balance between simplicity and readability could be better than this. Well, maybe you can make the "M" lowercase to remain consistent with the keyboard class... or if that's your programming style.

Conclusion

We have just added an important element to our WebGL graphics engine that takes it to the next level. We can now control our objects or camera with either mouse or keyboard. To demonstrate this in action you can take a look at the demo at the following URL:

http://www.tigrisgames.com/fx/index11.php

Just use the keyboard to move the view around. Of course in this demo I quickly hooked up keyboard controls to the main camera view that takes it position from our ModelView matrix. Whenever arrow keys are pressed, the translate transform for the ModelView matrix takes that in consideration because global x and y coordinates are changed. The result is illusion of a moving camera.

This is an extremely basic example. We're just getting started with controls. We'll get to advanced camera movement in the chapter on 3D cameras including the algorithm for generating LookAt vector which automatically points the camera in the direction of a given object or "follows" it.

I hope you enjoyed this mini chapter. That's really all there is to say about mouse controls. We wouldn't want to spend any more time with this. Let's move forward to our next subject.

Gem 22 - Keyboard Controls For Games

Rendering 3D objects on the screen is fun. But in a real game environment keyboard controls are essential. In this chapter we will learn how to write a simple and elegant keyboard controls system which we can later use to move objects and game characters.

Keyboard controls are often used for controlling our 3D camera around on the screen to simulate in-space navigation. This is so common that I had to include this chapter here. This way our future examples can be a bit more interesting and it just brings us one step closer to making games.

JavaScript keyboard events are designed around ASCII codes. You can go online to look up an ascii code for just about any key. Or you can write a single line of JavaScript code inside the keyboard event callback function that displays the ASCII code of the key that has just been pressed.

After a while of doing that, I've come up with the following keys. I chose some of the most commonly used keys in games: The arrow keys and WSAD. Let's define them.

keyboard.js
```
// ASCII codes
var KEY_LEFT = 37;
```

```
var KEY_RIGHT = 39;
var KEY_UP = 38;
var KEY_DOWN = 40;
var KEY_W = 87;
var KEY_S = 83;
var KEY_A = 65;
var KEY_D = 68;
```

I started a new file to include to the engine we've been building from the first page of this book.

The file is called keyboard.js and will needs to be included in your project.

I will also create a window.key object that will hold the global object responsible for tracking a key press on any of the keys listed above. In addition, we need to find a way of tracking the shift key.

```
keyboard.js (continued)
var isShift = false;
window.key = null;
```

Now we'll define the primary keyboard class itself. In JavaScript, whenever you want to create a new feature I often find myself starting it by creating a new object that has a matching name with what I am trying to accomplish.

In this instance, I decided to create a generic Keyboard class which we will initialize to gain control over any key we want. The reason each key is explicitly defined in Keyboard class, is that it results in much cleaner code. For example, we could refer to the left key as key.left. It's simply called "left" and attached to the main key object. I don't think that there is a more elegant way of doing this in JavaScript. All other keys we will define will follow the same pattern.

keyboard.js (continued)
```js
var Keyboard = function() {
    this.left = false;
    this.right = false;
    this.up = false;
    this.down = false;
    this.w = false;
    this.s = false;
    this.a = false;
    this.d = false;
};
```

Now that we have our basic data setup we need a way to initialize our Keyboard class and assign it to the global object instance key.

For this, I created a function InitializeKeyboard. It will be called only once during the initialization process right before we enter the main rendering loop in our WebGL application.

keyboard.js (continued)
```js
function InitializeKeyboard()
{
    window.key = new Keyboard();

    $(document).keydown(function(e) {
        if (e.keyCode == 16) isShift = true;
        if (e.keyCode == KEY_LEFT) { key.left = true; }
        if (e.keyCode == KEY_RIGHT) { key.right = true; }
        if (e.keyCode == KEY_UP) { key.up = true; }
        if (e.keyCode == KEY_DOWN) { key.down = true; }
        if (e.keyCode == KEY_W) { key.w = true; }
        if (e.keyCode == KEY_S) { key.s = true; }
        if (e.keyCode == KEY_A) { key.a = true; }
```

```
    if (e.keyCode == KEY_D) { key.d = true; }
    console.log(e.keyCode);
  });

  $(document).keyup(function(e) {
    if (e.keyCode == 16) isShift = false;
    if (e.keyCode == KEY_LEFT) { key.left = false; }
    if (e.keyCode == KEY_RIGHT) { key.right = false; }
    if (e.keyCode == KEY_UP) { key.up = false; }
    if (e.keyCode == KEY_DOWN) { key.down = false; }
    if (e.keyCode == KEY_W) { key.w = false; }
    if (e.keyCode == KEY_S) { key.s = false; }
    if (e.keyCode == KEY_A) { key.a = false; }
    if (e.keyCode == KEY_D) { key.d = false; }
  });
}
```

Here we are using jQuery to intercept the keydown and keyup events. jQuery helps us accomplish this in a cross-browser way so we don't have to worry about re-implementing this code for multiple browsers.

When a key is pressed, the key state is set to true. When it is released its state is set to false. We need both events to accurately simulate keyboard controls for games. They usually require both events.

I think we're done! From now on all you have to do is call InitializeKeyboard and place your key capture code shown below directly inside your main animation loop somewhere near the top:

```
// Main game animation loop:
setInterval(function() {

  // Take keyboard controls
```

```
if (key.left) { /* Move character left */ }
if (key.right) { /* Move character right */ }
if (key.top) { /* Move character top */ }
if (key.down) { /* Move character down */ }

// Process the rest of your game logic...

}, 0);
```

Want to test if a key has been pressed together with SHIFT? No problem. Just do something as follows:

```
if (key.left && isShift) {

    // Todo: perform special action when Shift is pressed

}
```

When you're moving left and shift key is pressed your character could run instead of walking. I think the idea is pretty straightforward here.

Tracking a Single Press

Sometimes in games you need to track the key just once. This gives the player control over how often to pick up or release an in-game item. Or a similar action.

You can simulate a "single press" event by tracking the key's state. Which is something unique to game development. It is not common for web applications to do this because they are usually not designed to run in a live real-time animation loop. But when it comes to games we sometimes need to check whether the key has been pressed just once.

Native JavaScript keyboard event system does not have an optimal way of doing this because from the start it just hasn't been tailored for real-time animation. We can in theory use a native event for this but it was originally designed for typing and not controlling game characters.

That's another reason this keyboard library decouples the press event into two categories. One on the way down and one on the way up. But this still gives us continuity of state. Once the key is pressed and not released, the state will be a continuous "true" on each frame. And that's not the effect we're trying to achieve with a single press.

The idea is to track a single press of a key. If the key is still being held on the next frame of animation, we do nothing even if the key's "pressed" state is still set to true. This "tapping" mechanism can be used for firing a laser gun at an interval defined by player and not necessarily when a frame-based counter expires. Some games require this type of action. Surprisingly, very often, as you may have found out if you've tried game development at least for a brief period of time. Let alone for over a decade.

All we're doing here is recreating the native JavaScript event and adapting it to real-time animation. It can be implemented as follows.

Note that an additional boolean key_leftPressed is required to make this happen:

```
var key_leftPressed = false;

setInterval(function() {
  if (key.left && !key_leftPressed) {
      // Todo: perform some in-game action: Fire a laser gun, etc.
      key_leftPressed = true;
```

```
  } else {
    key_leftPressed = false; // release key to restart the cycle
  }

}, 0);
```

This gives us better control over keyboard events for games over traditional JavaScript approach.

From now on in all of our future demos and examples in the book we will be using keyboard.js to provide keyboard controls for moving things around. It's a pretty straightforward library.

And of course, a complete set of controls for WebGL applications wouldn't be complete without mouse controls. And that's the subject of our next chapter. Once we wrap this up we will use keyboard and mouse together to change our view and model matrices to rotate either objects or 3D camera and finally make our demos a bit more interactive.

These are all very trivial elements of a JavaScript application. And they are not necessarily related to WebGL itself. But they are essential for making things more interesting and adding depth to the experience you will be creating in your own games.

Gem 23 - 3D Camera

Camera and world movement are achieved via matrix transformations to either the models in the world or the camera itself. We've already talked about matrices and even chose a matrix library that's now stored in matrix.js file as part of our WebGL engine so far.

In this chapter we will discover how to move around a 3D world using common techniques which also include a LookAt vector calculation (this is when a camera is looking directly at an object regardless of either camera or object's position in world space). This works great for adding different camera views to our game. For example, following the player's car in a racing game. We'll talk about this in a bit. For now let's focus on the basics.

In order to do this we will need to create a new JavaScript class.

The Camera Class

Traditionally the default camera is looking in the direction of negative Z axis. Our matrix library takes care of that by simply assuming it.

Remember that every time we add a major feature to our engine, it's probably a good idea to start a new class. This gives you ability to organize a large number of objects in a modular way.

For each object we have a "module", which is nothing more than a separate filename containing a class definition for describing a unique engine feature. Knowing this, let's add our camera class into the new file I started called camera.js

In JavaScript we can add a new class using the class keyword. It is just one of the at least 5 different ways of defining an object! When I started writing this book many of other modules were already written using function constructors. Each function in JavaScript by default is also an object constructor. In this instance, I'll add a new Camera class in that way. The rest of it is outlined in the source code below and then we'll take a look at each element in greater detail.

I am not going to overload you with complicated matrix math formulas that provide this functionality as filler text for the book. Instead, we will explore the 3D camera principles of primary interest and learn how to actually use them and what effect they have on the camera view. Once our camera class is completed, it will be used throughout the rest of the book to show how it can be implemented to arrive at some sort of practical purpose. For example, how to follow a racing car or some other object in our 3D game world which dramatically increases interactivity.

A completed example of how the camera works can be looked up on WebGLTutorial.org website where this library is actually being used. You can copy and paste the code from there. However, the rest of this chapter will go in detail on what that code actually does and how it was constructed.

The concept of camera is also extensively used in 2D platformer games as well. We can simply point our 3D camera in direction of the tile-based world and move it according to the current location of the main game character.

In particular, if we use WebGL for this purpose, we also get hardware-accelerated rotation and zoom effects which can produce tremendous improvements to the overall game look and feel. For example, creating a "smooth follow" feature for the main character instead of abruptly following the camera that feels almost mechanically tied to the keyboard's arrow controls.

Ok, enough of theory! Let's see what the class looks like.

```
// Main camera object class
// Note: The Camera class is dependent on
// matrix-generation functions located in <matrix.js> library
var Camera = function()
```

```
{
    this.x = 0;
    this.y = 0;
    this.z = 0;

    // Camera's direction vector
    this.direction = null;

    // This camera as represented by a "mat4" matrix
    this.ViewMatrix = null;
}
```

The camera has an x, y, z location in the world.

The direction vector is simply the direction in which the camera is looking at.

Method **LookAt** is a shortcut to setting the LookAt vector and storing it in ViewMatrix variable. But instead of integrating it into the camera class, I modified the CanvasMatrix4 class (because original lookat function in it did not produce accurate results with our current engine setup.) We'll see its source code implementation in a bit.

Let's go ahead and see all of the possible ways in which the camera can be used. Once we explore this subject in detail you will be able to create fly-by cameras, or achieve pretty much any camera placement you can possibly imagine.

As we've explored in a chapter about matrices movement in 3D space is interpretative. It means there isn't a single way of representing camera movement. For this reason, when not taught properly, camera operations may often appear perplexing.

First, let's take a look at the 3D camera perspective itself. Here we have visible near and far clipping planes. This is the area the camera can "see". You've seen this represented mathematically in an earlier chapter where we created a starfield demo.

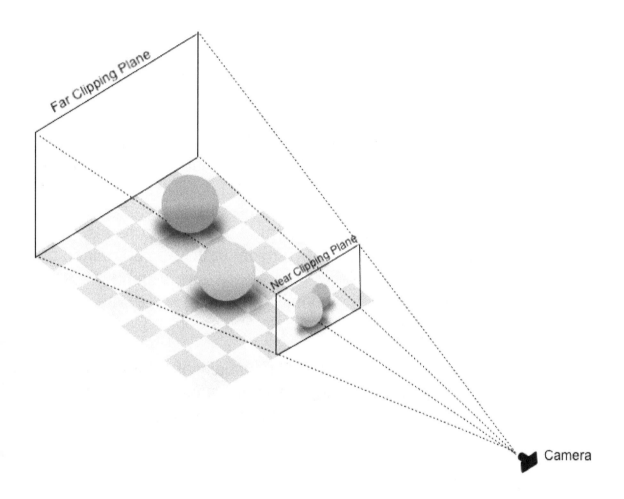

In this chapter we will demystify 4 different interpretations of camera operations that in one way or another determine what happens on the screen and how it happens. Breaking them down in this way will help us get a practical idea of how to gain full control over 3D camera.

These interpretations will be supplied with WebGL source code which will demonstrate each one separately in enough detail to start using them in your own games or 3D applications.

Doing that gives you ability to be the director in your own game world. Place the camera anywhere you want, and make it point to a specific direction while following a path. Or switch between different cameras to get a different view of the scene.

After some research you will end up with 4 different types of possible camera operations which I am listing below. 3 of them are extrinsic. The remaining one is intrinsic.

Intrinsic simply means that it relates to the format of the camera view itself and neither camera's position in the world nor the position of the objects in the world.

Intrinsic parameters are usually represented by a view cone also known as the view frustum. It's the pyramidal structure determined by the parameters of the focal point of the camera lens. When we change intrinsic parameters, the cone is affected in some way, either skewing or distorting the view, zooming in and so on.

Whereas changes to extrinsic parameters usually affect the objects outside the camera or when moving the camera itself which visually produces the same effect as moving the world in the opposite direction.

Projection (Intrinsic)
The view cone dimensions. This is where view frustum or the size of the view cone is changed. Used for camera effects such as zoom or projection adjustments that deal with the resolution and screen dimensions.

World (Extrinsic)
The position and angles of the objects in the world are transformed.

Camera (Extrinsic)
The position and rotation angles of the camera are transformed.

Look-At (Extrinsic)
The camera position and angles are calculated based on a target object. In this case the camera view "follows" an object represented by a vertex point (x, y and z.) usually lying directly in object's center or a place of interest on the object is arbitrarily chosen.

For example, you can make the camera follow the duck but focus on its eye. This camera style is often used in racing games like Mario Kart 8.

In this case, the camera coordinates are calculated backwards from the target object. To do this we need to cast a vector to the center of that target object and another one in an "up" direction. (A LookAt camera is determined by two vectors, not just one) and use this data to rebuild the camera view in a mat4 format so it can be further passed down the WebGL pipeline into the shader as such.

Gem 24 - LookAt Camera

The LookAt camera is perhaps one of the most useful camera views. It gives us ability to create a camera view from camera's position in space, an up vector and a direction vector. This can be used for implementing anything from car-chasing views to cinematic animations.

Calculating the LookAt vector is non-trivial. But it's not very difficult either once we understand what's involved. Let's take a look at this diagram that represents a LookAt camera visually:

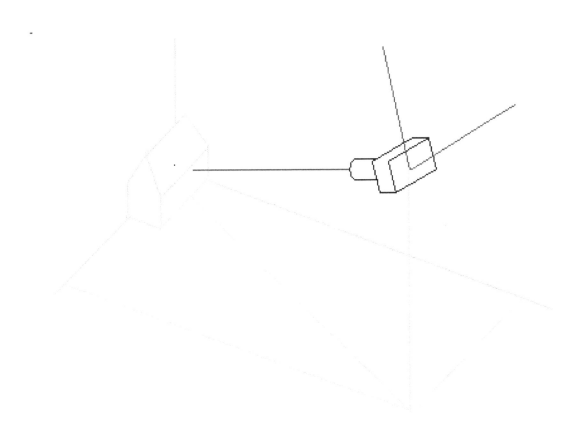

The **LookAt** camera is defined by 3 vectors pointing away from each other and separated by exactly 90 degree angle. It basically determines the camera's own local coordinate system. One of the rays points directly at a "target" object. The other two simply define the camera's "up" side. The up vector is usually computed in camera's local space. For example { 0.0, 1.0, 0.0 }, where the Y coordinate is pointing up by a unit vector of 1.0.

Much of standard functionality in 3D graphics programming is exactly the same in theory. But the details of implementation can get in the way and cause havoc, for the tiniest of reasons. Examples include swapping an x for a z here and there. Or using negative instead of positive signs in our equations. Miss one, or interchange one with the other, and the entire formula can collapse.

WebGL vector and matrix libraries were written by different programmers who thought differently about data sets, matrix order and a multitude of other details. For example, the Matrix library we included earlier in the book already has a lookat function. However, when I tried using it with our current engine build we have constructed so far in the book, it did not produce accurate results.

To circumvent this situation I created my own lookat function (and called it lookat2) and tied it to the prototype of the CanvasMatrix4 object. I completely rewrote the internal implementation and ensured that the code is cleaner to read. And more importantly, that it works accurately. In order to do all of this, I wrote the new version of the LookAt function with the help of the Vector class (vector3.js) we talked about earlier. This abstraction makes the code read almost like poetry.

Nonetheless, the entire operation is tied around two cross product and three dot product calculations. It's fairly computationally inexpensive provided that usually there is only one lookat camera switched on at any given time in our 3D scene.

```
CanvasMatrix4.prototype.lookat2 =

  function(posx, posy, posz, targetx, targety, targetz, upx, upy, upz) {

    var up = new Vector(upx, upy, upz);
    var lookat = new Vector(targetx, targety, targetz);
    var position = new Vector(posx, posy, posz);

    // Calculate the camera direction vector
    var vL = lookat.subtract( position ).unit();
    var f = new Vector(vL.x, vL.y, vL.z);
```

```
    // Cross product 1
    var vU = f.cross( up ).unit();
    var s = new Vector(vU.x, vU.y, vU.z);

    // Cross product 2
    var vF = s.cross( f ).unit();
    var u = new Vector(vF.x, vF.y, vF.z);

    // Assign results to this matrix
    this.m11 = s.x;
    this.m21 = s.y;
    this.m31 = s.z;
    this.m12 = u.x;
    this.m22 = u.y;
    this.m32 = u.z;
    this.m13 = -f.x;
    this.m23 = -f.y;
    this.m33 = -f.z;
    this.m14 = 0.0;
    this.m24 = 0.0;
    this.m34 = 0.0;

    // Calculate dot products
    this.m41 = -s.dot( position );
    this.m42 = -u.dot( position );
    this.m43 = f.dot( position );

    this.m44 = 1.0;
}
```

Here we first store the values up, lookat and position. These are simply passed into the function. The values are pretty straightforward. But the calculation that follows may not be.

First, we need to subtract position from the look at vector to get a new vector which will serve as the ray being projected from the camera's "eye" point to some target object. This also determines the length of the segment which will be used together with the up vector in the following way:

We will calculate the cross product between this new vector (f) and the up vector. And we'll then perform a second cross product operation. But this time between the newly generated vector (s) and and the direction vector (f).

Doing this will give us vectors that define a new camera matrix pointing in the direction of the target object. The camera will be pointing directly into the center of the given object.

Perhaps the CanvasMatrix4 naming convention (m11-m44) isn't so lucid after all. But basically when we write a value to this object inside a JavaScript object, it assigns a value to a property in that object. In this case we can see that CanvasMatrix4 class provides a property for each entry in the 4x4 matrix structure for a total of 16 items. We simply assign the results to m11 through m44 respectively where m11 means 1st row and first column. And m44 is the very last entry in the matrix grid (4x4 = 44.)

Creators of CanvasMatrix4 chose this naming convention over standard array implementation as a possible performance optimization so we don't have to deal with accessing arrays every time we need to perform a matrix operation.

Finally, all of the vectors involved need to be normalized. In other words, turned into unit-size vectors. Had we skipped this step your camera would move away from the target object soon as it would get really close to it, because the direction vector would be longer than the unit size. This produces a wonky zoom in/out effect. Normalizing vectors or turning them to 1.0 length vectors is a common operation in 3D graphics.

Practical Implementation

From the very beginning, this book was not planned as a reference of math formulas and long obscure mathematical derivations. Here we are focused on practical game design principles and their implementation with only brief source code explanations. Ones that are just enough to get the point across and start making something with it.

In that regard this section is perhaps the most exciting one so far. This is where an implementation of a LookAt camera with keyboard controls for recreating a racing game car chasing view will be demonstrated.

We already wrote the code for keyboard controls and PLY-format model loading. Moreover, we have also written a 3D collision detection function for determining an intersection between a line segment and a triangle. This will be handy for creating our car racing demo!

I will use all of this software we've developed up to this point with our new LookAt function to recreate a Mario Kart-like game in a future chapter. It won't have impressive graphics but it will have a few solid features:

Chase or "follow" camera.
Collision detection with arbitrary racing terrain.
Keyboard controls for our racing kart.

I won't be using any impressive 3D models there for the actual racing kart model. We can either use some of our earlier created objects (the cube, sphere, etc.) or load one from a PLY file. You can get creative here and make your own to make the game demo match the style of your choice. We'll have to leave this job to the artists.

But before we move forward with the racing kart demo, let's explore WebGL light. It'll make our level design appear a bit more interesting and less plain.

Gem 25 - Light And 3D Graphics

On this diagram we're looking at the standard OpenGL Light model. It's surprising how useful this knowledge is even to craftsmen outside of 3D computer graphics. It makes sense because 3D models are usually crafted by artists and not programmers.

Our job here, however, is to develop a graphics engine capable of loading and displaying such models. But your engine will not be very impressive or have that look of "professional" (or also known as "AAA") games without at least a semi-deep understanding of light theory as it pertains to 3D graphics. After this, we will dive into WebGL source code implementation details.

The same principles of light rendering apply to painted art. Here we're looking at a diagram consisting of 3 abstract light components:

Ambient Light - the average intensity and color covering the entire scene.
Diffuse Light - defined as the color of the light source.
Specular Highlight - the shiny, glossy reflection spot on smooth plastic and metallic objects.

When working with light in WebGL we are dealing with abstract representation of light rather than a perfect, correct model of light in the real world. However, WebGL offers enough horsepower to deliver hyper-realistic images by understanding and applying these 3 simple types of light.

Of course in nature there aren't any different types of light. These are all just abstract representations of it. Breaking down light into these categories helps writing efficient algorithms that simulate light as close as possible to reality.

We're now at a place in time where computer graphics have come extremely close to hyper-realistic depiction of nature and the world around us. Polygon-based graphics have reached this pinnacle sooner than real time ray-tracing graphics. But in a programmable shader pipeline provides almost ray-tracing like quality anyway. And it's more than acceptable for the purpose of creating games the graphics quality in which nowadays can match that of film.

Shaders provide simulation for each photon of light. But the process is kind of backwards. We are given access to each fragment (pixel) on the surface of a polygon. Which is only the result of a photon hitting some sort of a surface. Surface quality (shiny, dull, etc) in WebGL are created using materials. At first materials might appear too simplistic for creating anything that looks real. After all, materials are determined by the color of the object itself in combination with the color of the light being shined on that object. Specular highlight helps create illusion of either a plastic or metallic object. Or anything in between, like water, candle wax or wood for example.

When computationally represented they provide an accurate and extremely realistic picture. Even though as of this writing ray tracing is not in popular use, we're definitely getting there. As of this book, regardless the case, we will approximate light using abstract models when we think of implementing light in our WebGL application.

I can't help but to say "Let there be light, and there was light." Modern WebGL can certainly imitate light very well. What I'm saying is, adding light to your game is reminiscent of your game engine experiencing a full rebirth. It's an overhaul that has drastic impact on the final result. So don't get discouraged by making a sub-par engine at first. Adding light to it might change your opinion of your own engine fast. It makes that much of an impact.

Whereas flat-shaded, textured polygons define structural model for your game world, casting light on it, and especially adding specular highlights to secondary textures with normal maps can be done in just under a couple weeks of focused research.

While we cannot simply speak light into existence, we can still observe its certain properties and use them to create computer graphics. But before we do I've written this chapter to introduce you to basic principles of shading.

In fact, "shaders" were created to take these principles into action. And they will be instrumental for making all of these light effects possible.

Some light effects, such as blur and bloom are called "post-processing" effects are surprisingly easy to implement using (relative to the dramatic effect created by them) what's called a WebGL Framebuffer Object. We'll take a look at this a bit later. Let's slow down for now and start from the very beginning.

Model Specimen

Usually, one of the most common shapes is taken to represent a surface for observing how light responds to it from all of its angles. A sphere is such an object. It gives us a perspective on what the light will look like when it will hit any of the 360-degrees of the object.

You may have already seen other objects such as the "teapot" or the "bunny" which help us test what light rendering looks like on complex objects. Throughout this text here, we will take a look at how different types of light affect our generic sphere object.

Other chapters in this book demonstrate how to load pretty much any object from a PLY file that can be created in Blender. You can manually load them to experiment with other models you find online or with your own creations.

Starting Point

Knowing light and its properties is important. At least we can imitate how it works, without full knowledge. And that's good enough, we're not trying to be perfect here. All 3D graphics and effects are usually implemented using some kind of trick or optimization. And so you will be able to understand the basics of it after reading this tutorial, whether you're learning about it from GLSL vantage point and wish to learn how to write your own advanced shaders, or if you are looking for any basic knowledge about how light works in WebGL. So let's get started!

In the beginning, I will go over the types of light and toward the end of this chapter, provide a slightly more technical explanation with source code. This way we can gradually dive into the theory and supplement it with actual WebGL examples. Then a complete source code for a

3D sphere model will be provided to demonstrate principles we've just learned.

Sooner or later you will need to be able to load 3D models into your WebGL application. Also, we will write a sphere-construction function that takes a number of bands and other parameters such as its radius to automatically generate a 3D sphere using WebGL vertex data. We can then use this object to experiment with light sources and find out how they work.

What Light Is

Light is the most important idea behind visual representation of anything that a human being can visually perceive. The idea of perception of light lies in the fact that what you can see isn't based on the objects that you are viewing but on the rays of light cast from a light source and reflected from those objects. It's important to note that your eyes don't directly see objects as there is no physical correlation between your eyes and those objects.

All of this is theoretical, of course. We use the term light rays to merely abstract a more complex mechanism.

So the light rays commonly originate from an energy source such as the sun or a lamp in your room. It's important to note that theoretically a ray of light travels in a straight line and by the time you visually perceive an object, it is the rays of light reflected or scattered off that object that your eyes absorb. From now on you will have to think of light in terms of theoretical rays as described in this tutorial and not as just "something invisible that makes objects brighter". This becomes more important when you start programming your own 3D light graphics engine, as opposed to using the predefined set of OpenGL light-modeling functions.

So from this, the two rules to understand are:

Your eyes are mechanisms created to directly perceive or absorb the photons(more about photons in a second) of light and not the objects. And you are, as a programmer, destined to simulate this functionality on the computer screen.

A ray of light travels in a straight line.

The second point however, is not entirely correct, but can be correct at the same time -- let's discover the theory of light a bit further to understand what is meant by this statement. A side note on what is known about the light by scientists will help…

Light As Both: A Stream Of Particles And A Wave Of Energy

There are two ways that light could be thought of as. There is a theory of light particles described by PHOTONS. And there is a theory of light being a WAVE of energy. In ancient Greece the light was thought of as a stream of particles which travel in a straight line and bounce off a wall in a way that any other physical objects do. The fact that light couldn't be seen was based on the idea that the light particles are too small for the eye to see, traveled too fast for the eye to notice them or that the eye was just seeing through them.

In the late 1600s it was proposed that the light was actually a wave of energy and didn't travel exactly in a straight line being a stream of particles. By 1807 the theory of light waves was confirmed with an experiment that demonstrated that the light, passed through a narrow slit radiates additional light outward on the other side of the slit. So it was proven that the light has to travel in a form of a wave in order to spread itself that way, and not in a straight line. It is important to note that a beam of light radiates outward at all times.

The theory of light was developed further by Albert Einstein in 1905. He described the "photoelectric effect". This theory described activity of the ultraviolet light hitting a surface, emitting electrons off that surface. This behavior was supported by an explanation that light was made up of a stream of energy packets called PHOTONS.

To conclude, it is observed that the light can behave as both: a wave and also as packets of energy particles: PHOTONS. There is no solid explanation of the more complex underlying structure of how light works, as of yet.

The Color Of Light

In this section I describe what light is in more detail. Specifically, how color is being perceived by the viewer. As discovered in the previous section light is a wave of energy. The most apparent quality of light lies in representing color. Color is tightly connected to the concept of light. Let's see how.

The light that can be seen by the human eye is in general a mixture of all kinds of different lights scattered and reflected against the surroundings with different material properties. All physical matter is made up of atoms. The mechanics of reflection of photons off physical matter depends on various things such as the kind of atoms, the amount of each kind and the arrangement of atoms in the object that the photons are being reflected off.

Some photons are reflected and some are absorbed. When photons are absorbed they are usually converted to heat. The defining factors of the visual quality of a material lie within this matter absorption-and-reflection concept. The color that the material reflects is observed as that material's color. Also, the more light the material reflects the more shiny it will appear to the viewer.

Each different color is simply energy which can be represented by a wavelength. What's important to note is that color is only a wavelength visible to the eye. A wavelength is measured by the distance between the peaks of the energy wave. Consider this image.

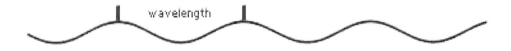

Light as a wave or wavelength.

The visible light is contained within the wavelengths ranging from 390 nanometers to 720 nanometers in length. At 390 nanometers the color is violet. A wavelength of 720 nanometers represents the red color. Everything in between is considered the visible light and the range itself is called the spectrum:

Light color spectrum, from ultraviolet 390nm to infrared 720nm.

The segment of the wavelengths between 390nm and 720nm is called the color spectrum. The wavelengths outside the color spectrum are not visible by the eye. Below 390nm (the wavelength of the violet color) the ultraviolet wavelengths are located. Above 720nm infrared wavelengths can be found. The prefix "ultra" means: beyond, on the other side of; the prefix "infra" stands for inferior to or beneath. ...hence the names.

As far as light programming goes, we are only concerned with understanding values within the color spectrum range unless we're programming some sort of an ultraviolet or infra red color wavelength simulation (which in fact we are not).

And therefore it wouldn't be convenient to describe everything about light that is currently known. That's rather a redundant subject, because what we're really after is learning how to construct and build some lit 3D shapes for our OpenGL application or video game.

So I will only put emphasis on the most important ideas that will help us understand light and light-programming better as it relates to programming with OpenGL. This means that we need to think of light in abstract form (ambient, specular and diffuse) to simplify the process.

In graphics programming, and perhaps other crafts which deal with representation of light, a few abstract terms which describe specific effects that light can produce on a surface of an object have emerged. These abstract types of light are described in the following section. Their terminology is crucial to a graphics programmer. Keep in mind that this is by far not the complete set of effects that light in general can produce, especially within the confines of modern OpenGL Shader Language (GLSL), and here will serves as a mere basics tutorial. I do believe, however that thorough understanding is achieved by knowing these basic principles, and knowing them well.

Abstract Types Of Light

The following terms describe different types of light that you must know when programming a 3D application which requires a light source. It is important to understand what effect each of these types of light create on the surface of rendered 3D objects.

These terms were created because certain effects that light produces on the objects needed to be described in order to distill the complex mathematical calculations of light. However, this doesn't mean that these exact types of light actually exist in nature, we just think of them as an abstraction of the effects that light can produce when cast on different materials. These effects are more than sufficient for creating incredibly realistic computer graphics.

It would be very time consuming to calculate the real mechanics of light and the way it works in nature so, this common set of light types was generally adopted by OpenGL: AMBIENT LIGHT, DIFFUSE LIGHT and SPECULAR LIGHT.

EMISSIVE LIGHT is differentiated from the rest, and is the type of light which is being emitted by an object, whereas the other three types of light are usually used to describe a light source. Let's take a detailed look at each of these types of light:

Ambient Light

Ambient light example in WebGL.

A 3D sphere lit by AMBIENT LIGHT only; appears to look 2D. Ambient light is the average volume of light that is created by emission of light from all of the light sources surrounding (or located inside of) the lit area.

When sun rays pass through the window of a room they hit the walls and are reflected and scattered into all different directions which averagely brightens up the whole room. This visual quality is described by ambient light.

Ambient light alone cannot communicate the complete representation of an object set in 3D space because all vertices are evenly lit by the same color and the object appears to be 2-dimensional as seen in the image above. Although the object displayed is actually a 3D sphere, it appears to be flat on the screen, when lit only by ambient light.

Diffuse Light

Diffuse light example in WebGL.

A diffuse light of red color is cast onto a black object defining its 3D shape.

Diffuse light represents a directional light cast by a light source. Diffuse light can be described as the light that has a position in space and comes from a single direction.

A flashlight held slightly above the lit object can be thought of as emitting diffuse light. In the image above a light source casting diffuse light of red color is located on the immediate left side of the object. When diffuse light touches the surface of an object, it scatters and reflects evenly across that surface.

To demonstrate how both AMBIENT and DIFFUSE lights work together to create a more-realistic looking object, imagine a 3D sphere with a dark red ambient light spread over it:

Ambient light example 2 in WebGL.

Now, by positioning a diffuse light source on the left side of the sphere, we get the following result:

Diffuse light example 2 in WebGL.

Notice how the sphere now appears to be 3D, rather than a flat circle. By combining the base ambient light and then shining light from a diffuse light source onto an object, we achieve a much more realistic illusion. In order to demonstrate how this technique is used to create realistic images, let's take a look at a screenshot of Toad, the character from Mario Kart 8:

An example of ambient and diffuse light used together to create realistic light on Toad, a character from Mario Kart 8.

Mario Kart 8. Copyright Nintendo.

Combining ambient with diffuse light sources is the same principle at work lighting 3D characters in Mario Kart 8. Try to ignore the red polka dot texture, we will cover texture mapping elsewhere in a tutorial on this site.

For now, simply notice how the ambient component of the hat (or is it part of his head?) is white or grayish. This is its base color. And the diffuse light source is projecting a bright white light onto it, supposedly coming from the sun.

There is a lot more going on in Mario Kart 8 graphics engine, visible on this screenshot. But we're not ready to go there yet. For now, let's move on to the next type of light, the specular light, or also sometimes known as specular highlight.

Specular Light

Specular light or highlight in OpenGL.

Specular reflection (or specular highlight) is displayed here in addition to the Ambient and Diffuse layers of light. You can observe how the object's 3D representation is greatly augmented by specular light properties. It's as if we can feel the material the object is made from. This could be a balloon, something plastic, with a smooth surface. The smoother the object is, the more defined this specular highlight will be.

Just like diffuse light, specular light is a directional type of light. It comes from one particular direction. The difference between the two is that specular light reflects off the surface in a sharp and uniform way. The rendering of specular light relies on the angle between the viewer and the light source.

Toad's head is made out of mushroom. So it is not very reflective. But Mario's hat is probably plastic. You can catch a glimpse of the specular highlight on it.

Here, this light is not very shiny, and barely visible, but it is indeed there. The shininess of the highlight can be dependent on object's material properties.

In order to create a hyper-realistic graphics Nintendo designers decided not to overdo the effect of the specular highlight here, by making it too intense, and dim it down instead:

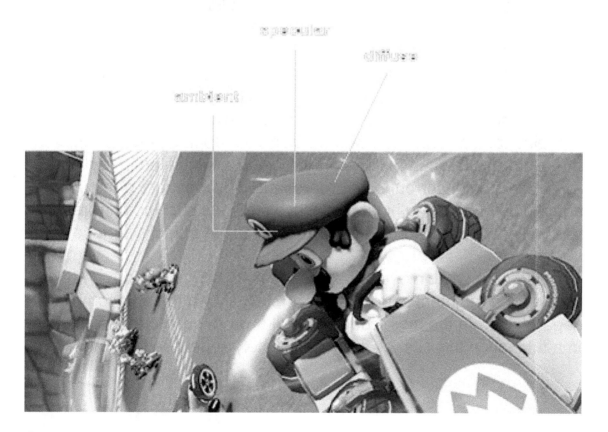

Specular Highlight Example, Mario Kart 8 courtesy of Nintendo.

We can only guess how Nintendo graphics programmers actually generated this effect. I am sure they used shaders, rather than some OpenGL command such as glBegin, glEnd and glVertex (that's the old way of doing things.) And I am sure they have in-house game engine tools that also help them adjust colors manually and arrive at a final result intuitively. But these are the building blocks of light representation on a 3D object, regardless of the API, or technique, the same principles apply.

We have just learned that from the point of the camera (the viewer of the scene) specular light creates a highlighted area on the surface of the viewed object known as specular highlight or specular reflection. The intensity of the specular reflection is dependent on the material the object is made of and the strength of the light source which contains the specular light component.

Object material colors can be imitated by adjusting all 3 components of the light we have just discussed. In addition, graphics programmers combine them with other techniques such as texture mapping, bump mapping (same as normal mapping,) environment mapping (this is when texture of the object is calculated in real time, as a reflection of surroundings represented by a sphere or a cube, commonly for creating highly reflective surfaces such as mirrors, or car bodies) that will add even more detail to the object's surface.

In modern OpenGL most of these effects are now done in a vertex shader or a fragment shader program, usually written and compiled separately from the main code. We will have to go into that elsewhere in a tutorial on this site, as it is a completely separate discussion.

Emissive Light

Emissive light is a little different than any other previously explained light components. The emissive light component is responsible for the object's material's property to reflect or absorb light. When applied to an object's material, emissive light acts to simulate the light that is reflected off the object.

With no additional light sources around, an object's color to which only emissive light component is applied has the same visual quality as an object with only ambient light applied to it. However, the mechanics of how any additional diffuse or specular light reacts with the surface of the same object with only emissive light applied to it is different.

Let's consider an object which emits an average amount of green color. On the image below emissive light component is applied to the sphere. And as you can see, the result is similar to the effect created by applying ambient light to the same sphere in the example above.

Emissive light in OpenGL is the kind of light that emits energy, rather than reflects it.

A 3D sphere reflecting green emissive light. The effect is similar to ambient light until additional sources of light are introduced into the scene.

As you already know, a light source can have all of the three components assigned to it which are the ambient light, the diffuse light and the specular light components. Let's see what happens when we apply a light source to the above scene. The light source we are applying has the following properties: red ambient light, red diffuse light and white specular light.

Emissive light (yellow) in OpenGL in combination with specular reflection.

If the above sphere wasn't emitting a light of green color, it would have appeared red in color. However, a green component of emissive light is applied to it. When the light source's "rays" of light hit the sphere's surface, the "source" and "destination" colors merge together producing a yellowish surface. As you know mixing green and red produce yellow.

The specular light component of the light source is white. The center of the specular reflection is white in the center, however as it spreads off it merges with the green and red colors, augmenting on yellow (which is green + red). Again, note that if there were no emissive light applied to the sphere, it would have appeared like the sphere shown under the section SPECULAR LIGHT above, all in red with a white specular reflection.

The way WebGL shades polygons to simulate light and how light properties are assigned to light sources and materials is explained in the following part of this tutorial.

Gem 26 - Light And 3D Graphics Part II

Light there was indeed… but how do we program it in WebGL? In pre-WebGL era, there was only OpenGL. In those days of old and renown OpenGL allowed creation of up to 8 simultaneous light sources to the scene. These light objects were created one by one using various light setup functions that started with gl prefix.

Programming was done in Immediate Mode. You may have heard of it before. WebGL does not support Immediate Mode. We now live in an era where glBegin and glEnd commands have been long removed and replaced with vertex buffer objects or VBO for short. VBOs came with the advent of shader technology quite a while ago. When working in WebGL we will be creating our light sources entirely within GLSL shaders. There is a library called LightGL that simulates Immediate Mode in WebGL, but you probably don't want to bother with it.

We still need to discuss a few points here before moving on. Light is a complex subject and to avoid making many common mistakes resulting in "Why didn't this work as expected?" situations we at the very least need to cover global ambient light, shading models and surface normals. (Especially surface normals.) I don't think without these principles it would be any easier to understand how light in WebGL actually works or easily avoid making mistakes.

In Immediate Mode GL_SMOOTH shading used to be the default shading model. It causes the computed colors of vertices to be interpolated as the primitive is rasterized, assigning different colors to each resulting pixel fragment.

GL_FLAT shading selected the computed color of just one vertex and assigned it to all the pixel fragments generated by rasterizing a single primitive. This produced models that exposed their rough edges. This is especially true of low-poly models.

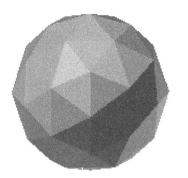 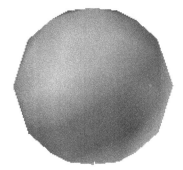

In either case, the computed color of a vertex is the combination result of light source color, position and the object's (or a polygon's surface) material. At its very basic most models lit by a semi white light will appear as they do on the images above.

Flat shading doesn't look that great on low poly models. However, if complexity of the geometry increases on the same model (let's say by continuous subdivision process) Flat shading starts to look closer and closer to Smooth shading. Let's take a look:

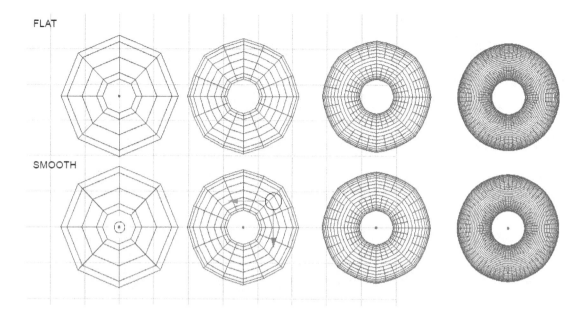

This is the wireframe of the same donut object. Let's shade both of them using either flat or smooth shading technique:

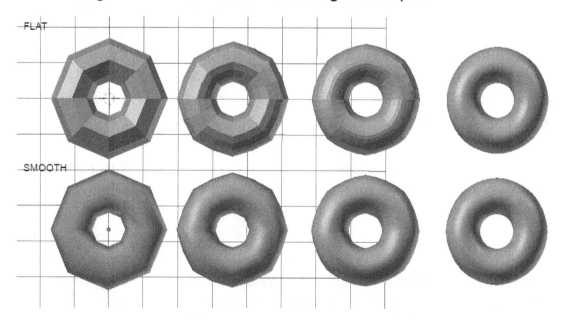

Here you will instantly notice that the last two models on each row look nearly identical in terms of how smoothly their surface is shaded. So why use smooth shading at all? Can't we just increase the number of polygons by subdivision and call it a day?

Of course, increasing geometry is a counterproductive tactic. The more polygons your model contains the more taxing it will be to the GPU. But smooth shading even on and after level-2 subdivision starts to look acceptable without having to render hundreds or thousands more polygons. And that's exactly the problem it is trying to solve. The advantages are hard to miss here. Practically all of the smooth shaded donuts in the second row look much better than its flat shaded counterpart. Note that the object geometry itself has not changed at all.

These are just examples of basic shapes. When rendering large 3D worlds these shading techniques become even more relevant in terms of producing higher quality image.

In the old days all we had to do is execute a few functions to flip a shading mode on or off. But the times are different now. Unfortunately in WebGL and any modern OpenGL pipelines we have to program shading manually. We have to write shaders containing algorithms composed of trigonometric formulas that calculate smooth or flat shading. There isn't a way around that. Good thing is that it's not as complex as it sounds.

A few other things will be needed. For example, we need to pass the position (in world space) and direction (a vector) of the light source into the shader.

This complexity creates the temptation of simply copying and pasting shaders from the Internet. But that also poses the danger of your GLSL program not properly compiling because the tutorial might have assumed a higher GLSL version that your graphics card driver does not support. Or the tutorial used a completely different approach to the overall pipeline design and things just won't match with yours. Not only that, doing this will probably not make you actually learn anything.

To solve the problem, I will explain this shader in detail. It's guaranteed to work in latest version of Chrome browser because the code was already tested while writing this book. And maybe we'll learn something new here and it will help getting better building your own shaders.

It took me several months to get better at writing my own shaders. But after a period of time I started to spot patterns. Shader logic has extreme layer of abstraction in them. If you don't understand something right away, chances are it will become obvious the more you work with them.

Global Ambient Light Model

In addition to specifying the ambient light amount to a light source or a material, it is possible to set the global amount of the ambient light which will be cast on all rendered objects in the scene. This method of lighting is called the Global Ambient Light and in itself is considered a lighting model.

Usually 3D worlds and game levels that start out using this model are first shaded completely by a balanced or dark hue of a particular color. For evening scenes, it could be a dark blue or gray. For daylight environment it could be a slightly brighter shade, but still on the dimmer side than 100% color value describing the surface material in original texture pixels.

Some pipeline techniques dim down the original texture a bit to avoid calculating Ambient Light in the shader. These textures which are usually saved in TGA format appear darker than you would expect in their original format.

When choosing ambient color you want something in between your brightest and your darkest expected color. For this reason often a value containing exactly 50% of each color channel from the RGB spectrum is chosen.

   vec4 ambient = { 0.5f, 0.5f, 0.5f, 1.0f };

This is normally done during the initialization part of your OpenGL application. However there are models that require a slightly darker shade, due to how consequent application of light illumination are applied later on. When shading is applied algorithmically, every once in a while you will bump into small calculation errors that can drastically change the final result. For example they can make the bright areas brighter than they usually appear in nature. For this reason in global ambient light intensity was R=0.2, G=0.2, B=0.2, Alpha=1.0 by default in older OpenGL implementations.

Smooth and Flat Shading Models

After setting up global ambient light the next step is usually setting up the shading model. I can't think of a good reason for choosing Flat Shading Model for your rendering. However, it can still be used for cases where object is inherently defined by its rough edges or 90 degree angles. A crate for example. But generally this is not the most commonly used model.

In most games smooth shading is the primary shading model for most objects in the scene. It produces objects that smoothly interpolate colors across vertices simulating a more realistic shadow effect. Usually an algorithm such as Gouraud is used but other models exist

(Hello Phong shading) that produce results that while technically higher-quality, barely distinct from one another, sometimes to the point of irrelevance.

Theoretically we can use Gouraud-shading. But shading can be handled in one of two ways. In the traditional Gouraud-shading technique the illumination is computed exactly at the vertices and the actual values are derived by interpolating them across the surface of the polygon.

In Phong-shading technique, the normal vectors are given at each vertex, and the system interpolates these vectors in the interior of the polygon. Then this interpolated normal vector is used in the lighting equation. Phong-shading produces more realistic images, but takes considerably mode time to compute for the reason that 3 normals are used per polygon, as opposed to just 1.

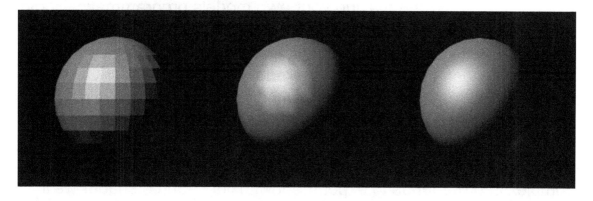

Here "flat", Gouraud and Phong shading models are shown in order from left to right. The latter two are both forms of "smooth" shading algorithms.

You can probably recognize these types of light rendering from video games that came from various eras from DOS games that used flat shading to N64 (Mario Kart) and modern hyper-realistic games. The reason each game era looked the way it did was because each shading method requires greater processing power.

Normal Vectors

In order to achieve any of the shading effects our model simply requires to have normal data stored at each vertex coordinate.

Normal vector calculations are crucial for an acceptable lighting result. While Phong shading is not 100% necessary, especially if you're working with WebGL which means that your game is tailored for mobile devices, if possible (not restrained by specs of your game) it is recommended that it is implemented because clearly it produces superior results. In computer graphics there is always a performance battle between "doing calculations at just the vertex coordinates" or interpolating across the entire polygon at the fragment level.

WebGL doesn't calculate normal vectors for you and this will be mentioned again below when we get to the Computing Surface Normal section. When making your own models programmatically by an algorithm, you are responsible for creating normal vectors yourself. But if you created your 3D model using modeling software such as Blender, the normals are already included in either OBJ or PLY files. PLY object loader is already discussed elsewhere in this book. And because normal calculations are required to make any feasible light rendering to work in WebGL, we will use the normal data from our loaded PLY objects. These objects don't have to be complex in order for us to experiment with light source shader we'll take a look at in a bit. Blender can generate basic 3D shapes such as cubes, spheres, cylinders, etc. with precalculated normals.

The Two Types Of Defining Light Properties In OpenGL (Light Source and Surface Material)

This section exists here because I want to explain something before describing how to define light sources and surface material reflective properties. Another temptation exists in believing that the color of the material is simply the color of the light that falls on its surface. But this is incorrect.

Theoretically, there are two types of light properties you should consider when programming shaders in WebGL. The first type of light properties is the one that describes a light source itself. Is it a light bulb? Candle light? Is it yellow? Or neon blue?

The second type of light properties is the one that describes the light reflected by the material of an object's surface. Here, the same RGB triplet goes into defining a material color that goes into determining the color of a light source. The resulting scene is a combination of both.

The color of each light source is characterized by the color, in RGBA format, that it emits and is defined by using a vec4 variable. The properties of the material the object is made of are defined by a similar vec4 variable. With different values describing the color of that material. This color is characterized by the amount of light that the material reflects.

Now, let's take a look at how to define a light source in WebGL. Basically, we want to combine Ambient, Diffuse, Specular and Emissive (if available, but usually not) lights together by multiplying them with the texture fragment in the shader.

Defining A Light Source

Before I go into the shader code I've yet to explain a few other things. This background theory will help us understand what shaders actually do.

Traditional OpenGL allowed a maximum of 8 light sources in a scene at once. Each of the light sources can be either enabled or disabled. All of the 8 light sources are initially disabled, and are enabled with a call to glEnable.

But in WebGL we have to write our own lighting code in GLSL shading language. Each shader is a compact program that will be ran on each individual fragment in your rendered 3D scene. The lighting formulas that go into each shader will determine the overall look of your rendered object.

We're no longer limited to just 8 light sources here. And techniques such as Deferred Lighting can be used to create hundreds of light sources that illuminate your scene.

Once you've figured out writing a shader for one object, it can be adapted for your entire scene. But in computer graphics a scene is usually composed of objects that contain multiple types of materials. For example, a boat can have wooden and metal parts. And objects are usually separated by material type during the rendering process.

When writing your shader you will determine Ambient, Diffuse, Specular and Emissive ingredients

Another diminutive difference when defining a light source (as opposed to polygon color) is that of the addition of the new variable 'float Alpha' as the fourth parameter in the array. In reality you would only specify this parameter for an EMISSIVE light component to modify an object's material's alpha value. Or if you're programming some kind of a advanced special effect.

An emissive light property is typically assigned to a polygon, not a light source. The float Alpha parameter is the polygon's alpha value. So what is this alpha parameter anyway? The alpha parameter is used to define the translucency factor of an object and could be used to simulate materials made out of translucent matter such as glass.

Alpha is also used to blend the lighted areas with the texture of a 3D model. Texture-mapping will be explained in detail in this book. The color format which describes the RGB values of color as well as the alpha value is referred to as the RGBA format. We will come across this value when setting up our texture maps. For now let's concentrate on how to specify the full range of properties for a light source.

Whenever we will write a shader for a specific lighting model we will need information about our light source:

```
// light source's position in the world
float position[] = { -1.5, 1.0, -4.0, 1.0 };

// overall color shade across entire object
float ambient[] = { 1.0, 1.0, 1.0 };

// the lit part of the object
float diffuse[] = { 0.6, 0.4, 0.1 };

// specular is a white bright shining spot on glossy objects
float specular[] = { 1.0, 1.0, 1.0 };

// a very dim glow
float emissive[] = { 0.1, 0.1, 0.1 };
```

These values will be combined with the material information which is usually stored in the 3D object itself after loading it from a file. It often includes texture map uv coordinates, vertex or fragment color and normal vector which indicates the direction in which a fragment is pointing at any particular location across the entire polygon.

This rounds up our discussion of assigning light properties to a light source. In the following part I will explain how to create a fully functional GLSL shader that will provide us with basic lighting that we will use across most of the demos presented in this book.

Some shaders have a completely different logic, depending on the effect they are trying to imitate. For example Environment Mapping (where each fragment is shaded according to a ray cast from it back into the surrounding sky) would require a completely different approach.

Materials In Real World

In nature, objects are lit by the sun which emits light of white intensity. White, as we know, is a combination of all colors. When this white light hits the surface of an object, some wavelengths of light are reflected and some are absorbed. The light that is reflected defines the color of the object we're viewing.

Different objects are made out of different matter which occupies different reflectance properties. For example, a red ball reflects only the red particles of light and absorbs all of the others. Under white light, all objects appear to be of their "natural" color because the white light contains all of the colors together, so the object always has a color to reflect.

However, try viewing the same red ball in a room with a blue light bulb as the only light source and the ball will appear to be black because there is no red color to reflect.

Defining Surface Material Properties

Before going further into the surface reflective properties, I have to point something out as this can confuse some of the beginner-level OpenGL programmers.

In WebGL, by assigning a material property to an object (defined by RGB color format), you are theoretically assigning the color which is reflected by that object. When assigning a color to an object you are merely assigning the property which describes that object's color. In other words it will not "react" with light and will remain just that - the object's color. This is the difference between assigning a color to an object and assigning a material property to an object.

Polygon Winding

Theoretically a polygon has a back and front face. This requires a bit more explanation.

How exactly do we know which side is the front (defined in WebGL as GL_FRONT) and which side is the back (defined as GL_BACK) of a polygon? The answer is simple. There are two ways of specifying a polygon in 3D space.

By specifying vertices one by one in clockwise direction and specifying vertices in counterclockwise direction. The direction you specify the vertices in is what describes which side is the front and which is the back. In the days of old OpenGL let you specify these rules with the glFrontFace command. In WebGL there are two functions gl.frontFace and gl.cullFace. We'll see a lot more of them in many examples of this book.

The principle which describes polygon's facing direction is called polygon winding.

This sets the default behavior. The CCW in GL_CCW is an abbreviation for CounterClockwise Winding. Let's take a look at the following image to better visualize polygon winding and move on with the surface material properties enlightenment.

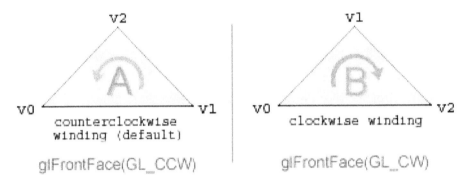

An example of clockwise and counterclockwise direction winding (default) to create Polygonal surfaces in OpenGL.

To define a polygon in counterclockwise direction, you first specify the first vertex - v0, continue defining its base by v1 and concluding the polygon with v2 as its peak point as seen in the example A.

With this configuration, the polygon will be defined as having counterclockwise winding and the visible, front side will be facing the viewer if GL_CCW (which is the default setting) is set with glFrontFace (or gl.frontFace in WebGL, of course).

If you try defining a polygon in clockwise direction, as seen in the example B, and GL_CCW is enabled, you will not see the polygon because it's face will be pointing away from the viewer. GL_CW flag is used in that situation.

There is a possibility to apply light to both of the polygon sides. In which case you don't have to specify polygon winding explicitly.

Material Properties

The AMBIENT component defines the overall color of the object and has the most effect when the object is not lit. The DIFFUSE component has the most importance in defining the object's color when a light is emitted onto its surface.

It is tempting to set AMBIENT and DIFFUSE components of the material to the same value. But to achieve greater realism and take opportunistic advantage of various forms of lightings (which there aren't many) the ambient component is usually set to a slightly darker shade than diffuse.

It is enough to define ambient and diffuse color components of a material for the object to appear realistically lit by a theoretical light source. However, this is not always the case. For example when modeling an object made out of metal it is desired for that object to have more emphasized reflective properties for it to look more like metal. These properties divide themselves into two categories: the SPECULAR component and the SHININESS component.

Specular Reflection Component

The SPECULAR REFLECTION component of the material defines the effect the material has on the reflected light. This functionality can be obtained by defining the GL_SPECULAR component of the object's material. This property adds a glossy surface to the object you are modeling.

Specular Exponent Component (Shininess)

An extension to the SPECULAR REFLECTION component lies in the use of "shininess" or the SPECULAR EXPONENT (Keep in mind, shininess is the second feature of the specular light component and not a unique light-type by itself). It is usually configured by some variable in the shader.

In the past in OpenGL it was defined by GL_SHININESS property of a material where you control the size and brightness of the specular reflection. The specular reflection is the very bright white spot which appears on objects with materials of high reflectivity. You really have to fiddle with both parameters to see exactly what effect they produce on a surface of a material. But you won't be fiddling with either one of them in WebGL without having to write your own custom shader to do it.

In conclusion, to completely define the specular component of a material you have to define both GL_SPECULAR and GL_SHININESS properties.

It is important to know that for the specular reflections to work you have to set both: the light source's specular light component and the object's material specular reflectance component.

And just when you thought we were done...

There is yet another important concept to understand when it comes to programming light in WebGL (And 3D graphics in general.) Even if all of your light sources are set in place and all material objects are defined to what you want them to be, it's still not quite enough.

For the light equations to work properly, it is required to know the direction which the polygons in your model are facing. This direction is defined by a normal (or a 3D perpendicular) vector in relation to the polygon's surface. The next section in this chapter covers this principle.

Computing Surface Normals

In order to display light correctly you are required to compute normal vectors for each polygon in an object. Neither WebGL nor OpenGL does this for us automatically.

While writing WebGL code for the first time plenty of times you will run into quirky problems. And lack of normals is just one of them. Either misconfigured or absent normal vectors are the cause of many problems you'll run into.

This is not limited only to light calculations but others as well such as bump mapping.

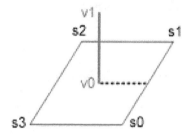

How is polygon surface normal computed.

The theoretical **normal vector** of the surface s0, s1, s2, s3 is indicated in red, defined by two points v0 and v1. If your book has black and white illustrations, this is the vector that's pointing up from the center of the rectangle.

A normal of a polygon is a perpendicular vector in relation to the polygon's surface. It is very useful in many implementations of 3D computer graphics. In particular when dealing with surface direction. Sorry, but WebGL doesn't compute normal vectors for you and this is something you have to do on your own.

C = A X B

B

A

But the good news is that Blender and other 3D modeling tools calculate and store normal data in file formats - OBJ or PLY, for example. And it just so happens that in this book we will deliver a fully functional PLY object loader function!

If your objects are constructed algorithmically, you are responsible for calculating normals on your own. But this is usually not a very difficult task, knowing basic trigonometry functions (cross product in this case) which we will get to later in the book.

Since all models in your 3D scene will be made out of polygons, it is convenient to have a function which calculates the normal vector of a polygon. But if you want to skip this step and use a Blender model, that's fine too.

A normal vector of a polygon is the cross product of two vectors located on the surface plane of the polygon (in the case below that polygon is a triangle).

And what we need to do is take any two vectors located on the polygon's plane and calculate their cross product.

The cross product will be the resulting normal vector. Mathematically the cross product of two vectors A and B is represented as A X B.

Let's take a look on the next page.

Polygon normal in a real world OpenGL application example

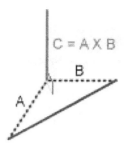

A normal vector C as the cross product of two vectors A and B.

The triangle's vectors A and B are taken here as an example. The result (the red vector; the one that's pointing up) is the normal vector which defines what way the triangle is facing. The pseudo code provided below calculates the normal vector of a given polygon.

The parameters are vertex_t v[3]; which defines the 2 vectors that lie on the polygon's plane and vertex_t normal[3]; which will hold the resulting normal vector. Keep in mind that if you are using counterclockwise winding (as this is the normally accepted default behavior) you must specify the points of v[3] in counterclockwise direction as well.

Pseudo code

```
   // This is how a vertex is specified in the base code
   typedef struct vertex_s
   {
       float x, y, z;

   } vertex_t;

   // normal(); - finds a normal vector and normalizes it
   void normal (vertex_t v[3], vertex_t *normal)
```

```
{
    vertex_t a, b;

    // calculate the vectors A and B
    // note that v[3] is defined with counterclockwise winding in mind
    // a
    a.x = v[0].x - v[1].x;
    a.y = v[0].y - v[1].y;
    a.z = v[0].z - v[1].z;

    // b
    b.x = v[1].x - v[2].x;
    b.y = v[1].y - v[2].y;
    b.z = v[1].z - v[2].z;

    // calculate the cross product and place the resulting vector
    // into the address specified by vertex_t *normal
    normal->x = (a.y * b.z) - (a.z * b.y);
    normal->y = (a.z * b.x) - (a.x * b.z);
    normal->z = (a.x * b.y) - (a.y * b.x);

    // normalize
    normalize(normal);
}
```

The final step of this function is to normalize the resulting vector and this is something I haven't talked about yet. Normalization of the normal vector are not the same thing. A normal vector can be any arbitrary length after calculation and usually is. Normalizing a vector is more often referred to as making a unit vector. It means bringing its length down to a unit length, which is achieved by dividing the vector by its own length.

The normalized (unit) vector is often used in many ways to achieve various effects in 3D graphics. For example, when dealing with 3D cameras, the unit vector is required to accurately calculate a "LookAt" (or "follow") camera view (the view that always points at a center of some other object even if it's dynamically floating around the scene.)

But it is also excessively used in calculating light.

The Need For Normal Vector

To normalize a normal vector means to reduce its length to unit size. A unit size is just 1. All of the calculated normal vectors are required to be a length of 1 to work properly with many 3D algorithms to avoid wonky results.

In the olden days it would be possible to tell OpenGL to normalize normal vectors for us with a call to glEnable(GL_NORMALIZE); but believe me, that would be more computationally expensive than doing normalization within your own code. In WebGL, we usually do this with the help of a JavaScript vector library. Which you will see implemented throughout several demos in this book.

So how exactly the normalization process is done? As stated above, all we have to do is reduce the size of a given normal vector to a length of 1. To accomplish that, first you have to find the length of a normal vector.

To find the length of any vector, you take all of the coordinate components (x, y and z) of that vector and square them. Add all of the squared components and find the square root (caution: one of the most expensive calculations in 3D graphics; if you can precalculate it using a static lookup table you probably should) of that sum. This sum will be the length of the vector.

Afterwards, divide each coordinate component of the vector by its derived length and you will get a vector which points in the same exact direction but of unit length. And the function normalize does precisely that:

Pseudo code

```
// This is how a vector is specified in the base code
// The origin is assumed to be [0,0,0]
typedef struct vector_s
{
    float x, y, z;

} vector_t;

void normalize (vector_t *v)
{
    // calculate the length of the vector
    float len = (float)(sqrt((v.x * v.x) + (v.y * v.y) + (v.z * v.z)));

    // avoid division by 0
    if (len == 0.0f)
        len = 1.0f;

    // reduce to unit size
    v.x /= len;
    v.y /= len;
    v.z /= len;
}
```

I'll provide a JavaScript library that takes care of these operations in this book when a situation presents itself where we actually need to use them.

In Conclusion

As this tutorial coming to an end let's overview some light principles we've covered so far.

The final appearance of shading on the object is reliant on the combination of the global ambient light; ambient light, diffuse and emissive lights theoret emitted from surrounding light sources and the lit object's material properties themselves.

The lit color of a vertex is the sum of the material emission intensity, the product of the material ambient reflectance and the lighting model full-scene ambient intensity - and finally - the average contribution of each light source in the scene.

Each light source contributes the sum of three terms: ambient, diffuse, and specular. The ambient light source contribution is the product of the material ambient reflectance and the light's ambient intensity. The diffuse light source contribution is the product of the material diffuse reflectance, the light's diffuse intensity, and the dot product of the vertex's normal with the normalized vector from the vertex to the light source.

The specular light source contribution is the product of the material specular reflectance, the light's specular intensity, and the dot product of the normalized vertex-to-eye and vertex-to-light vectors, raised to the power of the shininess of the material.

All three light source contributions are attenuated equally based on the distance from the vertex to the light source and on light source direction, spread exponent, and spread cutoff angle. All dot products are replaced with 0 if they evaluate to a negative value. Finally, the alpha component of the resulting lit color is set to the alpha value of the material diffuse reflectance.

And that's all. This concludes our discussion of light theory. Earlier in this chapter I also provided the source code of our basic shaders for flat and gouraud shading illumination: the very principles we covered here. This should be enough to get started.

Light is incredibly important. But truly, it is not just the light, but a combination of various techniques that will produce impressive visual quality for your 3D world creations. The rest of this book is dedicated to trying to bring and tie it all together.

Gem 27 - Multiple Viewports

WebGL supports multiple viewport rendering. You can choose a rectangular area on the screen into which you will output a scene. An example of a racing track shown from two different angles is depicted on the image below. Notice, both are rendered to the same canvas.

Creating a new viewport on the same canvas screen is done by gl.viewport function. We've already seen it in action before. It's a required call before writing anything to the screen even with a single view.

Let's set up the left viewport (note the half width):

```
// Set viewport for displaying camera
gl.viewport(0, 0, width/2, height);
```

And now let's setup a secondary view:

```
// Set viewport for displaying camera
gl.viewport(width/2, 0, width/2, height);
```

I'm using a wide canvas here of about 800 x 300 in dimension. Here width / 2 is 400 and height 300. Both viewports take up a unique rectangular space on the screen. It's really as simple as this. Calling drawElements after setting a viewport will render output into that area.

Multiple viewport views are often used for drawing multi-textured framebuffers containing texture, z-buffer, normal and other information for testing (in advanced graphics computations the offscreen framebuffer is rarely composed of just a single memory spot, rather it is a composite of several types of images).

Multiple viewports can be used for generating dynamic, real-time environment maps. By pointing the camera in 6 different directions from the current view it's possible to capture a dynamic cube map. This multi-texture cube map can then be passed to an environment map shader. This viewport technique can also be used for generating physically-based light rendering shaders.

Gem 28 - Rendering Multiple Objects

So far we've used the same texture.vs shader to render our game world and objects in it. But it has one limitation. The objects are not separate from one another. We're simply compounding them into the scene at their default location of x=0, y=0 and z=0. In games, objects rotate and move separately from one another.

An example of this is demonstrated on the following screenshot where a sports car (that looks a lot like an electric shaver) is rendered on the screen multiple times.

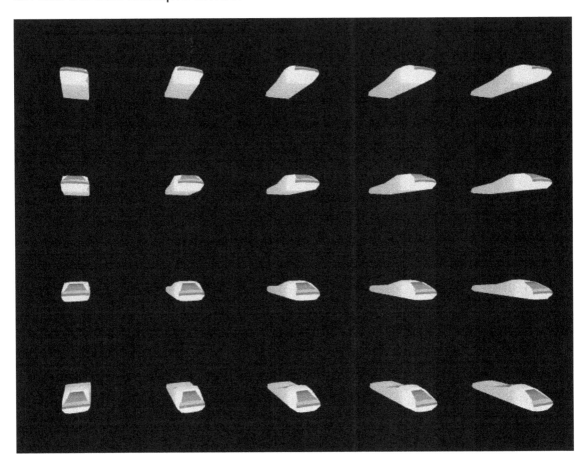

Here, each model is rotated individually. In other words, it has its own Model matrix. The same model is rendered using a 4 by 5 for-loop. View camera was moved back to glance at the scene from a distance.

How something like this can be implemented?

Separating Model from View

Up until this point we've created several shaders for basic rendering. Some of them did not have a camera view matrix. They were created simply to demonstrate the rendering pipeline at work.

Our most advanced shader so far is represented by the texture.vs and texture.frag pair that our engine is capable of loading automatically from a shader source directory.

But when we implemented the texture shader we were talking about the **ModelView** matrix because we simply wanted to move the camera around the scene. Our **ModelView** matrix was passed along with Projection matrix into the texture shader.

Now we're at a point where we will divide Model and View matrices into separate entries. For simplicity's sake that is exactly what they will be called in our shader. They will be represented by uniform variables of type mat4 just like all other matrices we've worked with so far.

We're still calculating **ModelView** matrix by multiplying **Model** by **View**. It's just, they are now separated. And doing that gives us the the ability to move individual objects on the screen. Usually, the View matrix is calculated first in our JavaScript game loop. It remains the same for the entire scene. This is our camera view. (So we're essentially moving **ModelView** into just View.) The Model matrix, however, is recalculated separately for each individual model that will be rendered in our 3D world. This **Model** matrix gives us the ability to control any given model's position and relative rotation around its own local coordinate system.

The shader formula from the texture vertex shader that once was:

texture.vs
```
uniform mat4 Projection;
uniform mat4 ModelView;

void main()
{
   gl_Position = Projection * ModelView * a_Position;

   ...
}
```

Will now be transformed to the following in our new move.vs shader:

move.vs
```
uniform mat4 Projection;
uniform mat4 Model;
uniform mat4 View;

void main()
{
   gl_Position = Projection * View * Model * a_Position;

   ...
}
```

Note: source code for all shaders explained in this book is available via my GitHub account:

github.com/gregsidelnikov/WebGLTutorials/tree/master/shaders

Originally the ModelView matrix wasn't separated because when it was created we were testing things out. But now we're moving toward a slightly more advanced implementation that will allow us to render multiple objects with unique matrix transformations for each.

Note the order of View * Model multiplication matters. Multiplication is done from right to left. First a_Position vertices are multiplied by Model matrix. Then they are multiplied by View and only then by the Projection matrix. This makes complete sense because it's like working with hierarchical data. Traditionally right to left is the order of multiplication in computer languages because of how this data is represented in computer memory registers.

And on the JavaScript side of things we now need to pass two matrices into the shader:

```
var Model = new CanvasMatrix4();
var View = new CanvasMatrix4();

// Generate View matrix
View.makeIdentity();
View.translate(0, 0, -2);

// Pass View matrix to the shader.
// Calculated only once per scene view
gl.uniformMatrix4fv(
gl.getUniformLocation(Shader.textureMapProgram, "View"),
    false,
    View.getAsFloat32Array());

    // Draw game world referenced to by "world_indices" array
    gl.drawElements(gl.TRIANGLES,
            world_indices.length,
            gl.UNSIGNED_SHORT, 0);

// Draw unique models in the scene
for (var i = 0; i < MODELS_MAX; i++) {
```

```
// Generate Model matrix per unique model
Model.makeIdentity();
Model.rotate(ModelList[i].rotate_Y, 0, 1, 0);
Model.translate(ModelList[i].x, ModelList[i].x, ModelList[i].x);
Model.scale(1, 1, 1);

// Pass Model matrix to the shader
gl.uniformMatrix4fv(
gl.getUniformLocation(Shader.textureMapProgram, "Model"), false,
Model.getAsFloat32Array());

// Draw a bound object referenced to by model_indices array
gl.drawElements(gl.TRIANGLES,
        model_indices.length,
        gl.UNSIGNED_SHORT, 0);
}
```

This example uses some elements of pseudo-code. Here imaginary ModelList contains data for each model's rotation angle. The View matrix is generated only once before entering the model rendering loop, within which,the Model matrix is updated on a per-model basis giving each model a unique placement in the world and a rotation angle.

The order is important. Model.rotate must be called first to rotate the model around its local axis. Only then Model.translate is called to actually move the object in space. Of course, unless you're trying to simulate orbiting planets or something that doesn't spin around its own axis. In which case the order of translate and rotate operations would be reversed.

When drawElements is called our shader goes to work. First we draw the view, outside of the model rendering for-loop. Every time we draw a new model we provide a new Model matrix based on that model's coordinates. The original View (outside of for-loop) and Model are cross-multiplied and this is what essentially separates individual models from the actual scene.

Passing Dynamic Values Into The Shader

Every once in a while you'll find yourself needing to pass some kind of a dynamic value into the shader from your JavaScript rendering loop. We've already done this with matrices. But what if you want to send a floating point array? Then, instead of using uniformMatrix4fv method we will use uniform3fv as shown below:

```
rgb = [1.0, 0.0, 0.0]; // Red
gl.uniform3fv(gl.getUniformLocation(
    Shader.lightProgram, "rgb"), rgb);
```

And in our light fragment shader we can apply this color to the entire model:

```
uniform vec3 rgb;

void main() {
   gl_FragColor =
      vec4(rgb[0], rgb[1], rgb[2], 1) *
      texture2D(image, vec2(texture.s, texture.t));
}
```

Multiplying a vector value representing the passed in color with the texture image will combine them together. This results in a textured model that looks shaded in a particular color that was passed via the rgb[3] array.

I modified our car spinning demo a bit and re-rendered the same view into 4 distinct screen quadrants. Each rendering loop of 20 cars (5 x 4) is now displayed using a unique color that was passed to the shader.

The screenshot depicting the result is shown below:

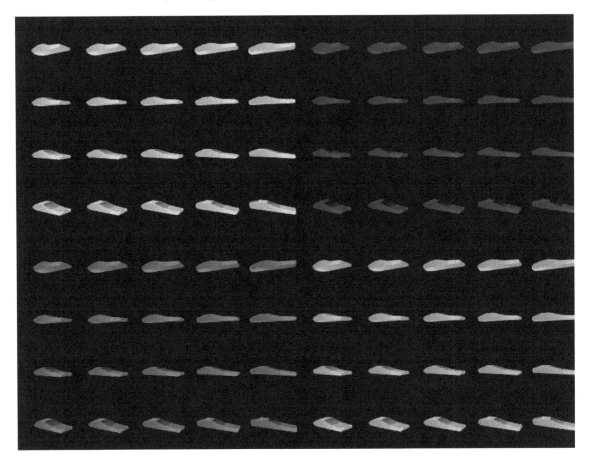

If you are reading this book in color this will look sort of like an Andy Warhol painting.

I know this is a simple example. And rows of spinning cars wouldn't do much. But I wanted to explain this principle because it's fundamental when you'll get to a point where you need to render different types of materials.

A single object made out of plastic and glass cannot be rendered in a single shader pass. You'll have to either switch the shader, just to render the glass area, and render the two elements separately, or fork out inside the shader itself by passing a flag value like "render_Glass = true" for example.

The example in this section demonstrated how to accomplish this. Of course, in a real world scenario, you'd replace color values with different surface algorithms but the idea is the same.

Gem 29 - Light And 3D Graphics Part III (Implementation)

We can now start actual implementation of our first light model by writing a new shader.

We'll start very basic here by creating a vertex and fragment shader pair for rendering a simple flat shaded scene. Later we will transform this shader to support smooth-shaded Gouraud-style rendering.

Light-based shaders require one additional piece of data that we haven't talked about until now. In fact, two pieces of data: the light position in the world and its direction. Both are represented by a 3D vector.

We can pass the position and direction of the light into the shader from our JavaScript program just like we did with other uniforms (in particular when we passed the ModelView matrix to the shader.)

But just to simplify and at the same time demonstrate another way of doing things, this time we will specify the light source data by hard-coding it into the shader source itself. You can easily make these values dynamic as well to create the illusion of a moving sun, for example, but in this particular instance it is not necessary. We simply want to create a basic scene lit by a single light source.

In this chapter we will take a look at a basic lighting model. We'll explore one of the most basic lighting techniques available in 3D graphics. This is what we will implement in this chapter.

Before we move on I need to mention that basic lighting models come in two flavors:

1. Directional Lighting
2. Point Lighting

Directional lighting usually comes from a very distant light source, such as the Sun. The light source is so far away that its rays hit the surface at the same angle throughout the entire object. Here all we have to do is specify the angle or direction vector. It stays constant for all vertices on the object when we actually calculate this value in the shader.

Point lighting is usually used to simulate smaller lights that appear in local space. For example, a light bulb or candle. Point lighting casts rays in all directions around it. When they hit an object, the angle between each ray and the surface fragment it hits are always different. Point lighting is calculated per-vertex. And then the color is interpolated between the surface of the polygon. This creates the illusion of a close-by light source.

In your 3D scene, your global illumination will be usually defined by Directional Lighting. Smaller lights will use point light technique.

Lighting The Scene

Until now we've only rendered few basic textured models that were loaded from PLY files. But we haven't setup any lighting models yet. In order to get started we need to define a light source.

There are two basic shading methods that we will explore in this chapter. That is the directional and point light techniques. They differ only by two calculations and produce slightly different output.

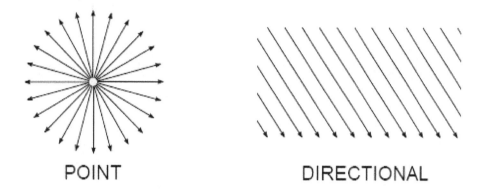

POINT   DIRECTIONAL

Point light casts light rays from a location somewhere in the world coordinates. Directional light uses a single vector to represent the slope at which light shines on the scene and is often used to imitate sunlight.

Gem Passing Light Source To Shaders

We've already covered rendering multiple objects uniquely placed in the world throughout the scene with their own position and rotation coordinates when we created shaders move.vs and move.frag by separating unified ModelView matrix.

We will take the vertex and fragment shader (move.vs and move.frag) pair and use it as a starting point to build our light shader on. First, let's create a basic flat-shaded scene.

One thing to note here is that flat and smooth shading do not require a different shader. This is because this effect is solely based on the direction of the normals as part of the object's composition. Blender allows smoothing the normals (by calculating them as an average at each vertex) or leaving them in their default direction which is what creates flat shaded effect. In fact, an object can be composed of a combination of smooth and flat shaded normals. The point is there isn't a magical setting you can turn on and off to enable either flat or smooth shading. It is determined by object's composition itself.

Any shader that requires lighting is likely to request a light source position and direction vectors. We can either create a light source position and direction arrays in our JavaScript program and pass them into the shader.

So, the first thing we'll do is pass that information to our shader as an array. We've passed uniform arrays to shaders before when we sent Projection, View and Model matrices to the GPU in other examples in this book. The same applies here. Except this time we're sending light coordinates.

We can hardcode these values directly into the shader, but I'll follow one of the examples we've already discussed where we passed values via an RGB array. Here, we'll do the same except with two new arrays containing light information: LightPosition and LightDirection. In the same way LightColor will be passed into the shader. In this case, we'll use a sharp white with just a hint of yellow just to see how our new shader affects the lit model.

Partial source-code shown:
```
var Model = new CanvasMatrix4();

Model.makeIdentity();
```

```
Model.rotate(car_angle, 0, 1, 0);
Model.translate(0, 0, 0);

LightPosition = [5, 5, -10];   // some placement
LightDirection = [x, y, 1];    // some other angle
LightColor = [1, 1, 0.9];      // bright white yellowish color

gl.uniform3fv(gl.getUniformLocation(
    Shader.directionalProgram, "rgb"), rgb);

gl.uniform3fv(gl.getUniformLocation(
    Shader.directionalProgram, "LightPosition"), LightPosition);

gl.uniform3fv(gl.getUniformLocation(
    Shader.directionalProgram, "LightDirection"), LightDirection);

gl.uniform3fv(gl.getUniformLocation(
    Shader.directionalProgram, "LightColor"), LightColor);
```

Here we have a LightPosition at some random placement of x=5, y=3 and z=-10 in world space. We also cast a ray from that position into direction of LightDirection. In this example, it is determined by dynamic variables x and y which in this demo we can control using the keyboard arrow keys. This is just to see how the scene light affects the entire view when a dynamic light source is present.

And here are our new shaders. I called the shader program directionalProgram. And the GLSL file pair is directional.vs and directional.frag. Let's take a look inside!

directional.vs
```
precision mediump float;
attribute vec4 a_Position;
attribute vec4 a_Color;
```

```glsl
attribute vec2 a_Texture;
attribute vec4 a_Normal;

varying vec4 color;
varying vec2 texture;

uniform mat4 Projection;
uniform mat4 Model;
uniform mat4 View;

uniform vec3 rgb;
uniform vec3 LightPosition;
uniform vec3 LightDirection;
uniform vec3 LightColor;

void main()
{
    gl_Position = Projection * View * Model * a_Position;

    vec3 normal = normalize(vec3(a_Normal));

    float NdotL = max(dot(LightDirection, normal), 0.0);

    vec3 diffuse = vec3(0.5, 0.5, 0.5);

    color = a_Color * vec4(LightColor, 1) * NdotL;

    texture = a_Texture;
}
```

Note also that in this shader we are finally accepting a new attribute. The a_Normal in **vec4** format will hold the normal vector for each vertex.

gl_Position. As usual we calculate our vertex position based on matrix modifications received from our JavaScript animation loop.

vec3 normal = normalize(**vec3**(a_Normal)).

Here we've taken normal data contained in attribute a_Normal and converted it to vec3 format. This is safe because normals usually store the X, Y and Z coordinates of the normal vector. We then convert this normal to a unit vector by calling built-in GLSL normalize function. This makes the normal a unit size. Meaning the vector is now 1.0 in length. Internally this is achieved by dividing the vector by its own length.

float NdotL = max(dot(LightDirection, normal), 0.0);

The dot product will help us determine the angle between the normal vector and the LightDirection vector. This makes a lot of sense because not all normals are directly facing the light source. Some are slightly turned away (gray illumination). Others completely away (absence of illumination).

The normals that more or less are facing the light source direction will be the brightest. And this is the type of a calculation the dot product operation allows us to do. GLSL shader has a native built-in method "dot" which we are using here to perform it.

Note that NdotL is a floating point magnitude, not a vector. It contains a value between 0.0 - 1.0. The final color will be multiplied by it. When that happens each color channel (r, g, b) is multiplied producing a shade of the original color found in texture multiplied by vertex color.

Except now it will be lighter or darker based on the value in NdotL. The light equation is linear here. Some of the time this algorithm can produce a value that are way too bright at certain light direction angles and camera view position. This is normal for standard implementation. But usually in games these values are tweaked using your visual intuition until you get a scene that looks visually better. In other words standard shading algorithms are rarely used as final.

We want to grab the max value between the returned dot product and 0.0. Because negative values will be generated by normals that are facing away from the light by clamping them to 0.0 we can simply discard them.

vec3 diffuse = **vec3**(0.5, 0.5, 0.5);

Here we have chosen a default diffuse color for our model. This is the color that will be used in absence of light (when normals are pointing away from the light source). You can experiment with your own values here. But this shade worked well when I was testing it. It created a nice realistic shading effect very similar to real life lighting on a rainy day.

color = a_Color * **vec4**(LightColor, 1) * NdotL;

Finally, the result is a conglomerate collection of different types of light sources multiplied by NdotL value that determines brightness of color at that vector. We simply store it in varying color variable and it will also be automatically passed onto our fragment shader.

LightColor is the bright white-yellowish color we passed from our animation loop.

Notice vec4(LightColor, 1) here is used to simply convert LightColor rgb array to a vec4 type so the shader can multiply them. Multiplication or other operations across different types is not allowed and will cause a shader compilation error. For example you cannot multiply vec3 by vec4. But GLSL has a clever casting mechanism implemented. Simply use vec3 value and add "1" as the second argument. Whenever you work with shaders you found online or copied from elsewhere, they may be written in different versions or formats of GLSL spec. Most of the time if a shader doesn't compile, check it for accurate type-casting. A lot of the time this will be the culprit.

And here is our directional light fragment shader.

directional.frag
```
precision mediump float;

uniform sampler2D image;

varying vec4 color;
varying vec2 texture;

uniform mat4 Projection;
uniform mat4 Model;
uniform mat4 View;

uniform vec3 rgb;

void main() {

  gl_FragColor =
    color *
    vec4(rgb[0], rgb[1], rgb[2], 1) *
    texture2D(image, vec2(texture.s, texture.t));
}
```

A small detail may have escaped you while reading this chapter. Even though we passed LightPosition into this shader, it was never actually used. I intentionally kept it for our next example where we will create a point light light source.

If you think about it Directional Light doesn't really need to have a LightPosition. Usually it represents sunlight and the sun is way too far away in order for the difference between rays to have any significant distinction. It's simply not necessary with this type of lighting.

So what does it actually look like? I loaded the car model into our existing engine so far and ran it through our new directionalProgram shader. This is what it looks like:

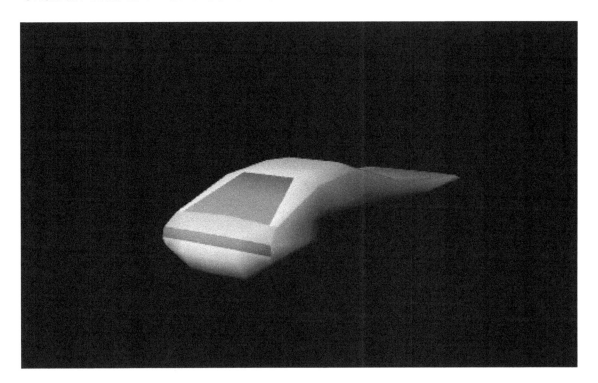

Here you can see combination of texture, vertex color (yellow hood, slightly seen from this angle here) and the directional light source illumination. I positioned the light closer to the back of the car and moved it a bit upward. The bottom of the car is completely dark, and diffuse color of 0.5f 0.5f 0.5f is used to shade that area.

Granted, this is not the most impressive 3D model. But I had to create something just for these examples. I went back into Blender and added a door and a back hatch. Adding detail helps a bit with realism. The variation of this model is depicted on following screenshot:

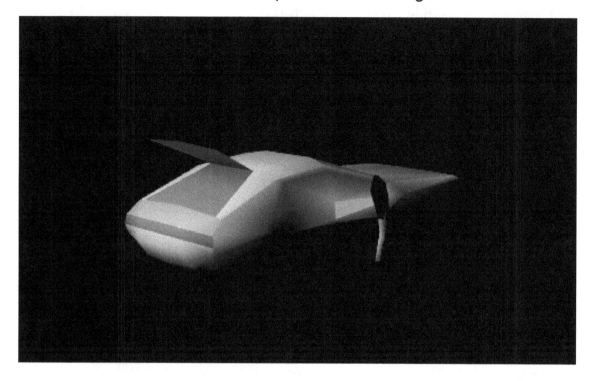

Here I modified the light source and made it more yellowish. The model is still lacking wheels. But because car wheels are usually rendered separately they are not yet included at this stage.

In the next section we'll discover how to add point light lights. There is only one difference between point lights and directional light. That is… we will be calculating the NdotL value (dot product performed on Normal and Light Direction) per vertex. Point lights visually produce a slightly different result and are normally not used for global illumination. They usually represent car lights, candles and small light bulbs in a dungeon. Or something.

But there is also another type of a point light shading technique. As many things are in WebGL, we can choose to do calculations per vertex or per fragment. Likewise, Point-Light per-fragment shading will be discussed as well. It simply produces more accurate results because shading calculation is performed at fragment (pixel) level. Per-fragment operations are usually more computationally expensive. But that's what GPUs are for. I started graphics programming in 2003 with a basic nVidia card. As of 2017 there literally not many slow cards out there anymore even at the low end of the spectrum. Quite a few support large textures of 4096x4096. Anyway, without going on too much of a tangent about graphics card performance, let's dive right into our point light shader algorithms. Given what we've explored so far in the book they shouldn't appear too complicated.

Point-Light Shader Per Vertex

Our point light shader will be a derivation of directional light shader. Its primary difference is now that instead of using light's directional vector, we are going to calculate one dynamically based on the vector between the light source and the vertex coordinate.

point.vs
precision **mediump** float;
attribute **vec4** a_Position;
attribute **vec4** a_Color;
attribute **vec2** a_Texture;
attribute **vec4** a_Normal;

varying **vec4** color;
varying **vec2** texture;

uniform **mat4** Projection;
uniform **mat4** Model;
uniform **mat4** View;

```glsl
uniform vec3 rgb;
uniform vec3 LightPosition;
uniform vec3 LightDirection;
uniform vec3 LightColor;

void main()
{
  gl_Position = Projection * View * Model * a_Position;

  vec3 normal = normalize(vec3(a_Normal));

  vec4 vert_Position = Model * a_Position;

  vec3 calc_LightDirection =
    normalize(LightPosition - vec3(vert_Position));

  float NdotL = max(dot(calc_LightDirection, normal), 0.0);

  vec4 ambient = vec4(0.3, 0.3, 0.3, 0.15);

  vec4 diffuse = vec4(0.7, 0.7, 0.7, 0.15);

  color = (ambient + diffuse) * a_Color * vec4(LightColor, 1) * NdotL;

  texture = a_Texture;
}
```

Here we will also first calculate the vertex position (this is different from gl_Position) and store it in the vert_Position vec3 variable:

```glsl
  vec4 vert_Position = Model * a_Position;
```

This is simply the vertex coordinate based on its Model matrix that was passed into the shader. If we take this vertex location and subtract it from the LightPosition vector we will arrive at the vector describing the angle of the theoretical beam of light hitting the object at that vertex location.

And then we calculate light direction dynamically in the shader for each vertex:

```
vec3 calc_LightDirection = normalize(
    LightPosition - vec3(vert_Position));
```

Note that we also have to normalize this vector for accurate results. That's all we have to do. Instead of a directional angle (the same for each vertex) we now have a slightly different value for any vertex on our model that will be hit by this point light source.

Finally, we do the same exact thing as we did in our previous shader. Calculate NdotL value based on this new light direction vector and the normal value that was passed from loaded model data.

```
float NdotL = max(dot(calc_LightDirection, normal, 0.0);
```

This will produce a dot product in the range of 0.0 to 1.0.

Finally I also added ambient and diffuse ingredients here. Here we simply add them up together and multiply by the original color of the vertex (a_Color).

The fragment shader is no different than previous one. In fact, it's simply multiplying the color we have just calculated above by the pixel data in the texture:

point.frag
```
precision mediump float;
uniform sampler2D image;
```

```
varying vec4 color;
varying vec2 texture;
uniform mat4 Projection;
uniform mat4 Model;
uniform mat4 View;

uniform vec3 rgb;

void main() {
   gl_FragColor = color * texture2D(image, vec2(texture.s, texture.t));
}
```

This is an example of a primarily per-vertex operation here. So the fragment shader is a bit vacant. All important operations are taking place in the vertex shader.

I created a quick Blender scene just for this demo. I put together a few basic boxes using the cube tool and arranged and rotated them at a slight angle throughout the entire scene.

The result of this shader effect is displayed in the screenshot below:

While shadows are missing from this example, it's a drastic improvement over any of our previous shaders. It looks like a low-lying light source illuminating the scene where each face facing the light appears to be brighter while faces pointing away from it are pitch dark.

Conclusion to 3D Topics

We've come very far from the very beginning where we initialized canvas in 3D mode. But we have not by any means exhausted everything there is about WebGL. So far, with this current knowledge we can make games that look like PlayStation 2.

This book took me about 2 months to write, working 10 hours almost every day including weekends. If you've ever written a book, or created something significant in scope (and hopefully quality) you'd know of "feature creep." This is when new ideas seem to keep coming non-stop. You want to implement them all but you have to stop somewhere. Otherwise the project will never be released.

It's the same with this book. It's not that there isn't anything left to talk about. I simply have to set a stopping point. We've covered most of the fundamental subjects that will help you get started with WebGL and begin making your own games.

I still have several subjects I want to cover which are currently still in draft mode. If you're reading this, chances are I am already working on the second edition of WebGL Gems. As an independent author I have control over the amount of content and length of the book. But as I mentioned, I simply had to stop somewhere so I can publish the first edition.

Amazon publishing allows me to update both the Kindle and Paperback version of this book. I believe that in about 2 more months I may be able to release an even better, thicker and generally upgraded version of this book. When this happens you will be notified, whether you made your purchase via Amazon, my free online programming newsletter or one of my websites. Write me a message to see if you quality for a free upgrade: greg.sidelnikov@gmail.com If you already purchased this book, chances are you pretty much do.

I want to thank you for reading up to this point and I hope that the material in this book has proven to be helpful. Until next edition of this book comes out, keep experimenting, look up shaders written by others and try making your own. We've covered enough material to start making basic 3D games and that is way more than I originally planned for this book.

But our adventure doesn't end here. To finalize the book, I wanted to cover 2D techniques because 2D games are in high demand these days. They are also generally easier to make. But how do we turn WebGL - a library that was exclusively developed for rendering 3D graphics - into a 2D game engine? This will be covered in the concluding chapters of this book that follow.

Gem 30 - 3D Collision Detection

It took me about 3 days to figure out collision detection algorithm. It's actually a lot more complex than doing collision in 2D coordinate system. Because this isn't a case of simply adding another axis and performing the same calculations. The whole approach is a bit different.

There are different types of collision detection when it comes to 3D graphics. However, the most important one of them all is the one explained in this chapter: 3D segment vs triangle collision.

Just like when we needed a Matrix library to deal with camera we will need a Vector library which will enable us to do cross-vector operations. A good one I found by doing a quick Google search was vector.js. It is really the same exact library I would have written for this book if I had to. It is minimalist, provides only the needed functionality and uses good naming convention. The vector class is simply named Vector.

We already have a 2D vector library. So I changed the name of this one to vector3.js. Once included we can start using the Vector class. Simply look up the source code in this new file from the demo available at the end of this chapter to get familiar with its methods.

But generally 3D vectors can be added, subtracted (from each other), multiplied and divided. You can also test if a vector equals another vector (this is when both vectors have a matching pair of the x, y and z coordinates in world space.)

Just like our 2D vector library from earlier in the book, we can also get length of a 3D vector or derive a unit vector by dividing a given vector by its length. This library provides all of this function. And in this chapter we will see how to implement it to aid us in achieving collision detection.

Without the 3D vector library we would have to add or subtract (and perform dot and cross products) by hand which would be a little redundant. Collision detection algorithms are excellent examples of showing importance of these two commonly used operations together.

How Does It Work?

We will cast a ray from its origin in some direction and test it against our level geometry. We will limit our collision algorithm to 3-vertex polygons (or triangles) but it can also be used to test **collision against an infinite plane**. Here, this part of the algorithm is depicted visually:

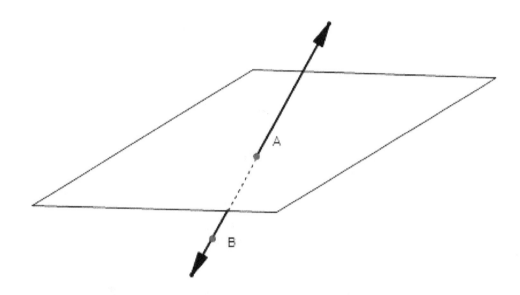

But it's just one of the two parts of the same algorithm.

In 3D graphics collision of a ray with polygon surface consists of solving two problems:

Did the ray intersect the plane shared by the triangle in question? Does the determined collision point fall inside the triangle area?

The second problem is depicted by the following illustration:

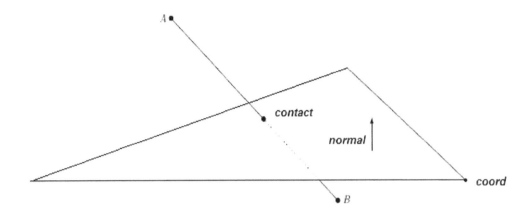

If we can solve these two problems we can safely assume that the cast ray collides with the given triangle. We can then calculate the collision point on the triangle's plane. This is the collision point which will be used to "place" our character or racing car on.

You get the idea :)

We cannot continue without first introducing a vector library. We can always write our own but chances are if it was explained in this book in detail it'd take up a good chunk of space. And it is not specifically a WebGL-related subject. What I will do is show you the JavaScript source code of the Vector library and then we'll write our collision function using it.

First, here is the full listing of our vector3.js library.

```javascript
function Vector(x, y, z) {
    this.x = x || 0;
    this.y = y || 0;
    this.z = z || 0;
}
```

```javascript
Vector.prototype = {
  negative: function() {
    return new Vector(-this.x, -this.y, -this.z);
  },
  add: function(v) {
    if (v instanceof Vector)
      return new Vector(this.x + v.x, this.y + v.y, this.z + v.z);
    else
      return new Vector(this.x + v, this.y + v, this.z + v);
  },
  subtract: function(v) {
    if (v instanceof Vector)
      return new Vector(this.x - v.x, this.y - v.y, this.z - v.z);
    else
      return new Vector(this.x - v, this.y - v, this.z - v);
  },
  multiply: function(v) {
    if (v instanceof Vector)
      return new Vector(this.x * v.x, this.y * v.y, this.z * v.z);
    else
      return new Vector(this.x * v, this.y * v, this.z * v);
  },
  divide: function(v) {
    if (v instanceof Vector)
      return new Vector(this.x / v.x, this.y / v.y, this.z / v.z);
    else
      return new Vector(this.x / v, this.y / v, this.z / v);
  },
  equals: function(v) {
    return this.x == v.x && this.y == v.y && this.z == v.z;
  },
  dot: function(v) {
    return this.x * v.x + this.y * v.y + this.z * v.z;
```

```javascript
  },
  cross: function(v) {
    return new Vector(
      this.y * v.z - this.z * v.y,
      this.z * v.x - this.x * v.z,
      this.x * v.y - this.y * v.x
    );
  },
  length: function() {
    return Math.sqrt(this.dot(this));
  },
  unit: function() {
    return this.divide(this.length());
  },
  min: function() {
    return Math.min(Math.min(this.x, this.y), this.z);
  },
  max: function() {
    return Math.max(Math.max(this.x, this.y), this.z);
  },
  toAngles: function() {
    return {
      theta: Math.atan2(this.z, this.x),
      phi: Math.asin(this.y / this.length())
    };
  },
  angleTo: function(a) {
    return Math.acos(this.dot(a) / (this.length() * a.length()));
  },
  toArray: function(n) {
    return [this.x, this.y, this.z].slice(0, n || 3);
  },
  clone: function() {
    return new Vector(this.x, this.y, this.z);
```

```
        },
        init: function(x, y, z) {
            this.x = x; this.y = y; this.z = z;
            return this;
        }
    };

Vector.negative = function(a, b) {
    b.x = -a.x; b.y = -a.y; b.z = -a.z;
    return b;
};
Vector.add = function(a, b, c) {
    if (b instanceof Vector)
    { c.x = a.x + b.x; c.y = a.y + b.y; c.z = a.z + b.z; }
    else { c.x = a.x + b; c.y = a.y + b; c.z = a.z + b; }
    return c;
};
Vector.subtract = function(a, b, c) {
    if (b instanceof Vector)
    { c.x = a.x - b.x; c.y = a.y - b.y; c.z = a.z - b.z; }
    else { c.x = a.x - b; c.y = a.y - b; c.z = a.z - b; }
    return c;
};
Vector.multiply = function(a, b, c) {
    if (b instanceof Vector)
    { c.x = a.x * b.x; c.y = a.y * b.y; c.z = a.z * b.z; }
    else { c.x = a.x * b; c.y = a.y * b; c.z = a.z * b; }
    return c;
};
Vector.divide = function(a, b, c) {
    if (b instanceof Vector)
    { c.x = a.x / b.x; c.y = a.y / b.y; c.z = a.z / b.z; }
    else { c.x = a.x / b; c.y = a.y / b; c.z = a.z / b; }
    return c;
```

```javascript
};
Vector.cross = function(a, b, c) {
  c.x = a.y * b.z - a.z * b.y;
  c.y = a.z * b.x - a.x * b.z;
  c.z = a.x * b.y - a.y * b.x;
  return c;
};
Vector.unit = function(a, b) {
  var length = a.length();
  b.x = a.x / length;
  b.y = a.y / length;
  b.z = a.z / length;
  return b;
};
Vector.fromAngles = function(theta, phi) {
  return new Vector(Math.cos(theta) * Math.cos(phi), Math.sin(phi),
Math.sin(theta) * Math.cos(phi));
};
Vector.randomDirection = function() {
  return Vector.fromAngles(Math.random() * Math.PI * 2,
Math.asin(Math.random() * 2 - 1));
};
Vector.min = function(a, b) {
  return new Vector(Math.min(a.x, b.x), Math.min(a.y, b.y),
Math.min(a.z, b.z));
};
Vector.max = function(a, b) {
  return new Vector(Math.max(a.x, b.x), Math.max(a.y, b.y),
Math.max(a.z, b.z));
};
Vector.lerp = function(a, b, fraction) {
  return b.subtract(a).multiply(fraction).add(a);
};
Vector.fromArray = function(a) {
```

```
    return new Vector(a[0], a[1], a[2]);
};
Vector.angleBetween = function(a, b) {
    return a.angleTo(b);
};
```

From now on this vector library will be included in all of our future demos in the book that require vector calculations.

Now that we have a reasonable way of doing Vector calculations in 3D space let's implement some of these methods to create the actual collision detection function.

Adding collision detection to the engine we're building gets us much closer to our goal of building a game engine. By just having this function implemented many doors open that, logistically, enable you to create almost any type of a video game that you can imagine where arbitrary objects need to collide with the terrain or walls, for example. Segment vs triangle collision detection is a pretty important element of any game. Without it your engine's creative capabilities would be thwarted.

If you have a good grasp on DOT and CROSS products, and collision detection, most of all of the other problems in general game development deal with shaders and visual quality of your game. But achieving something truly spectacular will always come from combining multiple features.

For example when I implemented collision detection in my own engine, together with "lookat" camera matrix math, I was able to make a basic version of a racing game engine where the car could travel across hills or otherwise elevated landscape and the view would accurately follow it.

That's good but how do we actually write the collision detection function? It's well-commented source code is provided below followed by a brief explanation.

```
var EPSILON = 0.000001;

function triangle_intersection(
    V1, V2, V3, // Triangle vertices
    O,       // O = Ray origin
    D) {     // D = Ray direction

    var e1, e2;  // Edge1, Edge2
    var P, Q, T;

    var det, inv_det = 0.0, u, v;
    var t;

    // Find vectors for two edges sharing V1
    e1 = V2.subtract(V1);
    e2 = V3.subtract(V1);

    // Begin calculating determinant -also used to calculate u parameter
    P   = D.cross(e2);

    // if determinant is near zero, ray lies in plane of triangle
    det = e1.dot(P);

    //NOT CULLING
    if (det > -EPSILON && det < EPSILON) return 0;
        inv_det = 1.0 / det;

    // calculate distance from V1 to ray origin
    T = O.subtract(V1);
```

```
// Calculate u parameter and test bound
u = T.dot(P) * inv_det;

// The intersection lies outside of the triangle
if (u < 0.0 || u > 1.0) return 0;

// Prepare to test v parameter
Q = T.cross(e1);

// Calculate V parameter and test bound
v = D.dot(Q) * inv_det;

// The intersection lies outside of the triangle
if (v < 0.0 || u + v > 1.0) return 0;

t = e2.dot(Q) * inv_det;

// Collision detected!
if (t > EPSILON) {

    var w = 1.0 - (u + v);
    var x = (w * V1.x + u * V2.x + v * V3.x);
    var y = (w * V1.y + u * V2.y + v * V3.y);
    var z = (w * V1.z + u * V2.z + v * V3.z);

    // return intersection point
    return [x, y, z];
}

// No collision
return 0;
}
```

V1, V2 and V3 are the triangle's vertices. O is origin of the segment. D is its direction. There is no point in explaining the actual mathematical derivation of the values here. It'd take way too many pages that could otherwise be spent on writing about WebGL functionality, which is what this book is about.

However, it's probably a good idea to go over the comments and see what each line does. Most of the cross and dot product operations solve the problem in an abstract way. I found that while it was easy to look up explanations of each step by just doing an online search, finding source code that worked accurately was a challenge.

I re-wrote this function from my OpenGL engine in JavaScript language. And from now on we will use it to check for collisions between a line and triangles. Note that all models we load with our PLY file format loader assume triangulation. Whenever you save a new object to be loaded into our engine, make sure that you have triangulated its faces first. In Blender this can be achieved by going in Edit mode on a selected object (press Tab) and then holding Ctrl and pressing T key.

Also note that our engine assumes Y axis going up in positive direction. And Z axis extending outward away from the camera in negative direction. By default, this is not Blender's configuration. So when saving your PLY file in blender, make sure to tweak its axis on the "save PLY" pane on the left hand side before clicking the Save button. Not doing this will result in an axis swap. And your model will be rendered vertically when it needs to be horizontal (for example.) This disparity between Blender's default settings can cause a bit of a headache.

Colliding An Object

We're now well-equipped to create an actual example where one object will collide with another. For this demo I created a pretty basic "staircase" model with a bump in its middle just to demonstrate collision.

We already know how to load multiple object, as it's been covered elsewhere in this book. Using those techniques I loaded a second object with is just a simple white sphere. I'll use it to collide with the staircase.

Here the sphere is actually located at x=0, y=0.15 and z=0 which places it slightly above the staircase. Now all we have to do is "drop" it and ensure that it stays on top of the surface or can travel up and down the stairs.

In order to achieve this, we need to for-loop through all vertices of the staircase model. We know that the model consists of triangles. In our previous examples where we loaded multiple objects we created a special global container window.ref_arrayMDL[m][e]. It's a multidimensional array where [m] holds the index of the model and [e] holds the index to a particular type of data associated with the model at index [m]. For example at [0][0] we can access the model's vertex list. At [0][1] its vertex colors, etc.

The rest of the available types of values are shown in source code below. Of course, they simply represent each compositional part of the model but vertices is the one we're looking for.

```
var vertices = window.ref_arrayMDL[i][0];
var colors = window.ref_arrayMDL[i][1];
var uvs = window.ref_arrayMDL[i][2];
var normals = window.ref_arrayMDL[i][3];
var indices = window.ref_arrayMDL[i][4];
```

When we loaded the model all indices were placed in linear order. For example indices in the example above points to an array that simply lists all indices from 0 to length-1 of the array. And while gl.drawElements function requires the indices array for drawing… what we need here is to simply parse through geometry of the loaded model. All we have to do is access its vertices array entry which is stored in window.ref_arrayMDL[i][0] where i is the loaded model's index. The staircase model in this demo was loaded first, so the entry in question will be [0][0].

Each set of 3 vertices on the list from this array defines each triangle in consequential order. Because our models are always loaded triangulated, we can be sure that every 3 vertices in the set refer to next triangle. This lets us easily loop through them.

Let's create a down vector from the sphere object, then loop through the vertices of our "staircase" model and rebuild each triangle in it as a set of 3 vertex variables v1, v2 and v3, as shown in the code below.

We then simply pass them to our triangle_intersection function we listed just a few paragraphs back. And if there is a collision, the function will return an array containing x, y and z point at which the down ray intersects with one of the triangles in the staircase model. If not, the function returns 0.

```
// Grab vertices of the staircase model
var vertices = window.ref_arrayMDL[0][0];

// Slightly above the sphere's center
var downRayPosition = new Vector(x, y + 2, z);

// cast down on Y axis
var downRayDirection = new Vector(0, -5, 0);

for (var v = 0; v < vertices.length; v += 9)
{
    var v3 = new Vector(vertices[v + 0], vertices[v + 1], vertices[v + 2]);
    var v2 = new Vector(vertices[v + 3], vertices[v + 4], vertices[v + 5]);
    var v1 = new Vector(vertices[v + 6], vertices[v + 7], vertices[v + 8]);

    var intersect = triangle_intersection(v1, v2, v3,
                        downRayPosition,
                        downRayDirection);

    // There was an intersection!
    if (intersect != 0) {

        var inx = intersect[0];
        var iny = intersect[1];
        var inz = intersect[2];

        // Adjust the sphere model's Y position to match intersection
        // on the Y axis, but also add sphere's radius 0.05 to make it
        // appear collide with the terrain
        y = iny + 0.025;
```

```
        window.collision = true;

        // end the loop
        break;

    } else {  window.collision = false; }


}
```

Surprisingly the collision detection algorithm is simpler than one would imagine it to be. It's just a matter of knowing and focusing on the right things.

Of course, this algorithm has room for improvement. We could eliminate unnecessary triangle tests here by passing the vertex data through another algorithm that will determine which triangles to test against and which ones are hopelessly far away or can be excluded following some other rule.

And another thing. The algorithm assumes that the model is static. In other words, the ball will only collide with the staircase as long as it remains in the same exact location it was originally loaded into. Rotating the model will not rotate its vertices as they appear in the vertex array at the time they were loaded from the PLY file. To fix this problem they will have to be passed through the Model matrix separately. That step is not shown in this demo.

We can now take a look at screenshots of the demo. I moved the camera view a bit to display what's happening here: The object itself was not moved nor rotated. I simply switched to a better view by moving the camera..

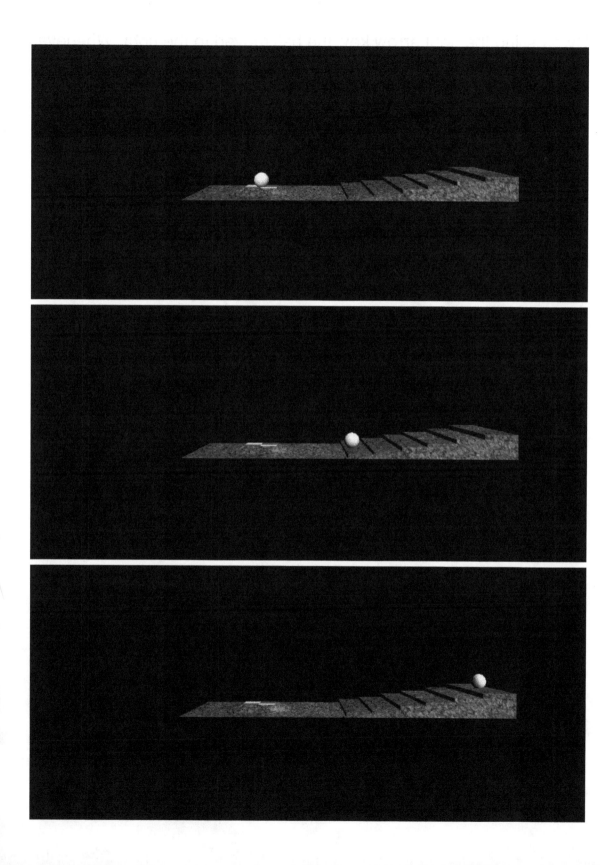

By pressing the right arrow key, the ball moved to the right. Whenever the ray intersected with staircase geometry a collision was detected. The ball was them moved to the collision point only on the Y axis, and a bit up in the amount of half of its diameter (which is its radius.) This way the sphere appeared colliding with the floor at its bottom contact point. Just as you would expect in a real case scenario.

I kept the lights on for this demo. So when the sphere moved from left to right, its illumination changed a bit. It just made this example look more interesting.

And that's that! I know all of what we've developed so far sounds incredibly simple. But I cannot stress this enough. Collision detection with camera follow algorithm (the LookAt camera) and some basic lighting shading effects is already enough for making just about any type of game possible. This is why I wanted to single out and focus on these important concepts. It only took us roughly 250 pages to implement them all. But in the end, these features gave us an opportunity to start making our own games. In the next chapter, I will put them all together to create a simple kart racing game. It wouldn't be fair to provide explanations for all of these subjects without putting the conglomerate together and showing you how powerful they already are at getting us closer to making real games with WebGL.

Platypus Kart

When I got my first PC at age of about 12 it was running on an Intel x386 processor with just 4 megabytes of RAM memory. Lots of games were available for this machine. Including hits like Need For Speed. Even NFS2 could run on it, either without sound or music. In order to get music to work you had to upgrade to a whopping 8 Megabytes of RAM.

When I was a kid I was totally intrigued by racing games. One of my favorite games was Quarantine where you took on a role of a bewitched taxi driver in an isolated city and took your customers to their destination while battling against Omnicorp. This game required 8 Megabytes of RAM, too. And I could only play it when my brother's friend visited us and actually brought an extra 4 Megabyte stick of memory with him. We would put it into our 386 and all of a sudden we could play Quarantine and many other games we couldn't with less memory.

When our friend was gone, taking his memory with him, we were back to Doom, Need For Speed 1, Battle Island and few other games. Ever since that time I've always been extremely interested in making my own games. As times went on, I thought about what game I should make. And apparently my old memories suggested I should make a driving game.

I've been fascinated with Mario Kart 8 ever since it came out. In fact, the reason I started writing this book was to get better at making my own hyper-realistic shaders. If you can get that implemented and with a little creativity, it would be possible to create worlds that look just like graphics from MK8. They are bright, colorful and have glowy lights (blur and/or bloom shader). In this section we will not be concerned with graphics-quality aspects of a racing game. That can always be added later in the creative stage when you construct your own levels in Blender or some other software. But we'll do what we can with what we've covered so far in this book.

We've already explored enough subjects that equip us with enough ability to make our own racing game. All we would need is a racing track model, some basic representation of our "kart", have it collide with the racing track, and add a follow camera right behind it using LookAt algorithm. I guess I'll just call it Platypus Kart. Because Platypus is just an odd creature.

Here is a scene of a newly loaded racing track I created just for this demo. Currently the camera is "looking at" the sphere. So whenever it is moved around, not only the sphere remains on the track, but the camera follows it, ensuring that it's always in the center of the screen.

But we now need to make the camera "chase" the car as it moves and accelerates. In order to make this happen we can cast a ray from the kart's current position in direction it is currently moving in. Velocity is stored in a new class I created for this demo called Automobile:

```
function Automobile() {
    this.x = 0;          // Position in the world
    this.y = 0;
    this.z = 0;
    this.velocity = 0; // Speed
    this.angle = 0;     // Angle of direction
}

var Kart = new Automobile();
```

Source Code

Below I am listing the source-code that takes everything we've made so far in this book and puts every single principle we've talked about to create a simple racing game demo. This is not a complete game. Just a starting point.

The source code itself is not very complicated at all. Surprisingly so. But clean code is always a result of focusing on and knowing how to use specific principles purposefully. Code doesn't have to be complicated.

First, let's wire our controls as follows.

```
if (key.left) Kart.angle -= 0.005;
if (key.right) Kart.angle += 0.005;
if (key.up) Kart.velocity += 0.0001;
if (key.down) Kart.velocity -= 0.0001;
```

Left and right arrow keys will control angle of direction of our car. Up and down keys will control acceleration. On every frame, the car will be moved forward along its angle of direction based on current velocity. We can also add friction that works against velocity by dampering it.

Here we also convert Kart's angle into a vector. This is achieved by a previously discussed function ang2vec from segment library which is now part of our engine. Converting the angle to a vector value helps us determine what direction to move the Kart in based on its angle. We talked about this in this book's section when we created a demo imitating "walking" on our map. Same principle applies here. Except now velocity is constantly applied on every animation frame. Note that ang2vec function returns a normalized unit vector. By multiplying it by Kart's velocity value we can determine how fast it should be traveling.

Per animation frame:

```
// Start main drawing loop
var T = setInterval(function() {

  if (!gl)
    return;

  // Take controls
  if (key.left) Kart.angle_velocity -= 0.005;
  if (key.right) Kart.angle_velocity += 0.005;
  if (key.up) Kart.velocity += 0.0001;
  if (key.down) Kart.velocity -= 0.0001;

  // Convert Kart's angle to vector coordinates
  var dir_xz = ang2vec(Kart.angle);
  var dir_x = dir_xz[0]; // on x-axis
  var dir_z = dir_xz[1]; // on z-axis

  // Move Kart in direction of its angle
  Kart.x += dir_x * Kart.velocity;
  Kart.z += dir_z * Kart.velocity;

  // Smoothly rotate the kart based on angle velocity
  Kart.angle += Kart.angle_velocity;

  // Friction forces work against us
  Kart.angle_velocity -= (Kart.angle_velocity * 0.0075);
  Kart.velocity -= (Kart.velocity * 0.005);
```

```javascript
// Clear WebGL canvas
gl.clearColor(0.0, 0.0, 0.0, 1.0);

gl.clear(gl.COLOR_BUFFER_BIT);
gl.clear(gl.DEPTH_BUFFER_BIT);

// Set "brick.png" as active texture to pass into the shader
gl.activeTexture(gl.TEXTURE0);
gl.bindTexture(gl.TEXTURE_2D, road.texture);
gl.uniform1i(gl.getUniformLocation(Shader.directionalProgram,
        'image'), 0);

// Create camera perspective matrix
Projection.makeIdentity();
Projection.perspective(45, width / height, 0.05, 1000);

gl.uniformMatrix4fv(gl.getUniformLocation(
    Shader.directionalProgram, "Projection"), false,
    Projection.getAsFloat32Array());

var View = new CanvasMatrix4();

// Generate view matrix
View.makeIdentity();

View.lookat2(
    Kart.x-1*dir_x, Kart.y+0.25, Kart.z-1*dir_z,
    Kart.x, Kart.y+0.25, Kart.z,
    0,1,0);

// Set viewport to Upper Left corner
gl.viewport(0, 0, width, height);
```

```
// Default ambient color set to "white"
rgb = [1.0, 1.0, 0.7];

LightPosition = [5, 3, -10]; // some angle
LightDirection = [-0.25, 1.75, 3]; // some other angle
LightColor = [1, 1, 0.9]; // white-yellowish

BindModel(1);
Model.makeIdentity();
Model.rotate(car_angle, 0, 1, 0);
Model.translate(0, 0, 0);

gl.uniform3fv(gl.getUniformLocation(
Shader.directionalProgram, "rgb"), rgb);

gl.uniform3fv(gl.getUniformLocation(
Shader.directionalProgram, "LightPosition"), LightPosition);

gl.uniform3fv(gl.getUniformLocation(
Shader.directionalProgram, "LightDirection"), LightDirection);

gl.uniform3fv(gl.getUniformLocation(
Shader.directionalProgram, "LightColor"), LightColor);

gl.uniformMatrix4fv(gl.getUniformLocation(
Shader.directionalProgram, "Model"), false,
Model.getAsFloat32Array());

gl.uniformMatrix4fv(gl.getUniformLocation(
Shader.directionalProgram, "View"), false,
View.getAsFloat32Array());

gl.drawElements(gl.TRIANGLES,
model_indices.length, gl.UNSIGNED_SHORT, 0);
```

```
// Draw Kart
BindModel(0);
Model.makeIdentity();
Model.translate(Kart.x, Kart.y, Kart.z);

gl.uniform3fv(gl.getUniformLocation(
Shader.directionalProgram, "rgb"), rgb);

gl.uniform3fv(gl.getUniformLocation(
Shader.directionalProgram, "LightPosition"), LightPosition);

gl.uniform3fv(gl.getUniformLocation(
Shader.directionalProgram, "LightDirection"), LightDirection);

gl.uniform3fv(gl.getUniformLocation(
Shader.directionalProgram, "LightColor"), LightColor);

gl.uniformMatrix4fv(gl.getUniformLocation(
Shader.directionalProgram, "Model"), false,
Model.getAsFloat32Array());

gl.uniformMatrix4fv(gl.getUniformLocation(
Shader.directionalProgram, "View"), false,
View.getAsFloat32Array());

gl.drawElements(gl.TRIANGLES,
model_indices.length, gl.UNSIGNED_SHORT, 0);

var vertices = window.ref_arrayMDL[1][0];

// At the sphere's center
var downRayPosition = new Vector(Kart.x, Kart.y+2, Kart.z);
```

```javascript
// cast down on Y axis
var downRayDirection = new Vector(0, -5, 0);

// Loop through all triangles in the model (could be optimized)
for (var v = 0; v < vertices.length; v += 9)
{
    var v3 = new Vector(vertices[v+0], vertices[v+1], vertices[v+2]);
    var v2 = new Vector(vertices[v+3], vertices[v+4], vertices[v+5]);
    var v1 = new Vector(vertices[v+6], vertices[v+7], vertices[v+8]);

    var intersect = triangle_intersection(
        v1, v2, v3,
        downRayPosition,
        downRayDirection);

    // There was an intersection!
    if (intersect != 0) {

        var inx = intersect[0];
        var iny = intersect[1];
        var inz = intersect[2];

        // Adjust the sphere model's Y position to match
        // intersection on the Y axis, but also add sphere's
        // radius 0.025 to make it appear collide with the terrain
        Kart.y = iny + 0.025;

        window.collision = true;

        break; // end the loop

    } else {  window.collision = false; }
    }
});
```

And finally, here is a screenshot produced by this code:

We can control the "kart" which at this point is just a sphere. The camera smoothly follows the direction in which it's going, while being positioned directly behind it. This creates a Mario Kart-like racing effect.

This "game" even supports curved road. Thanks to the collision detection algorithm.

The only true problem with the current approach is having to collide the sphere with all of the triangles in the level data. The map contains simple geometry but it's still pretty large considering that triangle_intersection function has to traverse each and single one of the vertices contributing to the level's geometry.

The current algorithm checks to collide with triangles that are obviously far away from the sphere to even be considered. And this taxes performance of the game. After all there are 2 cross product operations and 4 dot product operations per triangle! That's a lot.

To speed up the algorithm, you could calculate relative distance between the sphere and each vertex. If the average sum of vertices (center of the triangle) is too far away from the sphere (let's say 5.0 units of space or greater) then that triangle can be discarded from the collision test. In the current version of this game that's not yet implemented. For now, I'll leave the task up to you!

Also note that because our shader already supports vertex color, the road is nicely illuminated by an imaginary light source. To create this effect I simply vertex-colored the lit area in Blender while creating the racing track model. So, this isn't dynamic lighting. But if you think about it, it doesn't have to be.

Gem 31 - 2D Games

What a journey this has been so far! At the beginning of this book we started with creating a shader loading library. Then we learned how to draw triangles on the screen and loaded images that were applied as texture maps. We then loaded objects from a PLY file (with complete source included!) and applied some lighting to our scene.

We learned how to draw multiple objects and explored the possibilities for game design by discovering the collision detection function whose full source code along with a car racing example were also provided.

All of this was done by using 3D principles we've explored throughout the first part of the book. In this section we will learn how WebGL can be used for creating 2-dimensional games.

Making 2D games is all about rendering sprites on the screen. Traditionally, sprites are just images rendered on the screen. In WebGL we can imitate this behavior by creating a 3D rectangle that will always be facing the camera. There is no direct 2D support in WebGL other than this.

In this chapter we will also learn how to make our own font engine where each letter is represented by a square in a larger sprite sheet image. We will then take this concept and create frame-based animation which can theoretically be used for making characters walk across some sort of a 2D terrain.

We will convert the coordinate system to a 2D one (where positive Y is pointing downward, just like on traditional 2D game screens. A 2D collision detection function will also be provided as well. This should be enough to get started with writing your own 2D games using WebGL platform.

The great thing about making 2D games in a 3D environment is that you can supplement your 2D worlds with 3D objects to increase quality of your level design. For example you can add spinning windmills, fans, or other types of rotating objects. If you wish to make a purely 2D game that's fine too. It's just nice to know that we're not limited to flat 2D sprites.

First things first. And one of the techniques used in making 2D games in 3D is switching on the Orthographic projection. This is a projection that is used in architecture and engineering software for viewing a 3-dimensional object without 3D perspective enabled. In some cases this makes technical designing of an item (like a water pipe, for example) more convenient. Some 3D modelers use orthographic projection exclusively when designing their models. It's just a slightly different way of thinking about and viewing your 3D scene.

Orthographic projections are perfect for implementing 2D-based games. The Z axis is not completely gone. It's still there. It's just it's absent from the rasterization part of the algorithm. And no matter how far or close to the camera view our objects (sprites) will be drawn, they will appear the same size (their original size) regardless where they are on the Z axis.

Orthographic Projection

We've created perspective projection before in pretty much all of the demos in this book. In order to do that we used the matrix library CanvasMatrix which already included a function to construct a perspective-based camera. The orthographic projection can also be used via this class. It has a special function called ortho. It returns a matrix that can be then passed on to the shader, just like any other matrix we've used prior to this example.

Let's take a look at the ortho function:

```
CanvasMatrix4.prototype.ortho =
    function(left, right, bottom, top, near, far);
```

It's pretty simple. All we have to do is provide bounding coordinates that encompass the orthographic projection view. We still have near and far clipping planes, past which no graphics will be rendered.

Instead of sending perspective projection to our sprite shaders this time we will instead supply it with an orthographic matrix:

```
var Projection = new CanvasMatrix4();
Projection.ortho(-10.0f, 10.0f, -10.0f, 10.0f, 0.0f, 100.0f);
```

And later pass it onto the spriteProgram shader (explained in just a bit):

```
gl.uniformMatrix4fv(gl.getUniformLocation(
    Shader.spriteProgram, "Projection"), false,
    Projection.getAsFloat32Array());
```

This will create a "flat" 2D screen purposely missing perspective distortion.

Transforming 3D Coordinate System to 2D

WebGL wasn't made for games and by default provides a 3D world coordinate system in Cartesian space. This means x=0 and y=0 are directly in the middle of the screen. But 2D games are traditionally designed around a coordinate system where x=0 and y=0 are located in the upper left corner. No problem! We can convert this coordinate system to just what we need by translating the orthographic view left and up by half of the projection's width and height values.

But there is one more thing. WebGL coordinate system's Y increases going up. In 2D games we need the Y coordinate increase on its way down. To make this transition we will simply invert the Y coordinate during our calculations. Couldn't we have gotten away without any of these transformations and worked in original WebGL coordinate system? Of course! But if you're porting a canvas based (or any other 2D game that had traditional coordinate system) it's best to stick to the commonly accepted defaults.

Sprite Model

Because WebGL doesn't provide a direct access to the screen, the best and most efficient way of drawing sprites in this type of environment would be via creating a 3D model representing the sprite itself.

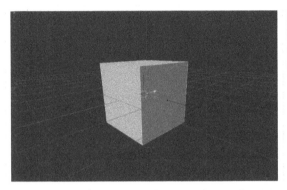 

This will be a square consisting of 2 triangles. You can either create one in Blender by making a cube and deleting all but 1 side or algorithmically by simply representing this square by an array of vertices. If you are creating one in Blender, make sure not to forget to triangulate your model.

I created this sprite object and saved it in sprite.ply. This is the "model" we will be rendering when we need to draw sprites.

I also chose a random but appropriate image for displaying as our sprite. It's a star! I found it by doing a quick Google search for free assets. I simply placed the file into our textures folder.

Remember, our engine is capable of automatically loading this image and storing it as a WebGL texture resource. It becomes an auto-magically generated variable window.star.texture because its filename was star.png.

This square will have texture coordinates (u and v) just like any other object we've dealt with thus far. And that's how an image will be mapped onto it. In the same way as before we will have to load and enable some type of a texture for using as the source image for the sprite being rendered. This texture can be either a single sprite or an entire sprite sheet containing all animation frames.

Sometimes the sprite sheet containing a map of images is also called an atlas.

In just a bit we will also explore sprite sheets which are basically large textures containing a grid of sprites. This way we don't have to load an image for each individual sprite object separately. Sprite sheets usually consist of 8x8, 16x16, 32x32 (sometimes larger) grids containing animation frames or a font's ASCII character table where each letter is represented by a small square inside the image atlas.

Drawing Sprites

I started a new shader just for rendering sprites. This will be the shader we'll turn on whenever we need to draw images on the screen. Note that the orthographic projection can be easily combined together with perspective-based rendering. The sprites will not be drawn separately. They will be simply rendered on top of what's already been rendered.

I called this shader pair sprite.vs and sprite.frag. In our shader library I called it spriteProgram. Every time we need to display some sprites we will turn this shader on.

sprite.vs
```
precision mediump float;
attribute vec4 a_Position;
attribute vec4 a_Color;
attribute vec2 a_Texture;

varying vec4 color;
varying vec2 texture;

uniform mat4 Projection;
uniform mat4 Model;
uniform mat4 View;

uniform vec3 rgb;

void main()
{
   gl_Position = Projection * View * Model * a_Position;

   color = a_Color;

   texture = a_Texture;
}
```

Here, we're not really doing anything we haven't before. Looks like a standard shader for rendering a regular 3D surface. We're only geometrically limited to a square.

sprite.frag
```
precision mediump float;

uniform sampler2D image;

varying vec4 color;
varying vec2 texture;

uniform mat4 Projection;
uniform mat4 Model;
uniform mat4 View;

uniform vec3 rgb;

void main() {

  gl_FragColor =
    vec4(rgb[0], rgb[1], rgb[2], 1) *
    texture2D(image, vec2(texture.s, texture.t));
}
```

The rgb value is for tinting the sprite just in case we want to color it a specific shade. By default white color will be passed to this value.

Scaling the sprite will be accessible via our Model matrix from our JavaScript program, so it is not necessary implementing it here.

Let's Draw Sprites

That's pretty much it. Let's try this out and draw 1,000 sprites on the screen.

```javascript
var View = new CanvasMatrix4();

View.makeIdentity();

// Move viewing camera back by 10 units
View.translate(0, 0, -10);

// Set viewport to Upper Left corner
gl.viewport(0, 0, width, height);

// Default ambient color set to "white"
rgb = [1.0, 1.0, 1.0];

BindModel(0);

gl.uniformMatrix4fv(gl.getUniformLocation(Shader.spriteProgram,
"View"), false, View.getAsFloat32Array());

// Draw 100 sprites, scaled down by 1/2 and randomly rotated
for (var yy = 0; yy < 10; yy++) {
  for (var xx = 0; xx < 10; xx++) {
    Model.makeIdentity();
    Model.rotate(xx + yy, 0, 1, 0);

    var rx = -10 + Math.random() * 20;
    var ry = -10 + Math.random() * 20;

    Model.translate(rx, ry, 0);
    Model.scale(0.5, 0.5, 0.5);
    Model.rotate(Math.random() * 360, 0, 0, 1);

    gl.uniform3fv(gl.getUniformLocation(
        Shader.spriteProgram, "rgb"), rgb);
```

```
    gl.uniformMatrix4fv(gl.getUniformLocation(
        Shader.spriteProgram, "Model"), false,
        Model.getAsFloat32Array());

    gl.drawElements(gl.TRIANGLES,
        model_indices.length, gl.UNSIGNED_SHORT, 0);
    }
}
```

And here is a screenshot produced by this code:

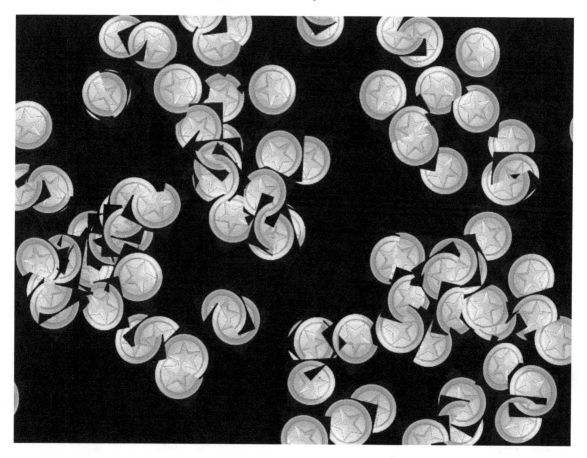

That's pretty much all there is to drawing sprites in WebGL.

Turning off Z-buffer

Note that orthographic sprites are still essentially going to occupy the same Z-buffer space with the rest of our geometry in the scene (if any.) For this reason it's a good practice to always draw sprites as the final step in the rendering pipeline. Turning off Z-buffer sorting ensures that the sprites we're drawing will be always rendered on top of existing view even if the sprites are technically "behind" any other objects already drawn on the screen.

Stretching

To stretch the sprite, let's say, by 2 units, you would do this by using scale function on the Model matrix as follows:

    Model.scale(2.0, 2.0, 1.0); // z is not required here

Scaling a sprite on Z axis makes little sense. For this reason we kept the last parameter 1.0 which is its default value. It makes no difference.

However, if you wish to scale your sprite only vertically or only horizontally, you'd apply the following parameters:

    Model.scale(2.0, 1.0, 1.0); // Scale horizontally by 2.0 units
    Model.scale(1.0, 2.0, 1.0); // Scale vertically by 2.0 units

Rotating

Rotation is also achieved in pre-shader step while calculating our Model matrix.

Model.rotate(15.0, 1.0, 0.0, 0.0); // rotate by 15 degrees on X axis
Model.rotate(15.0, 0.0, 1.0, 0.0); // rotate by 15 degrees on Y axis
Model.rotate(15.0, 0.0, 0.0, 1.0); // rotate by 15 degrees on Z axis
Model.rotate(25.0, 1.0, 1.0, 1.0); // rotate by 25 degrees on all 3 axis

Chances are, most of the time you will only be doing rotation on the Z axis. It's the only axis that it makes sense to rotate sprites on. Unless, you are looking to create some sort of an unusual effect in your game.

Transparency

GLSL fragment shaders provide a special and useful directive called discard. If you'd like to skip rendering a particular pixel (fragment) you can discard it based on its color value. Draw your sprite image as usual. Choose a "special" color that will not be rasterized to the screen. Then rewrite your sprite.frag fragment shader as follows:

```
void main() {

  gl_FragColor =
    vec4(rgb[0], rgb[1], rgb[2], 1) *
    texture2D(image, vec2(texture.s, texture.t));

  vec4 Magenta = vec4(1.0, 0.0, 1.0, 1.0);

  if (gl_FragColor == Magenta)
    discard;
}
```

Choose an unusual color such as magenta, that doesn't often appear in nature. The fragment will be discarded if magenta is found in your texture map. This will result in a sprite rendered with transparent parts.

Loading & Displaying Sprite Sheets

We've loaded and displayed sprites. But it's just like displaying a 3D object, which is something we've already done earlier in the book. What are some of the more interesting things you can do with sprite rendering in WebGL?

We can modify our sprite shader to work with the so called sprite sheets. I'll demonstrate this principle by loading a set of ASCII characters stored all in one texture. This will be our sprite sheet where each little square contains a single letters.

We'll pass the location of the square where each particular letter is located to the shader in terms of its row and column index on the sprite atlas. Here is the new font image:

Dropping font.png into our textures folder will automatically generate window.font.texture in our WebGL JavaScript engine.

This is a valid WebGL texture object. We will pass it to our shader by binding the texture to image uniform. Note the shader here being used is spritesheetProgram. Our new spritesheet shader which will be explained just below after this.

```
gl.activeTexture(gl.TEXTURE0);
gl.bindTexture(gl.TEXTURE_2D, font.texture);
gl.uniform1i(gl.getUniformLocation(
    Shader.spritesheetProgram, 'image'), 0);
```

Unlike traditional 3D textures which store vertex coordinates all over the place at an arbitrary location it's important that when creating sprite sheets that all sprites in them are stored in a grid.

It doesn't matter whether you want your square be 8 by 8 or 16 x 16 (or any other dimension) as long as a choice was made as to how many of these squares should fit into the sprite map horizontally and vertically. We'll call this the dimension of our sprite sheet.

For example the font map is 16 by 16 squares which is just enough to store the entire ASCII table. Coincidentally, each sprite in it is also 16 pixels in width and height.

Before showing the new font character choosing shader, let's assume that we will pass some new information to it so we can accurately pick the character square for any given letter:

```
// Which sprite from the spritesheet to display?
var column = 0.0;
var row = 1.0;
```

```javascript
// Sprite sheet grid is 16x16
var sheet_size = 16.0;

// Sprite dimension is 16x16 too (pure coincidence in this case)
var sprite_size = 16.0;

// Pass Model matrix to the shader
gl.uniformMatrix4fv(gl.getUniformLocation(
    Shader.spritesheetProgram, "Model"), false,
Model.getAsFloat32Array());

// Pass ambient color adjustment
gl.uniform3fv(gl.getUniformLocation(
    Shader.spritesheetProgram, "rgb"), rgb);

// Pass which column the character is in? (0-15)
gl.uniform1f(gl.getUniformLocation(Shader.spritesheetProgram,
    "column"), column);

// Which row? (0-15)
gl.uniform1f(gl.getUniformLocation(Shader.spritesheetProgram,
    "row"), row);

// Sheet's size (how many sprites across and/or down? 16 items here)
gl.uniform1f(gl.getUniformLocation(Shader.spritesheetProgram,
    "sheet_size"), sheet_size);

// The dimension of each letter sprite (16 pixels here)
gl.uniform1f(gl.getUniformLocation(Shader.spritesheetProgram,
    "sprite_size"), sprite_size);

// Draw the selected character
gl.drawElements(gl.TRIANGLES, model_indices.length,
gl.UNSIGNED_SHORT, 0);
```

In this code we have chosen a character residing in column 0 (first column) and row 1 (second row) using 0-based indices. Hmm. What's located in that square? The quirky left arrow, that's what! The shader explained in the following section will display this:

This is just one of the letters from the entire set. But at least, we were able to choose one from the sprite sheet by row and column.

Note that of course fonts are not the only things (and usually not primary things) that sprite sheet shaders are used for. They are commonly used for in-game character animation (birds flapping wings, character walking cycles, etc.) So how does this shader actually work? Let's take a look...

Spritesheet Font Engine

In this section I will introduce the new shader program consisting of spritesheet.vs and spritesheet.frag vertex and fragment pair. This shader will locate the correct area on the sprite sheet based on requested parameters.

spritesheet.vs
precision **mediump** float;
attribute **vec4** a_Position;
attribute **vec4** a_Color;
attribute **vec2** a_Texture;

```glsl
uniform sampler2D image;

varying vec4 color;
varying vec2 texture;

uniform mat4 Projection;
uniform mat4 Model;
uniform mat4 View;

uniform vec3 rgb;

void main()
{
  gl_Position = Projection * View * Model * a_Position;

  color = a_Color;

  texture = a_Texture;
}
```

Our spritesheet.vs remains the same as spritesheet.vs. That makes sense because we're not really dealing much with vertex coordinates here. It's spritesheet.frag that will do the important calculations in texture space.

spritesheet.frag
```glsl
precision mediump float;

uniform sampler2D image;

varying vec4 color;
varying vec2 texture;

uniform mat4 Projection;
```

```glsl
uniform mat4 Model;
uniform mat4 View;

uniform vec3 rgb;

uniform float column;
uniform float row;
uniform float sheet_size;
uniform float sprite_size;

void main() {

  // stride is 0.0625f when sheet_size is 16.0
  float stride = 1.0 / sheet_size;

  vec2 tex = vec2(stride * column + texture.s * stride,
                  stride* row   + texture.t * stride);

  gl_FragColor =
     vec4(rgb[0], rgb[1], rgb[2], 1) *
     texture2D(image, tex);
}
```

The primary point of interest is in the following two lines:

```glsl
// step is 0.0625f when sheet_size is 16.0
float step = 1.0 / sheet_size;

vec2 tex = vec2(stride * column + texture.s * stride,
                stride * row   + texture.t * stride);
```

Since we passed sheet_size (which is the number of sprites in the sheet either vertically or horizontally) we can calculate the stride of each in texture space by dividing 1.0 by the value stored in sheet_size. Which in this case was 16. (There are 16 by 16 letters in the sheet.)

We can then use this parameter to choose the little square we're looking for by multiplying stride by either column or row and adding the new value to texture.s multiplied by stride and texture.t multiplied by stride.

This works because in WebGL texture coordinates are calculated from 0.0 to 1.0 regardless of the actual size of the texture whether it's 256x256 or 4096x4096.

Printing Text

So we now have a way of printing any character from the font map. But how do we actually write a string of text? Text is usually indexed by ASCII character value. All we have to do is determine the numeric ID of a character and perform a linear calculation to convert it to column vs row coordinates. Knowing the number of sprites in the sprite sheets across and down doing this becomes pretty trivial.

But there is one other thing we need to worry about first. Our sprite sheet only choose characters by column and row. But ASCII codes are linear. So conversion is waiting to happen here.

I want to introduce a set of two special functions for converting from index-based to row/column based coordinates. These are pretty common operations in game development, and it's nice to have helper functions to accommodate for them:

```
function i2xy(index, mapWidth)
{
    var x = index % mapWidth;
```

```
    var y = Math.floor(index/mapWidth);
    return [x, y];
}

function xy2i(x, y, mapWidth)
{
    return y * mapWidth + x;
}
```

The function i2xy will convert an index based parameter to grid coordinates, provided we pass it mapWidth (the number of sprites in a column and/or row of a spritesheet.)

Additionally, JavaScript provides built-in function charCodeAt which grabs the ASCII code of a character in a string at a particular index.

```
var gl_text = "Hello from WebGL Text Engine!";
```

```
var c = gl_text.charCodeAt(i);
```

```
var ascii = i2xy(c, 16);
```

```
column = ascii[0];
```

```
row = ascii[1];
```

Function i2xy has successfully converted a character in a string at index position "i" to column and row location. We can now pass these new coordinates to our shader to retrieve the correct letter.

Here is the complete source code of the for-loop outputting our entire string to our view:

```
// Which sprite from the spritesheet to display?
var column = 0.0;
var row = 1.0;

// sprite sheet grid is 16x16
var sheet_size = 16.0;

// sprite dimension is 16x16
var sprite_size = 16.0;

var gl_text = "Hello from WebGL Text Engine!";

for (var i = 0; i < gl_text.length; i++)
{
  // Reset Model matrix for each letter
  Model.makeIdentity();

  // Rotate the sprite to ensure letter looks right side up
  Model.rotate(180, 0, 0, 1);
  Model.rotate(180, 1, 0, 0);

  // Move next letter in the string to the right by 1.5f
  Model.translate(1.5 * i, 0, 0);

  // Scale the character to some reasonable size
  Model.scale(0.1, 0.1, 0.1);

  var c = gl_text.charCodeAt(i);

  var ascii = i2xy(c, 16);

  column = ascii[0];

  row = ascii[1];
```

```
gl.uniformMatrix4fv(gl.getUniformLocation(
    Shader.spritesheetProgram, "Model"), false,
    Model.getAsFloat32Array());

gl.uniform3fv(gl.getUniformLocation(
    Shader.spritesheetProgram, "rgb"), rgb);
gl.uniform1f(gl.getUniformLocation(
    Shader.spritesheetProgram, "column"), column);
gl.uniform1f(gl.getUniformLocation(
    Shader.spritesheetProgram, "row"), row);
gl.uniform1f(gl.getUniformLocation(
    Shader.spritesheetProgram, "sheet_size"), sheet_size);
gl.uniform1f(gl.getUniformLocation(
    Shader.spritesheetProgram, "sprite_size"), sprite_size);

    // Draw this character
    gl.drawElements(gl.TRIANGLES,
        model_indices.length,
        gl.UNSIGNED_SHORT, 0);
}
```

And finally the results of these operations will output our string on the screen:

Sprite Sheet Animation Engine

Font engines are fun. But we can take them one step further and create a character animation engine based on the same principle. Instead of letters, each sprite will represent a single frame of animation.

A while ago while working on a mining game, I rotoscoped a walking person from a movie scene. I traced each outline and ended up with a fluid animation cycle. But that's not the image I want to show you in this example. The same game also had a slightly more impressive animation of a fire bursting out of a pipe.

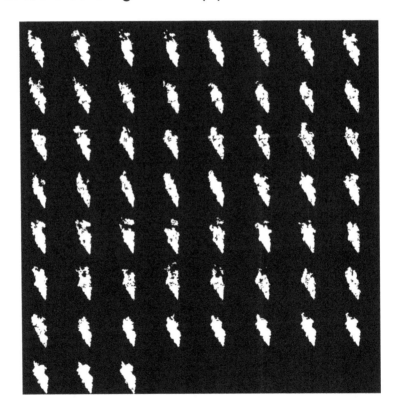

It has quite a number of animation frames! 59 to be exact. Let's scroll through all of them and pass them into our new shader to see what happens. This sprite sheets has 8 x 8 sprites in a grid. So all we have to do is change the sheet_size to 8 and sprite_size to 128 because that's the size of our flamey sprite.

Then, all we have to do is increment the animation frame by 1 until we reach 59. In the same way as we've done with the font engine we will use the i2xy function to determine location of the frame.

Finally, our code which is similar to the text engine from earlier, will look this way:

```
// Defined somewhere outside main animation loop...
var flame_index = 0;

// Which sprite from the sprite sheet to display?
var column = 0.0;
var row = 1.0;

// sprite sheet grid is 16x16
var sheet_size = 8.0;

// sprite dimension is 16x16
var sprite_size = 128.0;

Model.makeIdentity();
Model.rotate(180, 0, 0, 1);
Model.rotate(180, 1, 0, 0);
Model.translate(0, 0, 0);
//Model.scale(0.1, 0.1, 0.1);

// Rewind animation
if (flame_index >= 59)
    flame_index = 0;

var c = flame_index++;
```

```
var ascii = i2xy(flame_index, 16);

column = ascii[0];
row = ascii[1];

gl.uniformMatrix4fv(gl.getUniformLocation(
    Shader.spritesheetProgram, "Model"), false,
Model.getAsFloat32Array());

gl.uniform3fv(gl.getUniformLocation(
    Shader.spritesheetProgram, "rgb"), rgb);

gl.uniform1f(gl.getUniformLocation(
    Shader.spritesheetProgram, "column"), column);

gl.uniform1f(gl.getUniformLocation(
    Shader.spritesheetProgram, "row"), row);

gl.uniform1f(gl.getUniformLocation(
    Shader.spritesheetProgram, "sheet_size"), sheet_size);

gl.uniform1f(gl.getUniformLocation(
    Shader.spritesheetProgram, "sprite_size"), sprite_size);

gl.drawElements(gl.TRIANGLES, model_indices.length,
gl.UNSIGNED_SHORT, 0);
```

The flame animation is put into rotation until frame 59 at which point
the animation will rewind and start over. This technique can be
applied to pretty much any 2D sprite animation. From this point on an
artist can create sprite animations for walk or run cycles and place
them into each square. You could create animation arrays holding
frame index sequence, and every time the left key is pressed you

could choose "walk left" animation to display at your character location in the game world. The same could be done for "walk right" animation and so forth.

Conclusion

In this chapter we covered basic idea behind displaying 2D graphics in a 3D environment. This book is primarily about WebGL programming and not making games, but the best effort was made to include some of the common principles many game developers follow when making 2D games in WebGL.

Gem 32 - Playing Sound

I really don't want to spend much time talking about sound. Because this has nothing to do with WebGL itself. But in the context of game development I think it is necessary.

To reach some sort of balance between WebGL and game development principles, which is what I've tried to achieve throughout this entire book, I decided to show you a JavaScript library for playing sound that I use to build my own games.

Below what you're seeing is a complete source code listing for SoundStation class.

```
var SFX_JEWEL1 = 0;
var SFX_JEWEL2 = 1;
...
var SFX_COINDROP= 20;
```

```javascript
// Allocate sound buffer data
window.sfx = new Array(1000);
window.sound = new Array(1000);

var SoundStation = function(filename)
{
  this.that = this;
  this.context = null;
  this.audio = new Audio(filename);

  // Currently used only for background music volume
  this.volumeGainContext = null;
  this.musicVolume = 1.0;
  var that = this;
  this.play = function(__buffer_ID, repeatSound, contextGain) {

    // To turn all sounds off, uncomment this line:
    // return false;

    if (window.sfx[__buffer_ID] == undefined)
      return;

    var __buffer = window.sfx[__buffer_ID];
    var source = this.context.createBufferSource();
    source.buffer = __buffer;

    // tie to gain context so we can control this sound's volume
    if (contextGain)
    {
      this.volumeGainContext = this.context.createGain();
      source.connect(this.volumeGainContext);
      this.volumeGainContext.connect(this.context.destination);
      this.volumeGainContext.gain.value = 1.0;
```

```javascript
      } else

      // do regular connect (full volume)

      source.connect(this.context.destination);
      source.start(0);

      if (repeatSound)
         source.loop = true;
   }
   this.available = false;
   this.Initialize = function() {
      var contextClass = (window.AudioContext ||
         window.webkitAudioContext ||
         window.mozAudioContext ||
         window.oAudioContext ||
         window.msAudioContext);
      if (contextClass) {
         this.available = true;
         this.context = new contextClass();
         LoadSfx();
      } else {
         this.available = false;
      }
   }
   this.onError = function() {
      console.log("Sound.load('" + filename_url + "')... Failed!"); }
   this.load = function(__buffer_ID, filename_url) {
      var request = new XMLHttpRequest();
      request.open('GET', filename_url, true);
      request.responseType = 'arraybuffer';
      var that_v2 = this.that;
      request.onload = function() {
         that_v2.context.decodeAudioData(request.response,
```

```javascript
function(theBuffer) {
        window.sfx[__buffer_ID] = theBuffer;
        console.log("Sound.load('mp3')... Ok!");
      }, this.onError);
    }
    request.send();
  }
}

function LoadSfx() {
  console.log("LoadSfx()...");
  Sound.load(0, website.url +
"/property_stealth/games/gemini/sfx/jewel9.mp3");
  Sound.load(1, website.url +
"/property_stealth/games/gemini/sfx/jewel2.mp3");
  Sound.load(2, website.url +
"/property_stealth/games/gemini/sfx/swoosh.mp3");
  Sound.load(3, website.url +
"/property_stealth/games/gemini/sfx/plip1.mp3");
  Sound.load(4, website.url +
"/property_stealth/games/gemini/sfx/plop1.mp3");
  Sound.load(5, website.url +
"/property_stealth/games/gemini/sfx/soft_woosh.mp3");
  Sound.load(6, website.url +
"/property_stealth/games/gemini/sfx/synth1.mp3");
  Sound.load(7, website.url +
"/property_stealth/games/gemini/sfx/loaded.mp3");
  Sound.load(8, website.url +
"/property_stealth/games/gemini/sfx/expl1.mp3");
  Sound.load(9, website.url +
"/property_stealth/games/gemini/sfx/expl2.mp3");
  Sound.load(10, website.url + "/property_stealth/games/gemini/sfx/
crunch.mp3");
  Sound.load(11, website.url +
```

```
"/property_stealth/games/gemini/sfx/rocks.mp3");
  Sound.load(12, website.url +
"/property_stealth/games/gemini/sfx/glass1.mp3");
  Sound.load(13, website.url +
"/property_stealth/games/gemini/sfx/glass2.mp3");
  Sound.load(14, website.url +
"/property_stealth/games/gemini/sfx/glass3.mp3");
  Sound.load(15, website.url +
"/property_stealth/games/gemini/sfx/music.mp3");
  Sound.load(16, website.url +
"/property_stealth/games/gemini/sfx/beep1.mp3");
  Sound.load(17, website.url +
"/property_stealth/games/gemini/sfx/magick.mp3");
  Sound.load(18, website.url +
"/property_stealth/games/gemini/sfx/levelcompleted.mp3");
  Sound.load(19, website.url +
"/property_stealth/games/gemini/sfx/dice.mp3");
  Sound.load(20, website.url +
"/property_stealth/games/gemini/sfx/coindrop.mp3");
  Sound.load(21, website.url +
"/property_stealth/games/gemini/sfx/achievement.mp3");
  Sound.load(22, website.url +
"/property_stealth/games/gemini/sfx/coinloot.mp3");
  Sound.load(23, website.url +
"/property_stealth/games/gemini/sfx/coinpouch.mp3");
  Sound.load(24, website.url +
"/property_stealth/games/gemini/sfx/mellow_wahwah.mp3");
  Sound.load(25, website.url +
"/property_stealth/games/gemini/sfx/nevermind.mp3");
}
```

The long list of mp3 files would probably be replaced with your own set. Note that each sound file has an index value between 0 and 25 for all 26 sounds loaded.

In order to start using this class it first needs to be initialized as follows:

    var Sound = new SoundStation();

Afterwards, call the LoadSfx function before entering your main loop:

    LoadSfx();

That's all it takes to initialize sound station and load mp3 files. From this point on, you can play any sound you want from the loaded set by calling the following method on the main Sound object:

    Sound.play(SFX_COINDROP);

This example will play a "coindrop.mp3" file associated with sound id 20 (SFX_COINDROP).

A Note For Game Developers

The book has come to an end and it looks like we've reached the finish line. The purpose of WebGL Gems was to expose the reader to a wide variety of principles involved not only in WebGL programming but also game development.

I know that it is pretty much impossible to get the full picture of absolutely everything involved in the process of developing your own games. But I tried to focus only on the crucial parts that move the engine-development process forward the most. And this is why I created this guide as a starting point for game developers new to the WebGL library.

I was once asked a question on YouTube for my 2D game development video series, about what the steps should be for becoming a game developer after having sufficient knowledge of JavaScript.

I think the greatest choice that you will ever make will be between 1. Writing your own code and 2. Using Unity or UE3 engine. My personal approach is 1. simply because I want to understand how everything actually works. Curiosity is essential for nurturing the creative process.

Neither one is really better or worse than the other. But there are (dis-)advantages to both.

If you want to write your own code, you'll understand everything from ground up. This knowledge can also be useful when writing engines in Unity and UE3. Especially when you need to script something but don't know what a 3D vector is, for example.

But most people start game dev with 2D games. And it's all about drawing sprites on the screen, rotating them, or drawing transparent sprites. I think this is what I would recommend at this stage. Learn how to load images in JavaScript and use <canvas> to draw them either with native canvas image drawing functions or, of course with WebGL.

Game development is difficult to learn unless you know what the key areas of research are. For example, to make a 2D platformer, you have to understand the basics of creating and drawing a 2D grid-like map, keyboard controls and some basic 2D "sprite sheet" animation. It is really all pretty basic.

So now you have drawn your characters and your game world. It's time to implement collision detection. This is just a bunch of lines intersecting other lines. Or rectangles and squares intersecting circles, etc. There are already known algorithms for this. They are all explained in my tutorial series on YouTube as well as in this book.

You can take a look at the source code of Mosaic.js -- my 2D JavaScript game engine:
http://www.tigrisgames.com/mosaic

**This is a non-WebGL JavaScript engine. It contains libraries for most common function for creating video games. It can easily be transformed into a WebGL based engine -- by rewriting the rendering routines with WebGL implementation. And it's also one of the reasons I wrote this book in the first place. It was because I wanted to convert my engine to WebGL. Writing about it actually helped me with this process!

You can download the complete source code from the page. Current documentation is not so great, but there are some interesting bits on the homepage. Also, if you're going to make your own engine you'll probably end up with about 90% of the same code as seen in Mosaic.js or in this book anyways. You can take a look at it just to see what it entails.

So pretty much game dev is about creating (or choosing) a game engine. From that point on, it's about game design. So this is where you disassociate yourself from the actual code and step into the shoes of the game story writer, level designer, make character, and create dialog or whatever you conjure up :)

Hmm, one technique I learned that works really well is to break down the process into smaller parts. For example, figure out how to draw sprites (scaled, rotated and animated... or all at the same time). Now that you got this part working, you can start making a simple game.

I also recommend creating a challenge, like "make Tetris game in 1 week". Choose small games first, like pac-man, tic-tac-toe and so on. Start super small. Make the tiniest game possible with just few graphical elements.

www.ingramcontent.com/pod-product-compliance
Lightning Source LLC
Chambersburg PA
CBHW080608060326
40690CB00021B/4622